D1386026

Women in ᵁᵁ⸏ᵗᵃⁱⁿ

Wall-painting of a woman at Sparsholt.

Women in Roman Britain

Lindsay Allason-Jones

British Museum Publications

© 1989 Lindsay Allason-Jones

Published by British Museum Publications Ltd
46 Bloomsbury Street, London WC1B 3QQ

British Library Cataloguing in Publication Data

Allason-Jones, Lindsay
   Women in Roman Britain
   1. Great Britain. Society. Role of women, history
   I. Title
   305.4′2′0941

ISBN 0-7141-1392-1

Front cover illustration Bone hairpin modelled with a bust of a woman wearing an elaborate hairstyle. See also 48.

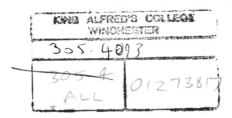
Designed by James Shurmer

Typeset in Ehrhardt
and printed in Great Britain by
Butler & Tanner Ltd, Frome and London

Contents

Photographic acknowledgements

The author and publishers are grateful to the following for permission to reproduce their photographs:

Antikenmuseum, Berlin. Staatliche Museen Preussischer Kulturbesitz 15
Audio Visual Centre, University of Newcastle upon Tyne 18, 27, 37, 41, 45, 56
British Museum 3, 12, 19, 23, 34, 43, 44, 48, 51, 54, 58, 59, 62
Bradford Art Galleries and Museums 4
Cadw: Welsh Historic Monuments. Crown Copyright 25
Cambridge University Collection 17
Cardiff City Council 2
Carlisle Museum and Art Gallery 38, 42
Corinium Museum 52
The Dorset Natural History and Archaeological Society, Dorchester, Dorset 31
English Heritage 35, 60
Fototeca Unione, Rome 67
Institute of Archaeology, Oxford 55
Michael Holford 66
Hull City Museums and Art Galleries 53
Museo Ostiense, Ostia 9
Museum of Antiquities of the University and Society of Antiquaries of Newcastle upon Tyne 6, 14, 39, 40
Museum of London 33, 46, 57
National Museum of Antiquities, Leiden 32
National Museum of Wales 26
Reading Museum and Art Gallery 63
Rheinisches Landesmuseum, Trier 30
Römisch–Germanisches Museum, Cologne (photo Ralph Jackson) 10
Römisch–Germanisches Zentralmuseum, Mainz 13
Shrewsbury Borough Museum Service 49
John Stanger 36
Sussex Archaeological Society, Fishbourne Roman Palace 65
The Vindolanda Trust 8
Warburg Institute 68
D. A. Welsby 16
West Sussex County Council Planning Department (Countryside Section) 28
Winchester Museums Service *frontispiece*
Yorkshire Museum 5, 11, 29, 47

Nos 24, 50 and 61 were taken by the author. The line drawings 1, 21, 22 and 64 were drawn by D. A. Welsby; no. 7 is by Tony Wilmott and no. 20 is by S. James (© British Museum).

Acknowledgements

A book of this type relies heavily on the work of other people and I would like to express my thanks to all the archaeologists whose detailed excavation and research provided the facts which support my comments and generalisations. In particular I am indebted to the following, with whom I have discussed their work: Dr Carol van Driel-Murray, University of Amsterdam; Dr Hilary Cool and Dr Jenny Price, Department of External Studies, University of Leeds; Dr J. P. Wild, Department of Archaeology, University of Manchester; Dr M. Henig, Dr R. S. O. Tomlin and Dr Hazel Dodge, Institute of Archaeology, Oxford University; P. T. Bidwell, Tyne and Wear Museums Service; Mrs Kay Hartley; Mrs Margery Hutchinson, Ancient Monuments Laboratory; Dr Theya Molleson, British Museum (Natural History); Dr M. Millett and Mr J. Casey, Department of Archaeology, University of Durham; D. Mackreth; Dr J. Richards, Department of Plant Biology, University of Newcastle upon Tyne; Dr S. Greep, Verulamium Museum; Dr G. Lawson, National Music-Archaeological Survey, Cambridge University; Professor A. Birley, Department of History, University of Manchester; Tony Wilmott, Central Excavation Unit; and Dr D. J. Smith. Specifically I must thank my sister, Dr Erica Allason-Jones, Department of Genito-Urinary Medicine, University College Hospital, London, Dr Ian Cameron, Leeds East District Health Authority, Professor W. Dunlop, Department of Obstetrics and Gynaecology, University of Newcastle upon Tyne, and Dr F. Miller for checking my medical facts, and Margaret Cox and Eleanor Scott for allowing me to read their unpublished theses and discussing their ideas. Mr and Mrs P. Smith were more than kind in allowing me access to the female burial on their property in York, as were my colleagues Miss Pat Southern, Dr M. C. Bishop, Dr K. T. Greene, Dr Karen Griffiths and Dr D. A. Welsby, Department of Archaeology, Dr Tony Spawforth, Department of Classics, University of Newcastle upon Tyne, and Miss Catherine Johns, R. Jackson and Dr T. W. Potter, Department of Prehistoric and Romano-British Antiquities, British Museum, who read various drafts. Their helpful comments, assistance and encouragement have been much appreciated.

Finally my gratitude must be expressed to Mrs Wendy Young who, once again, struggled with my handwriting to produce a readable text, and the staff of British Museum Publications who patiently guided me through the birth pangs of this book.

Preface

To begin by saying that this was an impossible book to write may be seen as a defeatist attitude, but to chronicle the lives, habits and thoughts of half the population of a country over four centuries could never be easy. In the case of Roman Britain the attempt has been made more difficult by the fact that only in the first few years of the occupation can we be said to be dealing with people who are clearly native Britons or specifically Romans of Italian descent. Even some of the earliest governors of the province came from Gaul or Africa, and as legionaries and auxiliaries retired and intermarried with the native population and merchants and slaves entered the country, so the population became more and more mixed. To talk about Romano-British women, even in the first century AD, as if they all had the same background, traditions and tastes is to oversimplify a complex situation. Any foreigner living in Britain could be described as 'British' by right of residence, while every inhabitant automatically became a 'Roman' when Britain became a province of the Roman Empire, and all were awarded citizenship by decree in AD 212. In Scotland the situation was particularly confused as the various incursions by the Roman army over the centuries meant that Scotland was occasionally part of the province but more often not.

In Britain the ways of the native Celts, for which we have little direct evidence, will have flavoured and dominated life, while the minorities may have kept together and continued their familiar practices with little effect on the majority. Even so, trends and fashions will have been brought in by new immigrants, and the wealthier natives will have looked to Rome for indications as to acceptable behaviour and the latest ideas. The cosmopolitan nature of Romano-British society may tempt us to use our knowledge of the life led by women in Rome as described by classical authors to fill in the gaps in the evidence from Britain itself. Indeed, the use of literary motifs in mosaics and wall-paintings makes it clear that works by such writers as Ovid and Pliny must have been widely read in the province, so that ideas which were familiar to women in Rome would have been available to their contemporaries in Britain.

However, although I have used quotations from classical sources to give some indication of both the Roman and Celtic attitudes towards women, it is dangerous to rely too heavily on literary evidence unless its relevance is supported by the archaeology: there are very few specific references to Britain in these sources. The difficulty of discussing women's rights, for example, illustrates our problem. Recent research has shown that each province in the Roman Empire had its own legal code based on an amalgam of Roman and native laws and assumptions about life in a province based on classical Roman law have often proved to be inaccurate and as we have little knowledge of the pre-Roman legal code in Britain, nor any idea of the extent to which the Roman code was adapted to fit native mores, even the most general discussion is fraught with difficulties. We are also quite unable to make any kind of estimate of the numbers of women in different classes of society – freedwomen, slaves, wives of military men, foreigners, and so on. In fact, as we have no census returns for the period we cannot even say confidently how many people there were in total in the province at any one time.

We do have a certain amount of information about some native women. Boudica and Cartimandua were mentioned by classical authors discussing the political and military affairs of the Empire, but their status cannot be thought of as typical for women in the province. Even in these cases the evidence is severely limited and on occasion contradictory. The bulk of the evidence concerning individuals comes from inscriptions – tombstones, altars, writing tablets and curse tablets – but this is slight. Of all the inscriptions surviving from Britain only about 10 per cent refer to women, and dating them is problematical. Many relating to women have previously been dated on doubtful premises, and none of the few surviving fourth-century inscriptions mention women at all.

The quantity and quality of the information in the inscriptions varies considerably from potted biographies to mere names. They are also strongly biased towards the upper- and middle-class Romanised population, for these were the people who could afford to erect imposing tombstones or dedicate altars. Of the women referred to in the inscriptions only some 15 per cent were of low status. Every female slave and freedwoman known by name and status in Roman Britain is mentioned in this book, but the thousands who must have lived in the province have disappeared without trace. Lead curse tablets found at Bath and other sites may do something to redress the balance for the less wealthy native population, but they hardly constitute overwhelming evidence: of 110 curse tablets from Bath with any decipherable text, just 16 mention women by name; of these 6 simply give a name, and only 3 could be said to give useful information about their status and position. Curse tablets found at Uley, Gloucestershire, promise to add to our information, but it may be some time before they are ready for scholarly publication.

The bias of the inscriptions is also reflected in the archaeological record: the lower the class the sparser its material remains. However, they still offer the most comprehensive body of evidence we have. It may be felt that the emphasis on material culture – dress, jewellery, cooking utensils, furniture and so on – gives a somewhat distorted view of the preoccupations of Romano-British women. However, an enormous number of hairpins and jewellery have been found in excavations and women are often portrayed on their tombstones holding mirrors. Although there can be problems in attributing some of this excavated material to the gender of its erstwhile owners, its sheer quantity strongly indicates that the women of the province were interested in their personal appearance.

Despite the problems of the evidence, I have attempted to present a fair view of the life and concerns of women in Roman Britain, even if these are not always to modern taste. My aim has been to stimulate discussion in what has been a neglected area in the hope that new information from excavations in the future may be interpreted with the female population in mind, and not just the male inhabitants, as has been the case in the past.

In order to keep references to a minimum, women cited in the text are listed at the end of the book with their source. Inscriptions discovered before 1956 are published in *Roman Inscriptions in Britain*, by R. G. Collingwood and R. P. Wright. Those found since have been published annually in either *Journal of Roman Studies* or in *Britannia*. The list does not include every woman known to have lived in Roman Britain, but none have been excluded who could in any way add to our knowledge of the period. The bulk of the exclusions are simply names scratched on pots.

The notes are restricted to classical texts and a few comments. Wherever possible quotes from the classical authors have been taken from the Loeb edition translations, as these are readily available in libraries and bookshops, and have the further benefit of carrying the original text and English translation side by side, allowing the reader to investigate the evidence at first hand. Works by modern authors which are referred to in the text can be found in the Bibliography, along with other publications which might be useful for further reading.

Introduction

The British Isles had been known to several generations of Romans before the first invasion by Julius Caesar in 55 BC. Among some sections of Republican society there was a belief that Britain was one of the Isles of the Blessed to which one journeyed after death, and the stories brought back by shipwrecked sailors and traders reinforced the idea of a fabulous land inhabited by shadowy beings. Even Tacitus was able to relate that, of the survivors of Germanicus' fleet who fetched up on the shores of Britain, 'not a man returned from the distance without his tale of marvels – furious whirlwinds, unheard of birds, enigmatic shapes half human and half bestial: things seen or things believed in a moment of terror'.[1] Although early visitors had not ventured far inland, the Roman authorities were aware of the many natural resources of the island, such as the grain, cattle, gold, silver, iron, hides, slaves and hunting dogs listed by Strabo.[2] This potential bounty may have provided some incentive to Julius Caesar, and later the Emperor Claudius, to invade the country. Caesar also considered it essential for the security of the European mainland to stop the tribes of Britain sending reinforcements to the Gallic and Germanic tribes in their struggles against the Roman army. The close connection between the people of Britain, Gaul and Germany can be traced back to the fifth century BC, and successive waves of immigrants and invaders across the English Channel meant that by the first century BC there were strong tribal links. Caesar noted that Diviciacus, whom he described as 'the greatest man in Gaul', had also been 'powerful in Britain',[3] while a number of Britons had served in the Gallic armies and rebellious nobles had found sanctuary in Britain after their unsuccessful resistance to Roman policy in 57 BC.

The two campaigns by Julius Caesar had little long-term political impact on Britain but they did open up the country to Roman trade, which in turn strengthened the cultural links between Rome and the British tribes via a Gaul which was rapidly becoming Romanised. Between the Julian campaigns and the Claudian invasion Roman ideas and culture were absorbed by the peoples of the south-eastern tribes, and information about the Britons, plus a steady supply of various commodities, were received by Rome in return. Britain was no longer seen to be a land beyond the edge of the world, and the way was paved for a determined attempt to include the island in the Roman Empire.

For various reasons it was not until the reign of Claudius that Britain was successfully invaded and became a province of the Roman Empire. The invaders of AD 43 found a country divided between powerful tribes who either lived in peaceful coexistence or were sworn enemies (1). These tribes all appear to have

1. Distribution of the native British tribes.

spoken the same language, which today is called Celtic. The meaning of the terms 'Celt' and 'Celtic' have altered over the centuries, but they are used in the absence of any better term to describe the native population of Britain before and during the Roman occupation. According to Julius Caesar, the tribes along the coast of south-east Britain were all Belgae who had emigrated from France and Belgium, but this may oversimplify a complex situation, and as the Romans expanded their control further north and west they found fewer people with any claim to either tribal or trade links with the Continental Belgae.

Despite our increased knowledge of Iron Age Britain we know surprisingly little about the female population before the Roman invasion, and the lack of evidence about the Celtic law codes, social mores and tribal government makes it difficult to assess the impact of Roman domination. It would be rash to presume that because the tribes in Britain have been described as Celts they behaved in the same way as the tribes of Germany and Gaul. Certainly they shared an ethnic tradition, but how far this affected the details of daily life is not easy to determine. Nor is it wise to rely on the accuracy of early writers, such as Julius Caesar or Tacitus, as their works have a political bias and as a result tend to dwell on the barbarity of the Celtic people in order to emphasise the civilisation of the Romans. Neither writer showed much interest in the women of the newly conquered province, and it was not until AD 51 that any female is mentioned by name. Regrettably, we have no information about the female members of the families of Togodumnos or Cogidubnus, or any of the other eleven British kings who surrendered to Claudius.

The number of inhabitants of Roman Britain has been variously estimated at four to five million but this may be a conservative estimate. Without census returns it is impossible to calculate the size of the population, nor can we estimate the ratios of the sexes. The proportion of men to women may have fluctuated over the centuries, and no doubt there were local variations as well. The invasion, for example, may have decimated the male population, particularly amongst the recalcitrant tribes, with the result that there may have been a considerable number of widows and unmarried girls in the first century AD. This balance may have been redressed during the Boudican revolt, when women joined in the fighting and thousands of women were slaughtered in Verulamium, Colchester and London. Later rebellions, and the transfer of troops abroad, will again have upset the balance between the sexes. Analysis of cemeteries gives a varied picture as to exact ratios: at Poundbury the ratios were equal, at Trentholme Drive, York, there were four men to every woman, while the Cirencester cemetery indicated a population of five men to two women. Lamyatt Beacon gave a contrary statistic of eleven women to every man. This varied pattern may be explained by the segregation of the sexes in cemeteries or by the preponderance of men which might be expected in a military area.

The cemetery evidence is more useful in giving a picture of the physical

2. Boudica and her daughters in heroic vein at Cardiff, as visualised in 1913–15 by J. Howard Thomas.

characteristics of the people. The average height of men was 5 feet 6 inches to 5 feet 7 inches (1.68–1.7 m) with the women consistently smaller at 5 feet 1 inch to 5 feet 3 inches (1.55–1.6 m) (the average height of a British woman today is 5 feet 4 inches, 1.625 m). This contradicts the classical writers' impression of the women of Britain being as tall and as well-built as their husbands. In particular, the contemporary descriptions of Boudica[4] bring to mind a Wagnerian contralto: 'in stature she was very tall, in appearance most terrifying, in the glance of her eye most fierce, and her voice was harsh; a great mass of bright red hair fell to her hips' (2).[5] There is no way of telling whether this is an accurate picture or merely propaganda. The preponderance of red hair among the southern tribes has been confirmed by traces of hair found in graves, but the physical attributes of the population will have varied from tribe to tribe. The Silures of the Welsh Marches, for example, are more likely to have been small and dark, while the tribes along the east coast may have shared the physical characteristics of their Gallic and Germanic relations. Within a few generations of the Roman invasion several women with African, Scandinavian and Mediterranean characteristics would have joined the population and throughout the centuries the intermarriage of native Britons to those of the other races of the Empire will have resulted in a mixed population with every colour of hair and skin being commonplace.

As more and more of Britain was absorbed into the new Roman province of Britannia, so the population become Roman in name, if not necessarily with full citizenship. There has been a tendency among modern writers to presume that because Roman law was valid throughout the Empire all the people of that Empire were subject to exactly the same legal and social restraints. The evidence of papyri from Egypt has shown that there were, in fact, local interpretations and variations on the central theme. In the provinces the interpretation of written law, particularly those laws which affected women – marriage, status and inheritance – would have been influenced by tradition, local custom and social moral values.

To add to the confusion, any discussion as to the status and legal rights of Roman women has tended to be biased by the literary evidence of the late Republic, and by our knowledge of the empresses and aristocratic ladies of Rome, which may bear scant similarity to the reality of life in a province. In Britain we have only the limited evidence of inscriptions, writing tablets and curse tablets to give any clues as to how rigidly Roman laws were followed, so to evaluate the status of women in Romano-British society we can only look at conditions in Rome and compare the limited evidence from Britain to judge the degree of similarity or disparity.

Throughout the Empire the population was divided between those who were free, freed or slaves, with various social subdivisions within the classes. The free population included those who were full Roman citizens with all the privileges which this brought; those who had the more limited Latin rights; and peregrines, as non-citizens were known. These different grades of citizenship or non-citizenship up to AD 212, when all those of free status were given citizenship, largely depended on where one lived, as we will see in chapter 3, but initially the majority of Romano-Britons will have had peregrine status, with full Roman citizenship accorded to only a few influential tribal leaders and their families.

At first glance the constraints on women in Rome might make the term 'free' appear misleading. A woman had no political status and no vote; nor could she hold political office or join the army, and in essence she remained a 'minor' all her life. No action taken by a woman had any legal validity unless it had the sanction of her father, husband or guardian. A Roman family had at its head the father who, as *pater familias*, had control over his wife, his children, his son's children and his slaves. On the death of the *pater* his wife and children became *sui iuris*, that is, independent of a *pater*'s control, and each adult son was promoted to *pater familias* in his own right. By Roman law no woman could be head of a family or exercise *potestas* (control), and it was the lack of *potestas* which limited a woman's legal role, as without it she could not own property, adopt a child, or exercise legal control over her children. For girls the initial control, known as *tutela impuberis*, ended when she was twelve and legally old enough to marry, but it was replaced by the *tutela mulieris*. Cicero voiced Roman opinion as to why this was necessary: 'our ancestors established the rule that all women, because of their weakness of intellect, should be under the power of guardians'.[6] Even an adult woman who became independent on the death of her father or husband was required at law to have a guardian appointed by her former guardian's will or by a magistrate's decision. These secondary guardians were usually brothers, paternal uncles or cousins, but could be appointed from outside the immediate family circle.

The duties of a minor's guardian included arranging, and consenting to, a suitable marriage, as well as administering property for his ward. An adult woman's guardian had less onerous duties, only being expected to give or withhold consent to her actions. Whether the role of guardian was a sinecure or not probably depended on the character of the people concerned, rather than on any demands made by the legal system, and a woman had the right to apply to the magistrates to have her guardian replaced if he proved unreasonable.

Was this male domination of women shared by the native British population? The careers of the first women known by name in the province, Cartimandua and Boudica, would appear to suggest not. The career of Cartimandua, ruler of the Brigantes, a large tribe or confederation of tribes who controlled the north of England, exhibited all the scandal and intrigue of a modern soap-opera. According to Tacitus she owed her position to 'the influence which belongs to high birth',[7] a position consolidated by her betrayal of Caratacus, leader of the Silurian tribe, after he had sought refuge with her following his defeat by Ostorius Scapula. Cartimandua was married at the time to Venutius, but the contemporary texts make it clear that it was she who held the reins of power and not her husband. She may have inherited her throne by native law, or have been installed as ruler by the Roman authorities. The former is the more likely explanation and may be supported by the behaviour of the wife and family of Caratacus when they were displayed as captives in Rome: according to Tacitus, when 'released from their chains, they offered to Agrippina, conspicuously seated on another dais nearby, the same homage and gratitude as they had given to the Emperor'.[8] Tacitus took this as an indication of the forwardness of the Empress Agrippina but the incident also says much about the British attitude to women: not only could a woman be a leader in her own right but the female consort of a ruler was of equal importance and entitled to respect.

Cartimandua did very well out of her act of treachery to Caratacus for 'from this came her wealth and the wanton spirit which success breeds'.[9] Domestic disharmony, however, also resulted, and she separated from her husband, taking Vellocatus, Venutius' armour-bearer, as her lover. Tacitus gives two versions of the subsequent events: in the *Histories* he suggests that 'her house was at once shaken by this scandalous act'[10] and as a consequence her husband was supported by the outraged populace in his attempt to remove her from office. In the *Annals* he commented that 'her enemies, infuriated and goaded by fears of humiliating feminine rule, invaded her kingdom with a powerful force of picked warriors'.[11] As she was already acknowledged as ruler this last comment might indicate that she had threatened to extend her influence to neighbouring tribes or other sections of the Brigantes. Even though a female leader was an alien concept to Roman thought, the authorities were still willing to support a female ruler if they felt it to be in their best interests to do so, and troops were sent to Cartimandua's aid. Venutius and his rebels were driven back, only to succeed in ousting Cartimandua in AD 69.

Although the exact sequence of the events in Cartimandua's life are confusing and open to several interpretations, it does appear that among the Brigantes a woman could be a ruler, hold property, divorce her husband, lead armies and be accepted as a force to be reckoned with.

The career of Boudica is even more complex.[12] She was the wife of Prasutagus, the leader of the Iceni tribe who had been confirmed as a client king of Rome after AD 47. She herself was descended from a royal house, although which one is not recorded, and was in her thirties when her husband died, leaving his kingdom jointly to his two daughters and the Emperor Nero. It should be noted that there was never any suggestion that Boudica had a right to her husband's throne in her own name, nor did she subsequently claim the throne for herself, but acted on behalf of her daughters, whose rights were recognised by the Iceni if not by the Romans. In making the emperor and his daughters co-heirs Prasutagus had vainly attempted to preserve his kingdom as an entity. The motives behind the Roman authorities' arrogant disregard for his last wishes are not far to seek or understand. While Cartimandua was a mature woman with an established claim to her throne, Prasutagus' daughters were young girls; their youth, and the fact that there were two of them, made each a potential focus of resistance and rebellion. An unstable client kingdom would not be to anyone's advantage, nor would it be conducive to peaceful provincial administration. An agreement between a client king and Rome was a personal arrangement rather than a treaty between two states, and on the death of the individual king the Roman authorities would feel no necessity to continue the arrangement into the second generation. Even so, it is hard to explain why Tacitus should report that 'as a beginning his widow, Boudica, was flogged, and their daughters raped. The Icenian chiefs were deprived of their hereditary estates as if the Romans had been given the whole country. The king's own relatives were treated like slaves.' This excessive behaviour has been blamed on the procurator, Decianus Catus, the high-handed attitude of the local officials and the low morals of the army veterans, but none of these explanations fully covers the events. Flogging was not a punishment normally meted out to free women for any criminal offence, while rape, far from being condoned, was a capital offence. The Emperor Hadrian was later to take a lenient view of those who, taking the law into their own hands, killed a rapist. A woman could not prosecute for rape herself but her relatives were entitled to do so and if they did not fulfil their responsibilities it was open to outsiders to press charges without the constraint of a time limit. According to the legal writer Ruffus, the result of a successful prosecution meant that 'a soldier who takes a girl by force and rapes her shall have his nose cut off, and the girl be given a third part of his property'.[13] For anyone to flog the widow of a client king and rape his daughters was not only reprehensible according to contemporary mores, but also an act of political folly and it is hardly surprising that the Iceni revolted, supported by the Trinovantes.

Cassius Dio's explanation of the revolt was that it was caused by 'the confiscation of the sums of money that Claudius had given to the foremost Britons' by Decianus Catus[14] and the calling in of Seneca's loan. He claimed that 'the person who was chiefly instrumental in rousing the natives and persuading them to fight the Romans, the person who was thought worthy to be their leader, and who directed the conduct of the war, was Boudica, a British woman of the royal family and possessed of greater intelligence than often belongs to women'.[15] He gave no indication that Boudica had suffered any personal indignity, nor did he refer to her daughters' claim to the Icenian throne.

The speeches of Boudica and the Roman commander, Suetonius, to their respective troops before battle, as reported by Cassius Dio and Tacitus,[16] are likely to be as historically accurate as the speech by King Henry V before the Battle of Agincourt as related by Shakespeare.[17] However, they do give an impression of the different Roman and Celtic attitudes towards women, and it is this difference which appears to have struck the classical writers. There is an inference that the Roman army was prepared to behave with forbearance and gallantry towards women as long as the women stayed at home, knew their place and did not meddle in affairs of state. It was the native woman's lack of womanly virtues which was felt to lie at the bottom of the trouble; not only were the tribes willing to be led by a woman but the female population joined in the fighting. Suetonius tried to rally his men by saying that the majority of those massed against them were mere women. Boudica took the same line with her troops, describing the heavy armour and weaponry of the legionaries as the defence of feeble men who were as weak as their womenfolk. British women were not only equal to their men but 'possessed of the same valour'.

Both classical writers refer to the British tribes being used to female leadership. We know of few Iron Age generals by name, so cannot estimate how many were women nor whether some tribes were more likely to be led by a woman than others. Apart from Boudica and Cartimandua, Tacitus also hints at a third female general, unfortunately anonymous, who led the Brigantes against a Roman fort and colony some time between AD 71 and 83. This cannot have been Cartimandua but may have been one of her successors, if Tacitus has not confused several incidents.[18]

It is clear that native women attached great significance to their tribal identity

3. The Snettisham gold torc. Cassius Dio described Boudica as wearing such a torc when leading her troops into battle as a symbol of her leadership.

4. Tombstone of Ved...ic.. at Ilkely: 'a tribeswoman of the Cornovii'.

and it was common for a woman to claim to be a member of a particular tribe. For example, at Ilkley Ved..ic.. (4) was recorded on her tombstone as a tribeswoman of the Cornovii, while at Templebrough Verecunda Rufilia's husband referred to her as a tribeswoman of the Dobunni. Both these women had married away from their native area and the references to their tribal origins on their tombstones shows the importance of an individual's tribal identity as well as making the point that this identity was not affected by marriage. To a Romanised woman it was more important to record one's status. At Lincoln Volusia Faustina (23) was remembered as 'a citizen of Lindum', and it is clearly her citizenship which is important rather than her birth or residence in Lincoln.

With such a tradition of female leadership and participation in events it is unlikely that British women would overnight relinquish all their rights and submit to the control of a *pater familias*, although several tombstones hint that the *pater familias* system was followed to some extent. The inscription at Old Penrith set up to Crotilo Germanus and Greca by their brother Vindicianus gives the impression that Vindicianus had assumed the role of *pater familias* after the death of their parents, while a soldier called Tadius Exuperatus, who was commemorated by his sister Tadia Exuperata on the same memorial at Caerleon as their mother Tadia Vallaunius, may also have seen his protection of the two women as the formal relationship of a *pater familias* to his wards. These references, however, may simply reflect the tradition of the extended family, with several generations living together. The tombstone of Aelia Matrona erected by her husband commemorated Aelia herself, as well as her son and her mother, and carries with it the implication that the whole family lived together. The tombstone of Mantinia Maerica also suggests that her mother lived in the marital home. Other households included sisters, nieces and cousins. To have three generations living under one roof was clearly not uncommon and may not have had any legal implications.

A curse tablet from Bath gives a somewhat different picture, as Veloriga is listed as the head of a family, equal in status to Trinnus, Marcellinus, Morivassus and Riovassus. Other women's names on curse tablets add to the evidence that even as late as the fourth century AD British women took part in transactions and owned property.

From an early period Roman women had the technical right to inherit and bequeath property, although at times this was subject to various restrictions. Wives had no right at Roman law to claim any of their husband's estate in cases of intestacy, although in practice most husbands seem to have tried to provide for their widows rather than rely on their nearest male relative to shoulder the responsibility for maintenance as well as guardianship. Julia Similina referred to herself as 'wife and heiress' of Titinius Felix, *beneficiarius* of the XXth Legion Valeria Victrix, but this is the only British example where a wife is specifically recorded as her husband's heiress. The number of wives who erected a memorial to their husbands, however, might indicate that they had inherited money, or at least had enough cash to pay for a tombstone and the right to carry out the transaction themselves.

Daughters are more often recorded as heiresses and they were fully entitled to claim on intestacy. A father might leave a married daughter a minimal share of his estate, taking the view that she had already had her share in the form of a dowry. Equally a daughter, married or single, might be left nothing in a will, in order to ensure that the property was kept in the male line. Martiola, from Penrith, an unmarried woman in her twenties, may have inherited considerable wealth when her father, Flavius Martius, a councillor of quaestorian rank in the *civitas* of the Carvetii, died at the age of forty-five.

To be eligible to make a will one had to be a free citizen and capable of attesting. As a consequence slaves, prisoners, the insane, congenital deaf-mutes and those who had been declared *infamia* as a punishment were excluded. One also had to be *sui iuris* and have reached puberty. Girls were considered to have reached adulthood at twelve (boys had to be fourteen), so the thirteen year old mourned by Vitellia Procula on a tombstone from York is likely to have been a daughter rather than a son: Vitellia describes herself as the 'heir in part' as well as the mother. Whether this child had inherited the estate from a father who left Vitellia Procula nothing or only a part of his estate is open to speculation. Another mother, also from York, who is recorded as inheriting from her offspring is Emilia Theodora, whose son Valerius Theodorianus died at the age of thirty-five years and six months. By Roman law a mother could in theory only be left the usufruct of a property but it was not uncommon for a mother to be left the estate outright. There is, however, a notable lack of inscriptions which refer to offspring inheriting from their mothers.

Other Romano-British heiresses are known by name, although we are left in doubt as to their relationship with their heirs or benefactors. It is likely that a certain Tiberia inherited from her father, although all that survives of his name is '-berius' and he could have been her brother. Lucius Ulpius Sestius inherited from Rusonia Aventina, but she was probably not his wife as a wife's property automatically became her husband's on marriage. Aurelius Mercurialis referred to himself on the tombstone of Julia Velva (5) as her heir, whilst mentioning that he had erected a tomb at York 'in his lifetime for himself and his family'. It would be odd for a father to see his relationship with his daughter as purely that of heir, and the lack of a common name between Julia and her heir suggests that she was neither his daughter nor his sister, yet there is the implication that she was part of the family. It is possible that she was Mercurialis' mother-in-law but the phrase 'lived most dutifully' is used most often to refer to wives or much loved freedwomen. Epigraphic evidence from Rome shows that freed-women were regarded as part of the *familia* and as such were entitled to a place in the family tomb. This is pure speculation, however. The lavishness of Julia

5. Tombstone of Julia Velva at York. She reclines on a couch with her heir, L. Aurelius Mercurialis, standing at its head.

Velva's tombstone might indicate that her estate was worth having, as does the appearance of Mercurialis standing at her side with a firm grip on the will.

Claudia Crysis, who died at Lincoln, was remembered by more than one heir, although they remain anonymous and their relationships are unspecified. The property of another woman, Pervinca, went to a certain Delfinus along with the estates of a large group of other apparently unrelated people. Why Delfinus should benefit from so many deaths is not stated but it is clear that Pervinca, who may have been a slave or a freedwoman, was as free to leave him her property as her male colleagues, and there is no suggestion that he was a husband, brother or father.

Literary references indicate that slavery was as much a fact of life in pre-Roman Britain as it was throughout the Roman Empire. A writing tablet from London in which Rufus recommended that Epillicus turn 'that slave-girl into cash'[19] recorded an everyday occurrence and both Rufus and Epillicus would have been astonished at any suggestion that their transaction was in any way immoral.

Some slaves may have accompanied their owners to Britain, but there was also an import and export trade by which slaves from different provinces changed hands. The fashion for giving slaves Greek names regardless of their origins makes this trade difficult to trace or evaluate, while the case of one Regina suggests that there was an additional domestic market. She was described on her tombstone as being of the Catuvellaunian tribe and the freedwoman and wife of Barates of Palmyra (6). For her to have been a freedwoman presupposes her to have been enslaved at some time, and in the late second century it is difficult to see how she could have become a slave unless sold by her parents. This practice was banned by law but evidence from Noricum (modern Hungary/Czechoslovakia) and other parts of the Empire suggests that it was widespread, as families found they could not afford to bring up all their children unassisted. It may also have been judged worth the risk that a girl would attract her master, who might as a consequence free her and marry her. Regina, unlike other freedwomen such as Calpurnia Trifosa, does not appear to have received Roman citizenship on gaining her freedom.

Roman law recognised the status of a slave and made due provision, particularly in the areas concerned with children and sexual relationships. Female slaves could be sold for breeding and it was considered sound commercial practice to breed one's own slaves for sale or use. Three children commemorated at Chester, Atilianus, Antiatilianus and Protus, may well have been *vernae*, that is children born to a slave woman on her master's estate.[20] A slave woman who produced a number of children might claim her freedom as a reward but she had no automatic right, for in this, as in all matters, she was dependent on the generosity of her owner. Any child born to a slave woman belonged to her owner and she had no claim to keep her children or have any say in their subsequent upbringing or education. Some Italian estate owners passed all *vernae* over to slave nannies to rear so that their mothers could return to work as soon as possible, whilst others split up families for financial gain.

Slaves could not contract legal marriages but in many households stable relationships were formed. The slaves themselves regarded these relationships as true marriages and British slaves are referred to with their wives on inscriptions and curse tablets: for example, Cunitius and his wife Senovara, the slaves of Cunomolius and his wife Minervina at Bath. These 'marriages', however, could be terminated by one or both of the partners being sold or freed.

After AD 52 if a Roman free woman had sexual relations with a slave without the consent of the slave's master she ran the risk of becoming a slave herself. If consent was given, the woman's status was still reduced to that of freedwoman, whilst any children resulting from the union might become slaves 'by agreement'. In Britain this may have affected the marriage of the free Roman citizen Claudia Martina to the slave Anencletus. Anencletus was not, however, an ordinary slave, but a slave of the Council of the Province, which gave him the

6. Tombstone of Regina from South Shields: 'freedwoman and wife of Barates of Palmyra', 'a Catuvellaunian by tribe'.

superior position of a civil servant. Claudia Martina's situation, therefore, may not have been as invidious as it appears.

In Britain the majority of female slaves may have been occupied in domestic work as maids, cooks, laundresses, spinners, weavers, wet-nurses, nannies or bath attendants, and the quality of their lives will have depended on the number of other slaves employed with whom they shared the work, and on the personality of their owner. In Italy there is evidence for a hierarchy among slaves in a household, and some of the supervisory slaves and ladies' maids owned slaves themselves. A large number of these superior slaves will have accompanied the imperial family on their visits to the province, whilst others will have formed part of the household of the governors and other high officials. For these people the fact of their slavery may have made little impact on their daily lives, but this was not always the case. The Elder Cato is known to have established slave brothels on his estates in Italy for the entertainment of his male slaves and, while it is not known whether this precedent was ever followed in Britain, slaves who fell into the hands of brothel owners, tavern keepers or gladiatorial trainers were truly to be pitied, particularly as they were unlikely to live long enough or earn enough to be able to buy their freedom. A female slave was also at the mercy of her male owner should he wish to take her into his bed. Whereas it was regarded as adultery for a married woman to have sex with a male slave, for a married man to have sex with a female slave was considered unexceptional, unless he was not her owner, in which case he could be sued by her master on the grounds that personal property had been damaged. If a female slave was raped the accused was not punishable by death, but again the slave's master could bring a charge for damages.

A female slave could obtain her freedom in several ways. Firstly, if she was over thirty she could be manumitted under the terms of her owner's will. During their lifetime owners could free slaves by verbal declaration before witnesses or by letter, or the slave herself could buy her freedom with money saved during her working life, or with a loan from a third party. The freeing of a slave by her master in order that he might marry her appears to have been common, although it was an opportunity denied to owners of senatorial rank. By an Augustan law a freedwoman married to her former master might not divorce him and marry a second time without his consent. It was also possible for a master to free his slave and live with her without going through a marriage ceremony: any children of the union would be illegitimate and take their mother's status, but this type of stable relationship, known as concubinage, was recognised, even encouraged, by Roman law. Concubinage allowed those unable to marry by law, such as soldiers, to have a long-term relationship, but might also be used when the girl's family was unable to raise a dowry. A married man was forbidden to keep a concubine and it was frowned upon for a bachelor to keep more than one.

Alternatively, a freedwoman, and on rare occasions a free woman, could live as a courtesan, whereby she was kept by a man but did not live under his roof. Courtesans were expected to register with the magistrates like common prostitutes, but were regarded as being of higher social standing. Most courtesans lived with their mothers or sisters and were considered to be cultured, well-read women. For obvious reasons it is impossible to estimate how many men in Roman Britain kept mistresses or even how many preferred to support a concubine rather than a wife.

Not all freedwomen were linked to their former masters by sex or marriage. By law a freed person was tied to their previous owner by a new relationship: that of patron and client. A patron was *tutor legitimus* to his freedwomen and could thus ensure that they died intestate, whereby he was entitled to first claim on their estates, over and above any children they might bear. If the patron allowed his freedwomen to make wills then he had little claim if they left him no part of their estates. Freedwomen, like freedmen, could become very wealthy, particularly if their patron set them up in business. Women could learn skills such as spinning, weaving, midwifery, metalworking and other crafts whilst a slave, and continue to practise their crafts after manumission. There was some argument as to whether a former slave could set up in business in direct competition with her owner, but the jurist Papinian was of the opinion that 'a freedwoman is not considered ungrateful because she practises her trade against the wishes of her patron'.[21] Exactly how many freedwomen set themselves up in business in Britain in unknown but there is a possibility that a number of crafts were carried out by either self-employed women or paid workers (see chapter 3). Collectives may also have been established, although there is no evidence that women in Britain, unlike those in Gaul, either formed guilds or joined them. In the other provinces there are a number of references to freedwomen joining the professions as doctors, accountants or librarians – opportunities not easily open to free women.

A freedwoman need not necessarily leave her master's household on gaining her freedom, and the majority appear to have continued to fulfil their old duties without a break and without any noticeable alteration to their lifestyle. Some even transferred to the heir's household on the death of their patron of their own free will, and it would seem from the many dedications of freedmen and freedwomen to their former masters and mistresses, and of patrons to freed clients, that many servants had an affectionate relationship with the families for whom they worked.

1. Birth, marriage and death

In Roman Britain, as for centuries before, the pattern of a woman's life was preordained. No matter what her social standing or ethnic origins might be, birth, puberty, marriage, children, the menopause, old age and death were the seven stages of female life which she was expected to follow and could do little to avoid.

A baby girl took her father's status if she was legitimate and her mother's if she was not, this status being determined at the moment of conception in the case of a child conceived in wedlock, but at the time of birth in the case of an illegitimate child. If the mother was of slave status and belonged to her owner at the time of giving birth then the child was deemed to belong to the owner, who could either rear her, sell her, or otherwise dispose of her, as he wished. If the mother happened to be free at the time of the birth, then her offspring would be born free.

Various rites surrounded a birth, one of which, according to Soranus,[1] was the laying of the new-born child on the earth and allowing it to cry for a while, before being washed and swaddled. The Germans, Scythians and some Greeks had a tougher attitude, condemned by Soranus, of plunging the baby into cold water in the belief that those who became livid or convulsed were not worth rearing.[2] Soranus also mentioned various superstitious beliefs surrounding the cutting of the umbilical cord, and it might be presumed from anthropological parallels that the native Britons had their own procedures and superstitions surrounding the birth of a girl.

A Roman family would name a girl on the eighth day and a boy on the ninth and the ceremony would be accompanied by rites of purification. During the Republic a Roman woman had only one name, the family name, and she was distinguished from her sisters by the use of terms such as 'the elder' or 'the younger' or by the use of numbers: *prima*, *secunda*. By the time of the invasion of Britain Roman women had acquired two names, the first being the family name, and the second taken from her father's name – for example, Fabia Honorata, daughter of Fabius Honoratus, or Aurelia Victorina, daughter of Aurelius Victor. In Britain the family name (*nomen gentilicium*) was often derived from that of the emperor from whom the family had first received the citizenship. This accounts for the large numbers of Julias, Claudias, Aurelias, Aelias and Flavias recorded in the province: they were not necessarily related.

On marriage a Roman woman might take her husband's name in the genitive, but this was not inevitable in Britain, where we have records of Aelia Ammillusima, wife of Marcus Trojanius Augustinus; Afutianus (son of Bassus) and his wife, Flavia Baetica; and Aurelia Eglectiane, wife of Fabius Honoratus who, as we have seen, followed conservative Roman practice when naming her daughter. Even so, some women appear to have been identified simply as the wife of a man; an altar erected at High Rochester was dedicated by a woman who referred to herself merely as 'she who is married to Fabius'.

Most Celtic families had assorted names: Lurio, a German, had a sister called Ursa, a wife called Julia, and a son called Canio; and Limisius had a wife called Aicetuos and a daughter called Lattio. Other offspring took their names from their mother, for example: Tadius Exuperatus and his sister Tadia Exuperata took their family name from their mother, Tadia Vallaunius, and the other, presumably, from their father. A lead tablet from Bath gives the family tree of Uricalus: his wife Docilosa, his son Docilis, daughter Docilina, his brother Decentinus, and sister-in-law Alogiosa. Why the children took their name from their mother rather than their father in this case is unclear as there is no suggestion that they were illegitimate.

British families appear to have had more choice of names available to them and were more imaginative when naming their offspring than orthodox Roman families. Celtic names can often be translated, for example, Boudica, 'victory', Cartimandua, 'white filly', or Grata, 'welcome', but many make it difficult for us to be certain as to the gender of the person concerned. This difficulty seems to have led to problems at the time: the female who is recorded as 'Tancorix, a woman' on her tombstone has the full sympathy of the present female author who is also blessed with an ambiguous Celtic name.

Nicknames and pet-names were used by Romans and Celts alike, indeed many Roman names originated in a private nickname. In Britain a four-year-old at Corbridge is remembered as 'Ertola, properly called Vellibia', and the name 'Ahteha' may also have been a pet-name. Slaves and freed women were often given Greek names, although they were not all of Greek origin: for example, Calpurnia Trifosa, whose Greek name Trifosa means 'delicious', whilst her nomen, Calpurnia, is derived from the name of her husband and former owner.

A legitimate child was expected to be registered within thirty days of its birth, and by the second century AD it was possible to register an illegitimate child. A birth certificate was available on request. From then on the childhood years of a well-born daughter would be spent in play and education, but other children might be put to work at a very early age. In Italy slave children acted as companions for their richer playmates or had jobs on farms or in workshops from as young as five years. Even in freed or free families children would be expected to help in the family business or sent out to work. There is documentary evidence in Italy and Egypt for girls and boys being apprenticed to craftsmen at the age of twelve or thirteen, but only those of freed status or slaves: free-born girls, even from the poorest families, do not appear to have been trained for a career in any formal way.

Soranus stated that menstruation started at the age of fourteen in most cases, and recommended that girls should be prepared for this from the age of thirteen by daily baths, regular gentle exercise and massage, as well as having 'the mind diverted in every possible way'.[3] Economic factors, particular diet, will have affected the age of menarche, and Soranus listed several professions, such as those of singing and dancing, where the strenuous exercise hindered menarche altogether.[4]

Soranus also recognised the problems of pre-menstrual tension: 'one has to infer approaching menstruation from the fact that at the expected time of the period it becomes trying to move and there develops heaviness of the loins, sometimes pain as well, sometimes also a flush of the cheeks ... and in some cases approaching menstruation must be inferred from the fact that the stomach is prone to nausea and it lacks appetite'.[5] There was little understanding of the causes or mechanism of menstruation, due to the fact that the function of neither the ovaries nor the Fallopian tubes had been recognised, although Soranus dismissed his colleagues' opinion that menstruation was nature's way of purging the female body of noxious substances, recognising that 'conception does not take place without menstruation'.[6]

How women coped with their menstrual cycle is not a question which can be answered confidently. The medical writers gave copious advice as to what should be done if periods were too irregular, too frequent, too painful, too heavy or non-existent, but gave no practical advice on hygiene. Possibly they regarded this matter as a mother's responsibility and not worthy of comment. There are references to tampons of lamb's wool in connection with contraception and medical treatment but not for monthly use. A suggestion has been made that leather briefs (7) were used as protection (see p. 114), but it is more likely that a form of washable linen 'nappy' was used, as in nineteenth-century Europe. It is interesting that the old wives' tale that menstruating women should not bathe may have started with Soranus, who otherwise gave sensible advice ahead of his time.[7]

From the time of Augustus the minimum age of marriage for females under Roman law was twelve, but some girls went through a form of wedding ceremony earlier. Tacitus mentioned that 'a girl who has married before twelve will be a legitimate wife when she becomes twelve'.[8] Hopkins' analysis of inscriptions in Italy indicates that 8 per cent of pagan girls and 3 per cent of Christian girls in his sample were married before the age of twelve, and that Aurelia Philmatio, who married at the age of seven, was not unique.[9] In the provinces girls appear to have married later: Tacitus, in his discussion of the Germans, said 'the girls, too, are not hurried into marriage',[10] while Caesar commented that for a German 'to have intercourse with a woman below the age of twenty is considered perfectly scandalous'.[11] Romano-British tombsones have not proved to be as helpful as those in Italy in ascertaining the age at which girls produced their

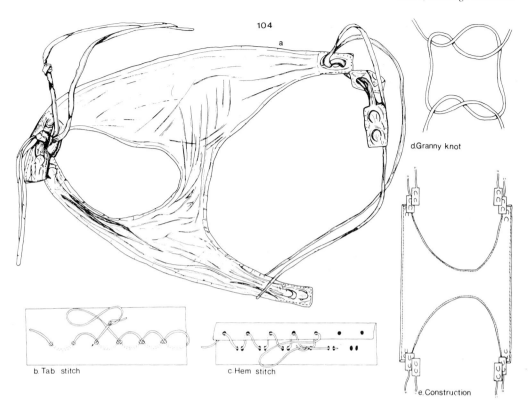

d.Granny knot

b.Tab stitch

c.Hem stitch

e.Construction

7. Drawing showing the construction of the leather briefs found in excavations at Queen's Street, London.

first child, but the majority indicate that girls usually postponed marriage until they were in their early to mid-twenties. Claudia Martina, at the age of nineteen, is the youngest wife so far known from a tombstone. Inscriptions, unfortunately, only give evidence for a particular level of society, but the skeletal evidence studied recently appears to produce a similar picture. At Poundbury Margaret Cox assumed from the age at which girls produced their first child that only 7.5 per cent of the female population had been married by the time they were seventeen, while 54 per cent had married by the time they reached twenty-one, and 62 per cent by the age of twenty-eight. This late age of first marriage and first child may have been due to economic conditions rather than moral traditions, with only the richer brides being able to marry in their teens, although an early marriage may have been seen to be 'the Roman thing to do'.

In wealthy families first marriages may have been arranged as in Rome, although a woman would have had more choice if she married a second time. An Italian mother had a duty to find her daughter a husband but how much say a Romano-British mother had in the choice of her daughter's husband, or

8. Jet plaque from Vindolanda
portraying a betrothed couple.

indeed how much say the bride had herself, is difficult to evaluate and may well
have depended on the characters of the people involved. In artisan circles and
among the freed, where dynastic considerations were of less moment, love and
lust will have played their usual part along with practical considerations such
as finance, and a proportion of the population may not have bothered with a
formal wedding ceremony at all. Slaves could only marry with their owner's
permission, although even then it was not regarded as a legal marriage: Senovara
could only call herself the wife of Cunitius as a courtesy title.

It was expected that a girl would be a virgin when she first married but that
her husband would not be. There was also a tendency for men to be much older

than their brides, particularly military men who were expected to wait until retirement in their forties before they married (see below, chapter 2). The marriage might be preceded by a formal betrothal ceremony at which both families made promises that the bride and groom would be married, and at which rings might be exchanged. There was no legal minimal age for betrothal: children could be betrothed from the cradle and there were many stories of men in Rome avoiding pressure to marry and father children by deliberately betrothing themselves to babies.

No religious ceremony was required to make a marriage binding or legal. The fact that a couple was married legally rather than simply cohabiting depended on whether there were witnesses or a written agreement that they intended to live as man and wife for the purposes of producing children. From the first century AD signed and witnessed marriage contracts became the norm, setting down the amount of dowry and other financial settlements, which facilitated matters should the marriage fail. In Rome the wedding was a civil ceremony performed at the bride's house, in which promises were exchanged and sacrifices made to the gods. Weddings did not become specifically religious in character until the acceptance of Christianity but it is possible that provincial marriages had a religious content. Unfortunately, nothing is known of the native British ceremonies, although it is likely that these differed from tribe to tribe.

Both the Romans and Celts were monogamous, although the wording of army retirement diplomas suggests that some cultures in the Empire recognised polygamy, and some foreigners in Britain may have had more than one wife. Of the Britons Julius Caesar noted that 'groups of ten or twelve men have wives together in common, and particularly brothers along with brothers, and fathers with sons, but the children born of the union are reckoned to belong to the particular house to which the maiden was first conducted'.[12] Caesar was not a trained anthropologist nor was he always reporting his own observations, but it is interesting that the idea that British women could have sex with male relatives other than their husbands was apparently still believed in Rome two centuries later, and that the Empress Julia Domna (15), when visiting Britain with her husband Septimius Severus, could still ask the wife of the Caledonian chieftain Argentocoxus 'about the free intercourse of her sex with men in Britain'. It is possible that the writers had misunderstood the situation and that, whereas under the Roman system a widow became technically the daughter of her new *pater familias*, under the Celtic tradition she became his wife, but in name only. Alternatively it has been suggested that the system followed was that of the Levirate, still practised in parts of modern Sudan, whereby widows capable of child-bearing are taken into the household of their husband's brother in order to keep the children within the tribal sub-group and to keep the family from dying out. This system has been practised throughout history by cultures where warfare resulted in many men dying young, leaving a high proportion of fertile widows. Whatever system was referred to one feels that Argentocoxus' wife got the best of the engagement in her reply to Julia Domna's impertinent question: 'we fulfil the demands of nature in a much better way than do you Roman women; for we consort openly with the best men, whereas you let yourselves be debauched in secret by the vilest' – a sly dig at the empress, whose private life was reputed to leave much to be desired.[13]

The subject of sex was openly discussed in Roman society before Christianity tightened its moral grip. Objects of domestic, religious or decorative purpose were often embellished with sexual imagery or scenes of sexual activity, reflecting the importance of fertility and its association with good fortune in Roman religious thought. The Roman sense of humour also contained much that was sexual or lavatorial. A number of writers provided information as to love-making positions, although invariably indicating that this advice was for the use of prostitutes and courtesans rather than respectable married women. The scenes of complex sexual positions decorating oil lamps and samian pottery, however, might indicate that married ladies were not ignorant of the possibilities.

Homosexuality between men was recognised to be common and was referred to many times in Roman law and literature, but female homosexuality was neither written about nor illustrated to any noticeable extent. Whether this reflects a lack of female homosexuality or simply indicates that lesbian activities were considered to be uninteresting by the classical writers or potters is not clear, but the latter is more likely to have been the case.

Soranus considered that the reason for marrying was to produce children and he suggested that women 'who digest their food easily, and have not loose bowels continually, who are of steady mind and cheerful' were the most likely to conceive.[14] Unfortunately, the Roman medical profession was not able to tell with any degree of certainty when a pregnancy had begun, nor was there any agreement as to the length of gestation. Aulus Gellius voiced the opinion that a child could be born after seven, nine or ten months, but never during the eighth month.[15] The difficulty of diagnosing pregnancy must also have been exacerbated by the number of women who, for dietary or other reasons, either had no periods at all or were very irregular.

Soranus included the care of the pregnant woman in his treatise on gynaecology, mentioning treatments for morning sickness and pica, that is the craving for 'things not customary, like earth, charcoal, tendrils of the vine, unripe and acid fruit'.[16] He listed the food which would benefit a pregnant woman and discouraged 'eating for two'. Gentle exercise was encouraged but he declared that 'sexual intercourse ... is always harmful to pregnant women'.[17] Miscarriages were commonplace and the wealthier women would secure the services of a midwife at an early stage to see them through pregnancy. The training and skill of midwives varied, and many rural women will have combined midwifery

9. Tombstone from Ostia, Italy, showing a woman in labour assisted by two midwives.

with witchcraft and the preparation of herbal medicines. Soranus gave instructions as to the attributes of the ideal midwife, which included short finger-nails and long fingers as well as strength of mind and body. Some midwives were slaves but the majority were freedwomen and several of Italian or Gallic origin are known by name.[18] The most superior were well-read women trained in many branches of female medicine who treated various gynaecological conditions in addition to pregnancy.

Home deliveries were the norm and were rarely under the supervision of a physician unless difficulties arose. Soranus advised that the prospective mother should lie on a bed during labour until the baby was ready to emerge, when she should be transferred to a special midwife's stool which had an opening in the seat. The midwife sat on a lower stool in front with an assistant behind the patient in case restraint was needed (9). Many of the contemporary medical writers' recommendations as to the correct procedures in complex deliveries might appal the modern reader, but it is impossible to generalise, as childbirth was an area where normal medical practices might be thrown to the winds to be replaced by magic and superstition. However, in Roman medicine the life of the mother was considered paramount, and in cases of difficulty the child was killed and dismembered in order to save the mother. Evidence for this practice in Britain has been found at Poundbury.

Death in childbed must have been all too common, and at Poundbury Margaret Cox has estimated that 51 out of 281 females (18 per cent) of child-bearing age had died shortly after childbirth. Lack of sterilised equipment and limited techniques will have resulted in a prevalence of uterine haemorrhage and gangrene, while crowded unhygienic facilities will have led to a high incidence of puerperal fever. The level of the midwife's personal hygiene would have been particularly significant.

A number of babies will have suffered trauma as the result of their rough treatment during birth and distressing malformations and deformities will often have resulted. Clear evidence of congenital disease is rarely found in skeletal remains as major abnormalities of the foetus will have resulted in miscarriage, stillbirth or infanticide. The minor malformations of *spina bifida occulta*, as opposed to the grosser form, have been found at Cirencester and York but probably had little effect on the lives of those with the condition. Ralph Jackson has suggested that dwarfism was more common than today as a result of intermarriage in small communities, but other congenital conditions may not have left any obvious trace on the skeleton.

Tacitus praised German women for breastfeeding their own offspring and implied that wealthy Roman women preferred to pass the responsibility on to wet-nurses.[19] Soranus was of the opinion that breastfeeding by the mother was to be recommended, although he believed that she should be allowed to rest for three weeks in order to regain her strength and that the baby should be breastfed by a wet-nurse in the intervening period. His list of essential virtues for the perfect wet-nurse include clear specifications as to the shape and condition of her breasts, physical condition and moral character, and he particularly recommended that she be a Greek 'so that the infant nursed by her may become accustomed to the best speech'.[20] He also recognised the danger of baby battering, as his strictures about wet-nurses being 'self-controlled, sympathetic, and not ill-tempered' was based on his fear that 'angry women are like maniacs and sometimes when the newborn cries from fear and they are unable to restrain it, they let it drop from their hands or overturn it dangerously'.[21]

Wet-nurses were slaves or freedwomen and their period of nursing could last as long as two years, during which time they might either live in the mother's

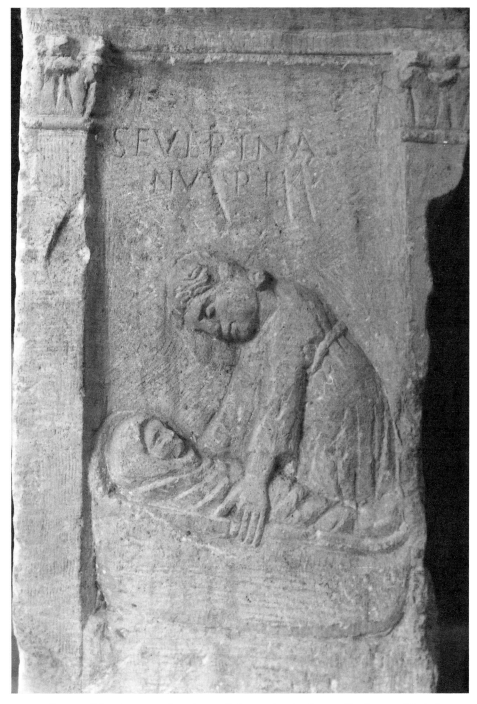

10. Tombstone of the wet-nurse, Severina, at Cologne, showing her tending her swaddled charge.

house or take the child into their own home. Wet-nurses often continued to look after the child after it had been weaned, and became respected members of the household. For nurse and mother alike Soranus was an indispensable guide, offering advice on weaning, teething, nappy rash and baby colds, and suggesting exercise by means of a 'little push-cart' and a chair on wheels to assist children in learning to walk.[22] Unfortunately his comments on potty training have not survived.

The evidence of tombstones suggests that Romano-British women did not produce large families compared with those in the medieval and post-medieval periods, who in similar circumstances and on a similar diet often produced as many as twenty or more offspring. The theory that the number of children a women bears leaves identifiable signs known as 'scars of parturition' has led a number of specialists to suggest that the skeletal evidence might indicate larger families, although few have suggested more than five children for any individual woman. Recently this theory has proved to be unreliable and estimates of fertility based on these measurements meaningless. This leaves us with the tombstone evidence and the number of babies' skeletons found in excavation, both of which seem to indicate a low birth rate.

It can be conjectured that this was not dependent on natural causes but that some form of contraception was being practised. Hopkins makes the sensible point that 'a general fall in fertility is a product of will plus technique, but the will is prior, if not to the discovery of contraceptives, at least to their use'.[23] If we accept that the women of Roman Britain had the will to limit the size of their families, what were the techniques available?

Aristotle, as early as the fourth century BC, had recommended cedar oil, white lead or frankincense smeared on the female genitals,[24] while Hippocrates suggested that women should drink *misy*, which was possibly dilute copper sulphate.[25] Pliny records 'a miracle: that is to rub it [cedar gum] all over the male part before coition prevents conception'.[26] He also recommended some antaphrodisiacs and treatments designed to cause impotence, but comments 'of all such preventives this only would it be right for me to mention to help those women who are so prolific that they stand in need of such respite'.[27]

Dioscorides in the first century AD put forward twenty prescriptions,[28] four of which are cautionary; three come under the heading of magic, such as asparagus used as an amulet; and seven are ineffective potions. Six of his recipes, however, contain elements which might have been effective to a greater or lesser degree. They are mostly mixtures applied to the genitals before coitus: peppermint with honey and water; cedar gum; axe-weed with honey; and alum, as well as two pessaries which may have hindered conception by blockage even though they contained no active spermicidal ingredient. Oribasius followed the same ideas as Dioscorides but added a pessary of cabbage to be applied after intercourse. Caelius Aurelianus, in the fifth century AD, endorsed an earlier

11. Tombstone of Flavia Augustina at York, the young wife of a military veteran. Both of their children died before their second birthday.

suggestion that the woman should hold her breath on receiving the semen.[29] Lucretius mentioned that a prostitute to avoid conception withdrew 'from the man's passion with her buttocks, and receives the moist fluid with all her breast relaxed. For thus she drives the furrow of the plough from the true direction of the path, and turns aside the blow of seeds from the vital parts'. 'But', he added, 'nought of this is seen to be needful for our wives'.[30] The only clear reference to the use of *coitus interruptus* occurs when Augustine lists it amongst the sexual perversions of the Manichees, and there is no evidence to suggest that it was practised as a contraceptive technique anywhere in the Roman Empire.

The best-known writer on the subject was Soranus, who appears to have researched contemporary practice with some thoroughness, as he cited fifty-nine medical authorities in his treatise on gynaecology. His sensible advice indicates that contraception was widely practised throughout the Empire and was not confined to prostitutes and perverted foreigners. He recommended avoiding intercourse at 'those periods which we said were suitable for conception',[31] that is, just after menstruation, advice still being given by Western doctors in the nineteenth century. He continued: 'and during the sexual act, at the critical moment of coitus when the man is about to discharge the seed, the woman must hold her breath, and draw herself away a little, so that the seed may not be hurled too deep into the cavity of the uterus. And getting up immediately and squatting down she should induce sneezing and carefully wipe the vagina all round; she might even drink something cold'.[32] Among his more practical suggestions were the use of vaginal pessaries, particularly wool soaked in honey, alum, white lead, or olive oil; and applications to both male and female genitals before coitus of cedar gum, vinegar, brine, or olive oil. These methods, if strictly followed, may have offered a degree of protection. The use of olive oil was still being advocated by Marie Stopes in 1931; in 1947 E. L. Koos revealed that the lower classes in New York City were relying on douches of water mixed with vinegar, lemon juice or alum; and lemons were still being used in parts of Glasgow as recently as the 1970s. Alum, vinegar and brine are all highly spermicidal and as such were recommended by Marie Stopes.

If the women of Roman Britain followed these efficacious methods there would have been a noticeable effect on the reproduction rate. However, they had no way of knowing which methods would work and which were useless: even Soranus was able to suggest sneezing whilst also recommending blocking the cervix. Pliny put forward several old wives' tales, and no doubt Britain had its share of old wives offering the amulets and potions of which Soranus spoke so scathingly. In matters of family planning a bride's mother would invariably have had advice to offer based on personal experience, as would friends and neighbours. The efficiency of a contraceptive, however, is not easily observable, and an individual's own fertility would affect their view of the matter. A couple might be convinced that their childless state was due to the woman carrying the dried uterus of a mule when in fact one or both of them might have low fertility. Another might argue that alum was useless on the grounds that they had used this method yet had six children, unaware of their own high fertility or their failure to adhere conscientiously to the method.

This confusion arose through a lack of knowledge of the physiological principles involved, particularly the difference between contraception and abortion. Soranus was perfectly clear: 'a contraceptive differs from an abortive for, the first does not let the conception take place, while the latter destroys what has been conceived'.[33] St John Chrysostom, on the other hand, in his *Epistle to the Romans*, admitted not knowing what to call a contraceptive, for it is 'something worse than murder . . . for it does not only destroy what is conceived but prevents it being conceived'.[34]

The Hippocratic Oath forbade abortion but eighteen of the medical writers mentioned it, of which fifteen gave methods. Soranus, for example, gave as much attention to abortion as he had previously given to contraception. His methods varied between being 'shaken by means of draught animals' to diuretic decoctions, poultices, baths in various substances such as a mixture of linseed, fenugreek, mallow, musk mallow and wormwood; and vaginal suppositories of wallflower, cardamom, brimstone, absinthium and myrrh in equal quantities with water. The *Digest* indicates no prohibition on abortion as such and although Septimius Severus passed a law which punished a wife who aborted without her husband's consent, it is clearly the deceit which is considered worthy of punishment not the act of abortion. In Roman law the foetus was seen as having neither a soul nor any individuality; its destruction, therefore, could not be murder, and although the sale of abortifacients was banned along with aphrodisiacs, it was under the law of poisons, because of the dangerous or lethal contents of some of the potions, rather than because of the moral issues involved.

In Rome abortion was an accepted form of birth control in fashionable circles but its use in the provinces is difficult to estimate. The Greeks dominated the medical profession throughout the Empire and all the medical men attested in Britain were of Greek extraction; so the methods of contraception and abortion described by Soranus and his fifty-nine sources are likely to have been familiar to their colleagues practising in Britain. There would also have been the backstreet practitioners who exist in every society to provide women with a way out of their difficulties. The methods listed above would all have been possible and available in Britain, particularly the use of bracken (*Pteris aquilina*), which Dioscorides avowed caused both childlessness and abortion,[35] while Pliny considered it to have antaphrodisiac qualities as well;[36] more exotic ingredients such as pomegranate seeds may have been imported. No doubt there were other native methods which went unrecorded in the medical literature.

A third method of controlling the size of families was infanticide. Soranus, in his section on how to recognise which babies were worth rearing, implies that those who failed the test should be disposed of.[37] His reasoning appears to have been based on purely medical grounds: he was concerned with those babies which were sickly or malformed. The literary evidence, on the other hand, indicates that babies were also exposed if they were not wanted for financial reasons. Plautus referred to the exposure of infants as a common occurrence,[38] and it was this practice which led to the alimentary schemes, or family allowances, for poor families in Rome which Pliny mentioned in his letters. Infanticide, however, was not confined to the lower classes. As the laws of inheritance divided an estate between the male children equally, a *pater familias* wishing to provide adequately for his offspring would keep his family small. Tacitus' comment in *Germania* that 'to restrict the number of children, or to kill any of those born after the heir, is considered wicked' carries the implication that it was not considered so in Rome.[39]

The number of infant burials found through excavations has led to the suggestion that infanticide was widely practised in Britain but the figures may not be significantly high. Comparisons between the archaeological evidence for Romano-British infant mortality and the statistics for other periods is complicated by the inaccurate use of terms such as 'perinatal' and 'neonatal' in archaeological reports and the lack of statistics for stillbirths before the Second World War. We tend to be biased in our opinion as to what is an acceptable death rate by modern figures: in 1975, for example, the perinatal mortality rate for England and Wales was 9.8 per thousand: that is, stillbirths and deaths within the first week; the neonatal rate (deaths within the first month) was 5.9 per thousand live births, and the infant mortality rate (deaths within the first year) was 9.4 per thousand live births. This reflects the recent advances in antenatal and postnatal care, but in 1920 the infant mortality rate in Bradford was 93 per thousand live births with no record of the number of stillbirths. The London Bills of Mortality for 1762–71 show that 66 per cent of children died before their fifth birthday, with 75 per cent of those dying before the age of two. Brothwell has recorded that 49 out of 328 burials (14.9 per cent) at the Dark Age site of Cannington were under a year old at death compared with 23 out of 174 burials (13.2 per cent) in the medieval period at Wharram Percy. Boon compared an infant mortality rate of 20–25 per cent at Roman Silchester with the rate of 11.6 per cent in England and Wales in the 1970s, but if the archaeological evidence includes the bones of stillborn children while the early statistics exclude them then we might conclude that a Romano-British baby's chances of survival were not too bad. Deliberate infanticide remains a possibility but there may be no more infants' skeletons than can be accounted for by natural events.

It was the excavation of Hambledon villa which produced the most emotive report of infanticide. Cocks recorded that 'the ground, roughly speaking throughout the northern half, was positively littered with babies. They number 97 and most of them are newly born, but an occasional one is rather older. A few were laid at length but the majority were evidently carried and buried wrapped in a cloth or garment, huddled in a little bundle, so that the head was almost central and the knee above it ... As nothing marked the position of these tiny graves, a second little corpse was sometimes deposited on one already in occupation of a spot, apparently showing that these interments took place secretly, after dark. The majority of the babies lay in the yard, north of the 3rd House'.

On the evidence of Barton Court Farm, where forty-one babies were buried in a separate area, we may now see the yard at Hambledon as the official infant cemetery. There is certainly no evidence for the burials being in any way illicit. The implication, made explicit elsewhere, is that the babies were illegitimate and were being disposed of by their mothers to avoid scandal. We do not, however, know whether illegitimacy carried any stigma in Roman Britain, nor is it likely that a girl could give birth in a rural community without the fact being widely known – that ninety-seven should do so stretches the imagination too far. Frere has suggested that the babies were the unwanted result of slave liaisons, but as slaves were marketable commodities it is more likely that an owner who did not wish to go to the expense of rearing a slave child would sell it on the open market. Mercatilla, for example, who died at the age of one year, six months, and twelve days, and is described as the freedwoman and foster-daughter of Magnius, may well have changed hands in this manner. Columella was of the opinion 'that [slave] women who are unusually prolific ... ought to be rewarded'.[40]

The discovery of an infant under the ramparts of the town at Winchester, as well as in the ramparts and ditches of other town sites, confirms that although Roman law forbade burial within city limits, children of less than forty days were exempt. The babies buried at Catsgore in stone-lined cists within the buildings or under the eaves had been interred with some ceremony and effort, and it can be argued that shaft burials were intended to help a child into the next world rather than that babies were sacrificed to sanctify the shafts or simply tipped down a handy rubbish pit. Several infant burials at Barton Court Farm, Winterton, Rudston and Catsgore were accompanied by animal skeletons, either dogs or sheep: further evidence that inhumation ceremonies were being carried out in a proper manner. It is more than possible that the funerary rites for a neonatal or perinatal child differed from those of an adult or even older children. The establishment of the infants' cemetery at Barton Court Farm might support this hypothesis, whilst the evidence at Trentholme Drive, York, which led the excavators to conclude that it was not the custom to inter neonatals at all, may also indicate that such infants had their own burial plot so far undiscovered.

The tendency for archaeologists to excavate only the buildings on villa sites may have overemphasised the incidence of infant burials compared to those of adults, who would be more likely to have been buried further afield. It is not known how many years or how many fertile women the ninety-seven babies at Hambledon represent. It is possible that this is not an excessive number of natural fatalities given an establishment of reasonable size over a number of generations. At Bradley Hill a preponderance of female infants has been taken as proof that girls were not regarded as worth rearing, but Bradley Hill is unusual: the majority of sites show a closer correlation to the natural ratio of births between the sexes: 106 males to 102 females. The ratio of infant burials to adult burials tends to remain constant throughout the south of England.

The burial of babies in or close to a dwelling may be because there was no legal obligation for them to be buried elsewhere – there is, after all, no legal requirement in Britain today for a stillborn child to be buried – or because they were regarded as being in some way attached to the house. Soranus mentions that a new-born baby should be laid immediately on the earth, a ritual which implies that the child was being introduced to the household gods or dedicated to one of the fertility goddesses.[41] If a baby died whilst the mother was still lying in or before it was weaned it is conceivable that it was judged to belong to the spirits of hearth and home: the connection between infant burials and hearths at Catsgore and Rudston should be noted here, and it may have been considered detrimental to the household if the baby was buried elsewhere. The discovery of domestic infant burials in pre-Roman contexts at Kingsdown Camp, Rotherley and Baldock suggests the continuation of belief from the Iron Age. There is also a marked geographical bias: the settlement sites in the north of England and Scotland do not produce infant burials and the more northerly villas contain intramural infant burials from the first to the fourth centuries, while the southern sites show a gap between the first and the fourth centuries. This may confirm that tribal traditions were a major factor in infant burial practices. The resurgence of infant burial in the fourth century may reflect the changes in religious thought in Britain linked to the spread of Christianity.

If a couple remained childless other than by design they could adopt or foster a child. According to Roman law only men could adopt and if this was done by *adrogatio*, that is by a legislative act, then the child had the rights of a legitimate child, but this was not recognised as a procedure in the adoption of girls. If the child was taken into the household without legal arrangements being made then she retained her status at birth. A number of children are recorded as being fostered in Britain, for example Mercatilla, foster-daughter of Magnius; Hyllus[42] at York; Hermagoras in the household of the tribune Honoratus;[43] and Ylas, 'dearest foster child' of Claudius Severus.[44] Their names appear to attest to their slave or freed status.

Childlessness was regarded as grounds for divorce and, except in cases of obvious male impotence, a barren marriage was blamed on the wife. Divorce was permissible on specified grounds only, all of which involved an offence committed by one of the partners. In the case of a wife's adultery divorce was obligatory, otherwise her husband was considered to condone the act and so lost any claim to the dowry as well as making himself liable to prosecution as his wife's pimp. Insanity was not grounds for divorce; on the contrary, if a woman was declared insane she could not divorce her husband, nor could her family obtain a divorce on her behalf.

By the first century AD divorce was not a difficult procedure technically. As the marriage had been formed by the two parties consenting to the match, so it could be dissolved by either the husband or wife renouncing their commitment. The only exception was a freedwoman married to her previous owner, who could not obtain a divorce without his consent. The dowry reverted to the wife's family on divorce but the husband could claim for retentions; for example, he was allowed a sixth of the sum to compensate him for his wife's alleged misconduct. It was essential to the woman's chances of a second marriage for the dowry to be returned intact, and there were several cases in Italy of a *pater* dissolving his daughter's marriage in order to reclaim the dowry or to avoid paying the final instalment. If the original marriage contract had been vague or if claims were made by either side to the household property, each could resort to the courts and one imagines that in the ensuing legal wrangle the divorce lawyers did very well for themselves.

Any children of the marriage were the financial responsibility of the husband, including a child born after the divorce. It was possible, however, for a mother

12. Betrothal rings from Richborough and Thetford, both with the clasped-hands motif.

to claim custody and have the children live with her. In this case her former husband was expected to pay maintenance for the children. His *potestas* remained inviolable. The husband was not responsible for his former wife's maintenance as she reverted to being her *pater*'s responsibility.

Loss of citizenship or enslavement resulted in the dissolution of a legal marriage without the need for divorce. If the husband joined the army the marriage was also regarded as null and void by the authorities although not necessarily by the partners involved (see p. 60). This latter stipulation will have affected a number of British families when the father was conscripted.

The majority of the medical writers state that the menopause occurred between the ages of forty and fifty, although Soranus extended the upper limit to sixty and Oribasius pushed the onset down to the early thirties. The latter recognised a correlation between the ages of menarche and menopause resulting in a set period of fertility for all women.[45] There was little written about the changes associated with menopause, possibly because most doctors were more concerned with the problems of fertile women, or because many of the symptoms of menopause were seen as a continuation of earlier problems or as psychological disturbances. Galen, for example, considered that hysteria, in its original meaning of 'affections of the womb', might often have a psychological cause.[46]

Other female ailments discussed in contemporary literature include inflammation of the uterus and vagina, prolapse of the uterus, closure of the womb and breast complaints. There were specialists in breast disorders of which mastitis and tumours are likely to have been the most common. There is little evidence for cancer of the breast, cervix or ovaries being major causes of death in the Roman period but identifying specific diseases from ancient descriptions can be fraught with difficulties.

Medical problems might be treated by diet, medicines to be taken internally or applied externally, or by fumigation with the vapours being introduced into the nostrils or vagina. In many cases the treatment may have been worse than the illness. A number of medical instruments, such as the vaginal speculum (13) and the uterine clyster, were designed specially to treat female complaints.

The complaints of old age are most easily recognisable in bone assemblages and osteo-arthrosis was prevalent: over 80 per cent of the adults at Cirencester, for example, showed signs of osteo-arthrosis, with more women affected than men. The implication that women led an active life with a great deal of lifting and physical exertion which took its toll in later life is supported by the appearance of nodules on the vertebrae which are the result of using the spine in carrying out heavy tasks. The higher incidence of arthritis in the neck among the female population of Cirencester has been interpreted as the result of carrying heavy weights, such as water pots, on their heads, while 'squatting facets', that is the development of impressions on bones at the front of the ankle joint which develop in people who spend an appreciable amount of time in a

13. Copy of the vaginal speculum found in Pompeii: dilation of the cervix was an approved treatment for hysteria.

squatting position, were more often found in the women at Trentholme Drive cemetery in York, suggesting that they spent long hours squatting over cooking fires or at their other work. Considering this evidence for an active lifestyle few female skeletons show fractures, although a woman at York with a badly healed right femur would have had a pronounced limp. This female showed a peculiar variation in her lumbar vertebrae which has tentatively been associated with her being a professional acrobat.

Osteoporosis will have been common among women of post-menopausal age but may not have become apparent in the skeleton unless they reached their sixties. The skeletons of the Lankhills cemetery, at Winchester, show variation in the survival rate of male and female skeletons which might indicate that the bones of elderly osteoporosis sufferers simply crumbled, leaving few recognisable traces.

Identifiable fatal diseases are difficult to recognise. Tuberculosis and leprosy may have been rife but so far only one skeleton, at Poundbury, has provided evidence for leprosy in Roman Britain. This cemetery also produced an example of Pott's disease, which is a result of tuberculosis, and other examples have been found at York and Cirencester. Venereal diseases, such as syphilis, may have been known, although the evidence is by no means convincing and descriptions of symptoms which might be identified as syphilis could be mistaken for other conditions, such as uro-genital tuberculosis. Certainly none of the classical writers warn the sexually active of potential medical dangers and it would appear that none were known.

Plagues regularly broke out in various parts of the Empire and are recorded as killing thousands of people. The effect of such outbreaks on the population of Roman Britain escaped comment by contemporary writers, although John Wacher has attributed the breakdown of town life in the immediate post-Roman period to pestilence, among other causes. As there was little understanding of the mechanism of disease it is probable that any epidemic would take its toll, particularly of the very young and the elderly. Complaints which modern science takes in its stride would often have proved fatal.

14. Pottery cup from South Shields, used for feeding infants and invalids.

Diet was a contributing factor to disease, particularly in the winter months when fresh fruit and vegetables were in short supply. The lavish meals and heavy consumption of alcohol of the upper classes would have resulted in their suffering from the 'executive' ailments of heart attacks, high blood pressure, ulcers and liver complaints. A diet rich with garlic, onions, wine and fish sauces would also have resulted in a high incidence of halitosis. At the other end of the social scale the diseases and deformities of the malnourished would have been prevalent, for example night blindness due to a lack of animal fats and oils, scurvy as a result of the lack of vitamin C, and rickets and osteomalacia from a deficiency of vitamin D in dairy foods and fish-liver oils. Poor diet would also have led to a tendency to catch diseases, with fewer reserves to aid healing. At all levels of society hygienic storage would always have been a problem and food poisoning a common complaint. Analysis of material from the sewers at York shows the inhabitants to have been riddled with worms and bowel parasites.

The use of stone to mill flour led, inevitably, to grit in the bread which wore down the teeth and exposed the pulp, but on the whole the diet was good for the teeth and dental caries was less widespread than today. Most skeletal assemblages reveal a parity between the sexes except at Bradley Hill, where the dental health of the inhabitants was particularly bad, but where the women's teeth were consistently in better condition than the men's. This may reflect a practice, common in many primitive societies, of the women eating a plainer diet with fewer sugars – the choicer, less healthy food being reserved for the men.

The life expectancy of a Romano-Briton has been the subject of many papers. Unfortunately the recent research in forensic pathology has indicated that the age of many skeletons over thirty-five has been wrongly assessed and as a result the statistics for adult deaths are inaccurate. The suggestion that few women survived past thirty-five or forty is likely to be a considerable underestimate, so further discussion of this topic awaits the improvement of scientific techniques. The evidence of the funerary inscriptions, however, shows a general spread of age groups with several women, such as Tadia Vallaunius and Julia Secundina living to sixty-five and seventy-five, while Claudia Crysis lived to the ripe old age of ninety. There may, however, be some evidence from Poundbury for a high death-rate among adolescent girls, suggesting that, contrary to natural expectations, Romano-British women did not live as long as their menfolk.

2. Women and the army

The women with military associations came from every social stratum and every province of the Empire but the most important woman in Britain at any one time would be an empress who accompanied her husband to the province. The number of emperors who brought their wives to Britain is uncertain but there is literary evidence to suggest that it was the norm for wives and children to be included in the imperial entourage: even Augustus had 'travelled to west and east with Livia as his companion'.[1] Sabina, for example, may have been resident in Britain whilst Hadrian inspected the frontier, as his biographer seems to hint that an unsavoury incident between the empress and Septicius Clarus, prefect of the guard, and Suetonius Tranquillus, 'director of imperial correspondence', occurred in Britain.[2] It was, however, Julia Domna (15), the Syrian wife of Septimius Severus, who made the most impact during her state visit whilst the imperial court was established at York during the Scottish campaigns. For once Britain was the centre of the Roman Empire rather than on the fringes, and contemporary reliefs show that the empress's hairstyle, clothes and manners were carefully copied by British womanhood. None of the other empresses are mentioned by name in connection with Britain, although it is reasonable to suppose that the governors of Britain who proclaimed themselves Emperor – Clodius Albinus, Carausius and his finance minister Allectus, and Magnus Maximus – would have had their wives by their side. The women's part in these rebellions is not recorded. In the later years of Roman rule several Britons became emperors of the Western Empire and the mothers, sisters and wives of Gratian and Constantine III may have had a considerable influence on the life of the province.

For 170 years after becoming a province of the Roman Empire Britain had a single governor who was recognised as a delegate of the Emperor with the rank of propraetor. The governorship of Britain was one of the most important posts and reserved for senior men of senatorial rank, ex-consuls. The post-holder was supreme commander of the army of occupation as well as the chief justice of the province, and in the absence of the empress his wife would be First Lady. There had been some debate in Rome in AD 21 as to whether wives should be allowed to accompany governors to provinces, as there had been some unfortunate incidents in the past. Caecina Severus had moved that 'no magistrate who had been allotted a province should be accompanied by his wife as 'there was point in the old regulation which prohibited the dragging of women to the provinces or foreign countries; in a retinue of ladies there were elements apt, by luxury or by timidity, to retard the business of peace or war and to transmute

15. Painting of the Emperor Septimius Severus with his wife, Julia Domna, and his children, Caracalla and Geta. Geta's face was erased after his murder by his brother in AD 212.

a Roman march into something resembling an Eastern procession. Weakness and a lack of endurance were not the only failings of the sex: give them scope and they turned hard, intriguing, ambitious. They paraded among the soldiers, they had the centurions at beck and call. Recently a woman [Plancina] had presided at the exercises of the cohorts and the manoeuvres of the legions'.[3] Despite this argument most governors continued to be accompanied by their wives, although a *senatus consultum* of AD 24 made a governor accountable for his wife's behaviour in the province.

One of the few governor's wives known by name to have resided in Britain is Pomponia Graecina, wife of Aulus Plautius, the leader of the invasion force of AD 43. She was accused years later of practising a nameless foreign religion which she was supposed to have discovered whilst in Britain, a slander which could hardly have become widespread if she had never been to the country. Domitia Decidiana, wife of Agricola, is not mentioned in connection with Britain, but Tacitus records that in AD 84, that is after being governor for six years, Agricola 'suffered a grievous personal loss in the death of a son who had been born a year before',[4] so that her presence must be presumed. Other wives may also be assumed on such tenuous evidence but they have not left their names, although we know that Pompeius Falco's wife had been the granddaughter of Agricola's predecessor, Julius Frontinus, and must have been familiar with Britain from childhood.

The first governors were Italian and probably had Italian wives, but over the years governors of Gallic, Spanish, Numidian and African origins were appointed who may have married in their home provinces or during the travels which were part of any senatorial career. A tour of duty could last up to seven years but the average was three; it was the Emperor Tiberius who extended the service period and by the end of his reign the governor's wife had become a recognised member of the provincial hierarchy. Her duties are unspecified but most will have accompanied their husbands on official visits and acted as the hostess at functions. Of the wife of C. Galenius, governor of Egypt, it was said that she would accept no petitions, would admit no provincials to her house, and was never seen in public – behaviour which was regarded as unusual as well as intolerably snobbish. Although unable to wield any official power a woman of character might be able to influence her husband and political events; one only has to think of the great political hostesses of the eighteenth and nineteenth centuries. This possibility had already been recognised, as it was generally considered improper for a governor's wife to accept favours or presents from client princes, and she had to take care that her behaviour did not jeopardise her husband's professional impartiality. Juvenal criticised those women who 'with unflinching face and dry breasts' participated in male discussions of politics and military activities.[5]

A large building on the river terrace in the area of Cannon Street station in London has been suggested as the governor's palace, built about AD 80. It seems to have had a large central courtyard with a fountain and an ornamental pool, and small rooms or offices ranged along its east wing. None of the reception rooms or the living quarters of the governor's family have been uncovered. It has also been suggested that the palatial villa at Fishbourne, built at the same time, was not occupied by the native king Cogidubnus as previously thought, but was the summer residence of the governor's family.

Around AD 197 Britain was divided into two provinces: Britannia Superior and Britannia Inferior, each with a governor, so there were now two 'First Ladies', none of whom, regrettably, are known by name. London continued to be the capital of Britannia Superior while York is likely to have been the capital of Britannia Inferior, with the legionary legate promoted to governor. The governor's *praetorium* in York, or indeed the residence used by the Severi as the imperial court, has not been found although a large building under the Old Station Yard may form part of it.

The reorganisation of the Empire by Diocletian led to further subdivision of Britain into Britannia Prima, Britannia Secunda, Maxima Caesariensis and Flavia Caesariensis, all governed by *praesides* of equal equestrian rank, although Maxima Caesariensis may have been promoted later, as there is a reference to a consular governor in the *Notitia Dignitatum*. Lincoln and Cirencester have been sugested as the capitals of the two extra provinces. About AD 370 a fifth province was created, called Valentia, with a possible capital at Carlisle. Unfortunately, nothing is known of the wives and daughters of any of these later governors, few of whom, indeed, are themselves known by name.

A governor of Britain was in charge of the army and responsible for justice in his province but had no control over finances. This was in the hands of an *equites* called the imperial procurator. One of these, Gaius Julius Alpinus Classicianus, died in Britain and was commemorated by his wife, Julia Pacata. Classicianus was a Gaul who succeeded Decianus Catus as procurator in AD 61, during the Boudican revolt. His wife was the daughter of Julius Indus, a famous Treveran noble, who had distinguished himself fighting on Rome's side in Gaul in AD 21. Both were, therefore, members of the new provincial aristocracy which had begun to play its part in the administration of the growing Empire. It is to be regretted that we know so little about Julia Pacata as she was clearly a woman of some courage, accompanying her husband to a province in the throes of a major and very bloody rebellion. Possibly she returned to Gaul after her husband's death.

Under the command of the governor were the legionary commanders known as legates, who were of senatorial rank. Of the 127 legates presumed to have been in office from AD 86 to 213, only twenty can be identified, and even fewer of their wives. At York the altar dedicated to Fortuna by Sosia Juncina is the only record of herself and her husband, Quintus Antonius Isauricus, legate of the VIth Legion. This has been dated to before AD 213, as after this date the legate would have been referred to as governor.

The legionary legates must have spent much of their time campaigning during the earlier decades of Roman rule, and their wives would have been expected to follow the drum and live in the *praetoria* of the legionary fortresses. Those at Caerleon, Chester and York must certainly have had legates' wives residing at various stages, but even the more temporary installations, such as Inchtuthill, may well have seen the families of legates at times. Of the legionary vexillation

16. View of High Rochester, home to Julia Lucilla and her husband, Rufinus, showing the bleakness of the countryside surrounding the fort.

fortresses only Longthorpe has been excavated to any extent, but the discovery of ear-rings and other female paraphernalia shows some women to have been in residence in the first century AD.

Anthony Birley has estimated that the number of equestrian officers serving in Britain at any one time must have been at least sixty, including prefects and tribunes. He has further calculated that more than five thousand men could have served as equestrian officers during the first two and a half centuries of Roman rule. Not all of these men will have married, nor of those married would the majority have had daughters, but the potential number of women of equestrian rank in Britain is still high. A few of these *equites*, such as Statius Priscus,[6] may have been born in Britain but the majority came from the other provinces. Equestrian officers were usually in their twenties or thirties, with either the necessary property qualification themselves or wealthy patrons to buy them commissions.

Two of the earliest fort commanders' wives to be known by name are Sulpicia

Lepidina, wife of Flavius Cerialis, the prefect of a cohort of Batavians, and her friend (or sister) Claudia Severa, wife of Aelius Brocchus. Cerialis was the senior officer at Vindolanda and we can be confident that Lepidina lived in the *praetorium* there as early as AD 100–5. This building was of timber and occupied a position on the eastern side of the south section of the *via principalis*. The lives of these women might be compared with those of the colonel's wives on the north-west frontier of India in the nineteenth century, or the American Midwest. The picture is one of some discomfort, a certain amount of danger and a great deal of boredom and loneliness. There would be few women in the immediate area of the fort in the first century AD other than the domestic staff of the *praetorium*, and certainly none of the same class as the commanding officer's wife, so a visit to another fort must have been eagerly anticipated.

Many of the females commemorated on tombstones or other inscriptions may have been the wives or daughters of commanding officers: Aurelia Romana and her sister Sabina, for example, were probably the daughters of the prefect at Greta Bridge, while Anthony Birley has suggested that Vettia Mansueta and her daughter Claudia Turianilla were the wife and daughter of the commanding officer at Carvoran. Two women who are known to have been married to senior military men are worth discussing in some detail: Aurelia Eglectiane and Julia Lucilla. Aurelia Eglectiane was the wife of Fabius Honoratus, the tribune of the 1st Cohort of Vangiones, a large infantry unit, at Chesters in the late second century. The family is known from a tombstone, possibly post-dating AD 161, mourning the death of their 'most sweet' daughter, Fabia Honorata. The age of the child is not given but the phrase 'most sweet' was usually reserved for toddlers. The *praetorium* in which they lived was placed between the head-quarters building (*principia*) and the east gate. Part of this building was exca-vated in the nineteenth century and found to have had a roughly built hypocaust heating system and a separate bath suite.

More is known of Julia Lucilla from her husband's tombstone and their freedman's altar to Silvanus Pantheus. She refers to herself as '*clarissima*', that is, of senatorial rank, although this was not strictly true as her husband was only an equestrian and she would have lost rank on her marriage. Her husband, Rufinus, had been prefect of the 1st Cohort of Lusitanians and also of the 1st Cohort of Breuci, before taking over the command of the 1st Cohort of Vardulli at High Rochester north of Hadrian's Wall. The date of his command is not known but may have corresponded with the Severan campaigns at the end of the second century and the early years of the third. His career had also included the sub-curatorship of the Flaminian Way and Doles, as well as the sub-curatorship of Public Works, and it was possibly during this term of office in Rome that he met his wife.

Julia Lucilla's life at the outpost fort of High Rochester (16) illustrates how the wives of officers often found themselves in the military arena, living in remote areas far from civilisation. The exposed position of High Rochester and the unsettled nature of the surrounding countryside would have meant that she would have been unable to venture far on her own – even the soldiers' bath-house was inside the fort walls. We know that her household included a slave called Eutychus, who may have been freed by her husband's will and who refers to his 'dependants' in his dedication to Silvanus Pantheus. The name Eutychus is Greek, which may or may not reflect his origins, and it is likely that he and his wife and children had accompanied Rufinus and Julia Lucilla on their journey from Rome rather than having been inherited from the previous commanding officer. Little is known of the *praetorium* at High Rochester in which all these people lived except its probable position by the west gate.

When Rufinus died at the age of forty-eight he was buried in the cemetery outside the fort where other officers' stone-built tombs have been uncovered. Julia Lucilla will not have been the only soldier's wife to have buried her husband in a foreign land, nor Aurelia Eglectiane the only mother to have left behind a child buried in a military cemetery. It is probable that Julia Lucilla went back to her family in Rome when she was widowed but it is not known whether widows and orphans were expected to find their own way home or if the army made any provision. As the *praetorium* was a 'tied house' a widow would have had to remove herself and her household before the next incumbent took office, and this may have caused difficulties on occasion.

The best known of the fort *praetoria* is at Housesteads (17) although, unfortunately, none of the women who lived there are known by name. The building began as an L-shaped structure but was later extended to the more common courtyard plan. The kitchen, with a large oven, was in the north-east corner, and a bath suite was inserted into the north range some time in the second century. Several of the rooms were heated by hypocausts and there was a lavatory in the west range. It has been suggested that the eastern end of the south range contained stabling with servants' quarters above. The courtyard form of *praetoria* was established throughout the Empire and reflected middle/upper-class housing plans in Italy. The *praetorium* at Housesteads seems to have been comfortable and the mistress of such a house would have had little to complain about as far as her quarters were concerned.

Both the legions and the auxiliary units relied on their centurions, each of whom was in direct command of eighty men. Most centurions had risen from the ranks although there were exceptions. The post offered a permanent job with no compulsory age of retirement and a steady, substantial salary. They were, on the whole, intelligent men who had some education and were capable of dealing with paperwork. They were often transferred from legion to legion and province to province as situations developed which required men of experience, and as they had always been allowed to marry, their wives must have been among the most travelled women in the Empire. Several are known by name

17. Housesteads fort from the air. The courtyard house of the Commanding Officer's family is just inside the south gate, while outside are the excavated inns and shops of the *vicus*. Houses and other buildings can be made out as rectangular marks in the ground outside the gates and above the cultivation terraces.

who visited Britain fleetingly: Claudia Marcia Capitolina, whose husband had served with the VIth Victrix at York before being transferred to Arabia with the IIIrd Cyrenaica and whose son had been born whilst they were resident in York; and Salviena Metiliana, whose husband, born in Cologne, died at Lambaesis in Algeria after a tour of duty in Britain, possibly at Housesteads. Such women thought little of packing their belongings and taking their children across continents. Papyri from Egypt suggest that it was common for centurions to go on ahead when they were transferred, leaving their wives to arrange for the transport of the goods and chattels. One can imagine that these were redoubtable women who stood no nonsense and could deal with any situation.

As the centuries of infantry were commanded by centurions so the twenty-four or sixteen *turmae* of a cavalry *ala* were commanded by decurions. Only one decurion's wife is known by name: Aelia Comindus, wife of Nobilianus, who died at the age of thirty-two at Carrawburgh. Luckily more information is available about the families of centurions. The most senior centurion's wife about whom we have any evidence in Britain may have been Januaria Martina, whose husband, Vivius Marcianus of the IInd Legion Augusta, may have been *princeps praetorii*, that is a centurion of senior rank who was the chief administrator in the governor's headquarters. Certainly his tombstone at London shows him to have been a man of some consequence. Aurelius Super, centurion of the VIth Legion, who died at York at the age of thirty-eight, may also have been a senior man to judge by the elaborate coffin paid for by his widow, Aurelia Censorina.

A woman of possibly African origins, Vibia Pacata, was married to Flavius Verecundus, centurion of the VIth Legion Victrix, whose own birthplace appears to have been in Pannonia (modern Hungary). How this couple of widely divergent origins met and what they thought of their posting at Westerwood, on the Antonine Wall, is unknown, but this perhaps serves to emphasise the travels of centurial families and that foreign women were to be found as far north as the Antonine Wall. Other centurions, such as Aurelia ...illa's husband Gracilis, came from Upper Germany to lead auxiliary units. He held a commission with the XXIInd Legion which was never stationed in Britain. The legion of Flavia Baetica's husband, Afutianus son of Bassus, is not recorded, nor is his place of origin, only that he was centurion of the 2nd Cohort of Tungrians at Birrens.

The centurion resided in the suite of rooms at the end of each barrack block but it is not clear whether his wife and family lived there as well or had accommodation outside the fort. Some of the more exposed forts had no external settlement and provision must have been made for housing the centurial families within the walls. The centurion's quarters were not small, often measuring 20 to 30 feet (6–9 m) square internally, and would have been considered adequate for family housing.

The tombstone of Marcus Aurelius Nepos, centurion of the XXth Legion Valeria Victrix, shows his wife as if standing a few paces behind him in an unusually subordinate position. Her name is not known – a space left for it was never filled. Possibly she remarried or moved away, and again one questions what happened to centurions' and decurions' widows. They would have been even less able to finance their own transport back home than the wives of commanding officers and one wonders where they would feel home to be after a lifetime of travel. Possibly they gravitated to the *vici* or towns frequented by veterans and some will have remarried. Maritima, the widow of Julius Marinus who died at the age of forty, and Aurelia Censorina, whose husband died at thirty-eight, are both likely to have been in the prime of life and could have faced a long widowhood.

Below the rank of centurion soldiers were forbidden by law to marry during their military career. Exactly when this restriction was first brought into effect is not clear but that it was in force before the invasion of Britain is indicated by Cassius Dio's statement that 'he, Claudius, gave the rights of married men to the soldiers, since in accordance with the law, they were not permitted to marry'.[7] The reason for the ban can only be conjectured but probably arose from the theory that a soldier would be more disciplined, mobile and efficient if he was not hampered by a wife and family. The ban continued until the reign of Septimius Severus when, according to Herodian, 'to the soldiers he gave a very large sum of money and many other privileges that they had not had before; for he was the first to increase their pay and he also gave them permission to wear gold rings and to live in wedlock with their wives'.[8] The date of this edict was AD 197 and the phrasing can be interpreted in two ways: either that the soldiers were allowed to marry legally or that they could now cohabit with their wives. There had been no hindrance at any time to soldiers forming less formal arrangements with local women.

The many tombstones set up by soldiers' widows or in memory of soldiers' wives are all presumed to date to after AD 197, as theoretically there could be no soldiers' wives earlier. However, a tombstone is not a legal document: its inscription reflects how the couple saw themselves, not how the Roman legal system viewed the situation. It would seem improbable that the native Celts would have allowed hundreds of their daughters to cohabit with soldiers without insisting on some form of wedding ceremony; if a woman had been married by native custom she, and her relatives, would regard her and describe her as a wife, even if the union was not recognised by Roman officialdom. Some of these tombstones, therefore, may predate AD 197, and the edict may simply have regularised a situation which the army was well aware existed already: Anthony Birley has estimated that 40 per cent of military diplomas of auxiliary soldiers recognise an existing relationship with a woman, and a legal opinion given as early as the time of Hadrian presumed that soldiers would be married, as it 'decided that a son under paternal control, who is in the army, could be the heir of his wife'.[9]

By refusing soldiers permission to marry legally the State simply avoided responsibility for their dependants. There was no legal requirement for the army to provide food or accommodation for the women or children, or concern itself over their protection. There is some evidence that the dependants of serving soldiers, particularly auxiliaries, followed them on campaign: Cassius Dio refers to 'not a few women and children' straggling behind the marching column of Varus,[10] and Caesar mentions carts filled with female luggage at the back of his convoy.[11] These camp followers will have walked or travelled in waggons, sleeping in tents or under carts, living off the country and earning money by performing services such as cooking or mending, or entertaining. The Roman army was not the only army in history to have had families with it on the march, and it is always a mystery how these families survived. As there were women and children at Waterloo, so there may have been women and children at Mons Graupius, the battle against the Caledonians in Scotland in AD 84. If one was attached to a military man one's only chance of continued support for oneself and one's children would be to follow wherever he went, although if a unit had permanent winter quarters the women may have felt it worth the risk to remain at the base.

In the case of installations with permanent garrisons, settlements grew up outside the gates and these were known as *canabae* at fortresses and *vici* at forts. There has been some argument as to whether these were provided by the military or grew up unofficially. Some show a formalised layout and may be housing for veterans, while others straggled along the roads leading to the gates. Some forts, such as Melandra and Ribchester, had fortified *vici* which may suggest that they grew in importance, attracting merchants and craftsmen until they were thought worthy of protection. This is a move which Barri Jones has considered to be associated with the legal recognition of *vicani*, the local councils.[12]

There is no uniformity in the size of the building plots nor in the type of house construction in *vici*. Many have long rectangular buildings varying from stone-founded wattle-and-daub dwellings to wooden shacks. Many of them were occupied by traders and these houses were open at the front with living accommodation at the rear. By AD 197 many of the inhabitants of *vici* will have been second or third generation: there are a number of inscriptions which refer to people born *ex castris*.[13] The legal status of these people was very uncertain, as children born during their fathers' military service were illegitimate and could have no claim if their fathers died intestate. As a soldier could not register the birth of a child, even if his offspring were provided for in his will, they might have difficulty in proving their identity. Furthermore, a woman could not reclaim her dowry on the death of her husband if the State had not recognised her marriage, nor could her family prosecute for adultery. Even more unsatisfactory was the ruling that a marriage contracted legally was considered dissolved if the husband joined the army, and any subsequent children were considered illegitimate. This may have affected the 5,500 Sarmatians who were conscripted some time between AD 169 and 180 and sent to Britain, as well as units such as the *numerus Hnaudifridi* and the 'Tigris bargemen', and those raised in Britain.

In theory the removal of the ban on marriage should have affected the accommodation of the now legal wives and children. The discovery of individual buildings, referred to as chalets, which replaced the barrack blocks of forts in the third century, has led to their identification as married quarters, particularly as there is some evidence that many *vici* were abandoned at about the same time. The analysis of the small finds, however, shows that female artefacts appear in forts along Hadrian's Wall with some regularity in the second and

18. The dresses of Romano-British women were fastened by chained brooches like this unmatched pair from Newcastle upon Tyne. Finds of female accessories at such military sites indicate the presence of women in the forts at an early date.

early third centuries (18) but tail off in the fourth, the opposite of what might be expected. Footwear also indicates increasing numbers of women and children in military areas during the second century, the size distribution in the third century according with a normal urban population. The chalets, on the other hand, show few traces of female occupation, although at Malton several infant burials were found under the floors of possible chalets. If they are married quarters the picture given is of a very depleted garrison as buildings which had previously housed eight or ten men would only hold one man and his family. If they are not married quarters, and the *vici* are also abandoned, then exactly where the wives and children of the late third century lived remains a mystery.

Several tombstones refer to married legionaries, such as Julius Julianus of the IInd Legion Augusta and his wife Amanda, or Flavius Agricola of the VIth Legion Victrix and his wife Albia Faustina; others mention foreign auxiliaries: Aurelius Marcus of the 2nd Cohort of Dalmatians mourned his wife Aurelia Aia, who came from Salonae in Dalmatia (modern Yugoslavia), and Pusinna set up a tombstone to her husband Dagvalda, who was a Pannonian.

19. Military retirement diplomas, such as this example from Malpas, Cheshire, reveal that even before AD 197 many soldiers were married, some to more than one wife.

Wives were not the only female dependants: Lurio, a German, lost his sister Ursa, who seems to have followed him to Britain, his wife Julia and his son. Felicius Simplex, a legionary in the VIth Victrix, lost his ten-month-old daughter Simplicia Florentina, while Secundus of the IInd Legion Augusta was mourned by his mother. It is not clear how the army viewed female dependants who were not wives but who had a legal claim on their menfolk, such as sisters and mothers. Soldiers must often have found themselves in the role of *pater familias* on the death of their fathers and thus responsible for all their unmarried female relatives. Some may have considered that sending money home was an adequate discharge of their duties but others must have taken their responsibilities more seriously and preferred to have the women close to hand. Tadius Exuperatus, who himself died on 'the German expedition', appears to have been born in the *canabae* at Caerleon and taken charge of his mother Tadia Vallaunius and his sister Tadia Exuperata on his father's death.

Not all the soldiers recorded by name were ordinary soldiers; many had specific duties, such as Vacia's brother, who was a staff-clerk at Great Chesters, and Gaius Valerius Justus, a record clerk of the XXth Legion at Chester, who mourned his 'most chaste and pure wife' Cocceia Irene. Julia Similina was the widow of a *beneficiarius* of the legate of the XXth Legion, while the *singularis consularis* of the Cavalry Regiment of Sarmatians at Ribchester lost his wife, his son and his mother-in-law, Campania Dubitata. An *imaginifer*'s daughter is recorded at Kirkby Thore. There must also have been women married to sailors with the *classis Britannica* but none of their names have survived.

When a soldier retired he was granted certain privileges which were recorded on a diploma. A fine example was found at Malpas, Cheshire, in 1812 (19). This is datable to AD 103, and grants Reburrus, a Spaniard, among other soldiers serving in Britain under Lucius Neratius Marcellus who had served twenty-five years or more, Roman citizenship for themselves, their children and their descendants, and recognises their marriage 'with those who are their wives at the date of this grant, or in the case of the unmarried, any wives they may subsequently marry, provided they only have one each'. This last clause highlights the interesting situation that, whereas the Romans were monogamous, many of the provinces of the Empire had a tradition of polygamy and many of the auxiliaries might well have had several wives before being drafted or have expected to marry more than one after retirement. This clause, of course, does not stop multiple marriages but ensures that only the children of one wife are recognised as legitimate and so entitled to the citizenship.

The units referred to on the Malpas Diploma include Thracians, Pannonians, Gauls, Spaniards, Germans, Belgians, Dalmatians and Portuguese. Not all of these will have returned to their country of origin after discharge, and some will have settled in Britain. Likewise veterans of British units serving abroad, such as *cohors I Brittonum milliaria*, will have settled in Dacia, Pannonia and Upper Moesia, marrying local girls unless their British wives had followed them abroad. Legionaries were originally granted land on retirement but by the time Britain was a Roman province this had been replaced by a cash bounty. There is evidence of land grants to some veterans at Colchester, Lincoln and Gloucester in the first century, as the State tried to establish official settlements, but this was rarely successful – the boorish behaviour of the veterans at Colchester, for example, was a contributory factor to the dissatisfaction which led to the Boudican rebellion. By the reign of Nero it was becoming clear that veterans preferred to settle near their old forts rather than be rehoused in 'new towns', and the population of *vici* swelled as a result.

Some veterans barely survived their discharge: Flavia Peregrina's husband Crotus, son of Vindex, died at Templebrough at the age of forty: he may have been invalided out because if he had served his full term he would have had to have joined up at the age of fifteen; possibly he lied about his age. Other veterans lived to a ripe old age: Onerata's husband Valerius Verecundus, at the age of seventy, was a young man compared to Cassius Secundus who died at eighty leaving a widow at Chester, or Julius Valerius, who had passed his hundredth birthday when his wife Julia Secundina and his son Julius Martinus erected his tombstone. Julia Secundina's tombstone also survives, recording her death at the age of seventy-five. Clearly Julius Valerius had married a much younger woman on his retirement and possibly had lived at Caerleon all his married life.

Marrying a veteran might be considered an excellent match for a girl, as veterans were reasonably well off, having earned a good salary for over twenty-five years, as well as receiving a cash handout if a legionary. One's children also received full Roman citizenship and there were sundry other perks. This led to a number of families in *vici* and towns with young children whose fathers were in their forties or fifties whilst their mothers were only in their twenties. A typical, if rather sad, family is recorded on the tombstone of Flavia Augustina at York (11), whose husband, Gaius Aeresius Saenus, suffered in his retirement from the loss of his wife at the age of thirty-nine and his son and daughter in their second year.

There is substantial evidence that ordinary soldiers could have slaves: Victor the Moor, for example, seems to have been the slave of a soldier of the *ala I Asturum*.[14] The majority of these slaves were male and possibly performed the functions of batman, but female slaves were owned by centurions and other officers. The most interesting is an anonymous woman who was the slave of M. Cocceius Firmus, centurion of the IInd Legion Augusta at Auchendavy. She is known, from a reference in the *Digest*, to have been condemned to cook for the convicts at the salt mines as a punishment for some unspecified crime.[15] Whilst serving her sentence she was 'captured by bandits of an alien race' and sold. Cocceius Firmus presumably thought that, despite her criminal record, she was worth recovering and repurchased her but sued the Imperial Treasury for the purchase price on the grounds that the State should have taken better care of his property whilst she was in its charge! One presumes that most of these slaves lived in the *vici*, although those belonging to the commanding officer will have lived in the *praetorium*.

Other women who were present at forts were the wives and daughters of the merchants and craftsmen who were attracted by the ready market provided by the army and the security offered by proximity to a military installation, and set up in business in the *vici*. One of these merchants may have been Barates, husband of Regina (6), although it is not clear whether he was a maker of standards or a standard-bearer. Other traders, such as Antonianus at Bowness-on-Solway[16] and the Jewish merchant Salmanes at Auchendavy,[17] may have travelled from *vicus* to *vicus* taking their families with them as Salmanes appears to have done, or made one *vicus* a home base. The women of these traders would have been expected to serve in the shop or assist in manufacturing, and it is regrettable that we know nothing of the butcher's wife at Vindolanda, or the women who lived in the *mortaria* and samian shop at Castleford. Many women are recorded as living in *vici* but it is not always clear if they were the wives, widows or daughters of soldiers or veterans or were attached to the civilian population. Some of these women are British, for example, Verecunda Rufilia of the Dobunni (Cirencester), who is attested at Templebrough, but others are foreigners, such as Titullinia Pussitta, a Raetian (from modern Germany/Austria) who was at Netherby.

Vici must have been noisy, bustling, cosmopolitan places, teeming with people of all nationalities. It was also in the *vici* that travellers would have found overnight accommodation and where soldiers would have come in their off-duty hours. Taverns and cafés have been identified at several sites – one inn at Housesteads revealing the seamy side of *vicus* life, as excavation revealed the skeletons of a murdered man and woman buried in the floor. Prostitutes, acrobats, singers, dancers and jugglers would also have inhabited the *vici*, entertaining the troops as well as the locals who flocked there on market days to sell their produce.

3. Women of town and country

It may seem to be an obvious comment that the life of an urban woman differed from that of a rural woman but in Roman Britain the differences were fundamental. The initial impact of the Roman invasion on the life of a country woman outside the battle zone appears to have been minimal. In most areas she would have continued to play her traditional part in the agricultural and social life of her community and the cultural changes experienced by her urban sisters were only slowly assimilated, if at all. The rural population's hesitancy in accepting the Roman lifestyle is reflected in its domestic architecture: in the first century, while the townswomen were settling into their Continental rectangular houses, the women of the country continued to live in the traditional circular hut of the Iron Age.

The huts were made from the building material most readily to hand: boulders or rough-hewn blocks where stone was plentiful, or timber, wattle-and-daub or cob in other areas. The roofs would have been thatched with straw, reeds or heather, or covered with turves. Most reconstructions have a central hole in the roof to allow smoke to escape, but experiments at Butser have shown that this arrangement, coupled with Britain's windy climate, results in roof fires. It is more likely that the roof covered the whole house and smoke escaped as best it could through the thatch.

It is easy to imagine these buildings as small, rather squalid dwellings, but many were as large as 40 feet (12.19 m) in diameter, covering an area greater than a pair of modern semi-detached houses. Such a house would probably have been occupied by an extended family or several related families, with similar groups living in other huts in the compound created by a ditch-and-bank, wooden palisade, or stone wall.

These settlements were based on a self-sufficient agricultural economy, and aerial photographs have revealed the majority to have had associated field systems. Women living in rural settlements would have been fully involved in growing crops and tending animals. Indeed, the distribution of decorative finds such as bangles and beads, and domestic items such as querns from the settlements, compared with the spearheads, arrowheads and other military objects which dominate the hillfort assemblages, may hint at the existence of a predominately male warrior class living separately in army camps, with food production almost entirely in the hands of the women living in extended family groups with their children and the elderly. Women may also have been responsible for gathering food as well as growing it, not only harvesting wild crops but also hunting and fishing. This picture of the pre-Roman rural economy

20. Reconstruction of an Iron Age settlement at the Cat's Water site, Fengate (after Pryor). Circular huts in small compounds continued to be built and inhabited into the second century in some parts of the province.

is, however, speculation based on anthropological parallels rather than firm archaeological evidence.

After the invasion there was a general upheaval in these rural settlements which will have affected the lives of their inhabitants. Some were destroyed by enemy action whilst others were demolished to make way for forts and military zones. One wonders what happened to the occupants of these settlements; evidence from Egypt is beginning to suggest that the army occasionally offered some degree of compensation, and there may have been an official rehousing programme which moved the displaced rural population into the towns and *vici*. Other settlements were incorporated into the great imperial estates in areas such as Salisbury Plain and Cranbourne Chase. The men, women and children who lived in these areas would have been enslaved and their lands confiscated to provide food for the military.

The surviving farmers would have been expected to concentrate on providing food for a greatly increased non-productive population, both the army and the new town-dwellers. Farms which had previously been worked to provide just enough for the family's annual needs, with some surplus as insurance against a bad year, started to expand. With the breakdown of the Iron Age warrior class more men will have been employed in agriculture, and as the increased yields

67

led to greater prosperity, despite corn taxes and other dues, so the women will have become further removed from the day-to-day sowing and harvesting. In the more remote upland areas, however, where it was difficult to scratch a living from the soil, many subsistence farms must have continued to be run by owner-occupiers or tenant farmers with every member of the family expected to work from dawn to dusk from a very early age.

In the military zones, particularly the northern frontier, small villages were occupied into the third century at least, and there are indications that the population diversified into industrial production, supplying the military personnel with small items of metalwork, jewellery and other craft goods. Analysis of the finds from villages around the northern frontier compared to those from the forts has shown that this was a one-way process. Few artefacts of 'Roman' manufacture were purchased by the native population, either because they were not to native taste or because they were too expensive. The native goods, however, found a ready market among the soldiers and *vici* inhabitants. How involved the women were in these industrial processes is unknown; possibly they continued to concentrate on the production of food and left it to the men to supplement the family's income, but most of the artefacts required simple technology and there is no reason to suppose that the women were not as skilled as the men, particularly if the numerous spinning and weaving accessories imply a cottage industry rather than the provision of home needs.

In the lowlands villages in the more modern sense of the word began to be built, with rectangular houses of timber or timber-framed wattle-and-daub, later replaced by stone structures. Some of these buildings apparently housed people of some affluence: at Park Brow the houses had glazed windows and door-keys, demonstrating that the contents were of some value rather than that the inhabitants were becoming less trustworthy. The smaller villages tended to replace earlier Iron Age habitation but a number of the larger ones were on new sites. The village below Thundersbarrow hillfort, for example, may represent the enforced removal of the local populace from their fortified enclosure into an undefended, less troublesome village. Other villages grew up in mining areas or pottery production centres and, although most villages continued to have associated field systems, many of them had a mixed population of farmers and industrialists and were not totally reliant on agriculture.

Individual families prospered in the lowlands away from the military areas and as they grew financially more secure, so their houses developed from the purely functional to the more elaborate. These new farms were known as villas, an ambiguous term used by Roman writers to cover all rural buildings from small farmsteads to palatial establishments, with only the slightest connection with agriculture, owned by aristocrats and officials who used them as summer retreats from the pressures of town life.

The variety of villas built throughout the four centuries of Roman occupation makes it impossible to describe an 'average' villa. In an attempt to give some idea of villa life, therefore, an example of a basic agricultural villa, Sparsholt, might be compared with the more palatial site at Bignor. Excavations at Sparsholt (21) have indicated that the occupants in the early second century lived communally in a large aisled hall made of flint with stone bonding courses. The thatched roof was supported by wooden posts and the building was lit by a clerestorey in the nave. As the residents became more prosperous partitions were built to provide some privacy and two of the new rooms were embellished with mosaic floors. The influence of Roman standards of civilisation resulted in a bathroom being made, although initially this only had a portable bath and the hypocaust heating system appears to have doubled up as a corn dryer. It was some years before a brick-built bath suite was erected.

In the third century a second house was built at right angles to the first, which continued to be occupied. This building was a single-storeyed dwelling in the Continental manner, with a verandah running along the front and windows placed near the tiled roof. Inside, the house was divided into separate rooms with the central front door leading into the main reception room.

21. Plan of Sparsholt villa showing the original aisled building to the right (after D. E. Johnston). The later house provided more comfort and privacy for its inhabitants.

The plan of Sparsholt reflects the changes in agricultural life throughout the first two centuries of Roman rule. The lack of privacy in the original aisled building suggests a communal life with few noticeable differences between the life of the farmer's family and its workforce, or perhaps a family-run establishment relying solely on its members for labour. The development of separate rooms points to a new class distinction between the farm-workers and their employers, as well as increased prosperity seen in the provision of wall-paintings (28), mosaics and a bath suite. The building of the main house may be an extension of this development, with the family living in separate quarters and the labourers living in the aisled building, or an expansion into two nuclear families, possibly different generations working together, or even a new owner or tenant with more Romanised ideas requiring a more modern house. Despite these concessions to modernity, Sparsholt seems to have remained a reasonably prosperous farm well into the post-Roman period but never rose to the ranks of the wealthy. The mistress of such a farm would have been fully occupied, as were the female occupants of small medieval manor houses, supervising the kitchen garden, managing the house, providing meals for the immediate family and the farm-hands, and rearing her family. The more her house expanded, the less involvement she would have had in the farm. Her daughters will have been expected to help in the house and on the farm from an early age, training for their later role as wives on similar farms in the neighbourhood. These women will rarely have visited towns, except on occasional market days, and will have lived restricted but busy lives.

The owners of Bignor, by contrast, may have led a leisured life of culture and travel. The villa was built on a south-facing slope commanding extensive views, and the lack of other villas in the area has led to the assumption that it eventually formed the centre of a large estate, possibly farming 2,000 acres (810 ha.) of arable land as well as pasturage on the Downs.

Little is known of the timber-framed house destroyed by fire in the early years of the third century, but the first stone house, built around AD 250, was a simple rectangular building, probably housing a similar family to the contemporary occupants of Sparsholt. The Bignor family, however, was more successful and as their financial situation improved so the house was enlarged (22). At first the extensions were modest: a portico along the east front and two projecting rooms (numbered 2 and 3) which turned the cottage into a middle-class winged corridor villa, complete with a private bath suite and piped water from the two adjacent streams. The villa at this stage, although large, was not palatial and it may have been a change of ownership or a sudden increase of wealth which led to the installation of the impressive fourth-century mosaics whose subjects point to the owners' high level of education, and the provision of such luxuries as a summer dining-room with a central hexagonal fountain (Room 1).

22. Plan of Bignor villa (after S. S. Frere). Bignor was one of the largest and most elaborate of the British villas but it still retained an agricultural role, the buildings in the outer courtyard being used as barns and byres.

The building was always of one storey, although the slope of the ground led to a split-level plan with short flights of steps in some of the corridors. The number of small rooms as well as the reception suites indicates that a large number of people were housed here and, no doubt, an extensive staff was required to run the establishment. Both in the house and on the farm slave women will have been used for various tasks. Literary sources describing life in similar large villas in Italy indicate that these tasks would have been very specific and limited in their scope: a woman would have been responsible for doing the laundry, or looking after the hens, or peeling the vegetables, and she would have had a clearly defined place in the hierarchy of servants, both slave and freed.

The women of the owner's immediate family would have had little to do with the day-to-day running of Bignor other than issuing orders to the housekeeper or steward. In fact, the mistress of the house may rarely have been in residence, dividing her time between her town and country houses, and supporting her husband in the political and administrative duties of a provincial aristocrat.

In its final form Bignor was one of the largest villas known in Britain, covering 4.5 acres (1.8 ha.), and this size and the quality of its interior decoration point to a more substantial income than could be accounted for by agriculture alone, although it is clear from the buildings in the outer courtyard that agriculture was still important to the economy of the villa. The owners of Bignor are unknown, as are most of the villa dwellers, but there is a tentative suggestion that the fifth-century owner was Ambrosius Aurelianus, the antagonist of Vortigern in AD 437.[1] A woman known to have owned similar vast estates in Britain was the heiress Melania, although it is not known if she ever visited them or where they were located.

The lack of inscriptions from rural sites at any time has meant that few women living in villages or villas are known by name, except by graffiti on pottery, for example: Matugena, Secunda, Bellicia and Vitia. An exception is Aurelia Concessa, 'a very pure girl', whose tombstone was discovered near Flixborough. The inscription records that she was buried 'on the estate'. Most villas had burial plots nearby but tombstones are rare: Sulicena buried at Wotton-under-Edge and Julia Ingenuilla at Nailsworth were also country dwellers, while Candiedinia Fortunata, Titia Pinta and Cosconia Mammiola appear to have been wealthy women dividing their time between York and their northern villas at Adel, Eastness and Sutton-under-Whitestone Cliff.

The Roman was an essentially urban being: political activities, social life and commerce all revolved around the town. Iron Age Britain, by comparison, was agricultural and the majority of people lived in small groups. A few larger settlements existed, which Latin authors referred to as *oppida*, but this term was not accurate, simply the nearest equivalent title for a phenomenon which was alien to Roman life: the *oppida* of Iron Age Britain were not towns in the sense of administrative centres. Throughout the Empire Rome made the establishment of towns a priority, not only because they were seen to be a vital factor in civilising primitive people, but also because they simplified the administration of a new province. By breaking up the tribal strongholds and evacuating the defendable hillforts potential centres of rebellion were dispersed and the people more easily taxed, educated and policed. The effect on the population, particularly the women, must have been extensive. The status of an individual woman was no longer dependent on her husband's or father's financial and social standing in an agricultural community but was affected by the status of the town in which she lived, as well as the standing of her male relatives within the town.

To establish towns more was required than merely rehousing the population in larger groups. Urban living demanded a completely different lifestyle which had to be learnt by example. Model towns known as *coloniae* were established, populated by legionary veterans, the earliest of which was Camulodunum (modern Colchester). This town, according to Tacitus,[2] was provided with all the main official buildings of a Roman town: a forum, a theatre and a temple to the Deified Emperor. Other *coloniae* were placed strategically at Lincoln and Gloucester so that the maximum number of native Britons could witness the benefits of urban living.

The classical accounts of the Boudican revolt give some indication of how rapidly towns had been established in the first seventeen years of Roman rule. During this time the female urban population had grown as the womenfolk of veterans, merchants and traders as well as camp-followers moved in. It was against these women that much of the hostility of the Boudican troops was directed, as those who were of Roman origin were seen as the enemy, while those of native origin were regarded as collaborators and traitors. Cassius Dio relates that: 'The worst and most bestial atrocity committed by their captors was the following. They hung up naked the noblest and most distinguished women and then cut off their breasts and sewed them to their mouths, in order to make the victims appear to be eating them; afterwards they impaled the women on sharp skewers run lengthwise through the entire body'.[3] Some of the milder atrocities perpetrated on these women brings to mind the humiliations meted out to female collaborators in post-Second World War France. It clearly took more than seventeen years for the intermarriage of Roman veterans and native women to be accepted.

The inhabitants of *coloniae* would have been regarded as the élite. The majority were Roman citizens, although many of their wives would have been provincials, and a number of non-citizens, known as *incolae*, would also have been residents. One of the urban upper class, and the only Roman knight recorded by name from the province, was Macrinus or Macrinius. His tombstone was erected at Colchester by his widow Valeria Frontina and two men who may have been his sons or freedmen. According to Anthony Birley, his name and that of his widow indicate that they were both descended from first-century veteran colonists.

As well as the 'new towns', existing settlements were promoted to the rank of *municipium* by grant. A *municipium*, and thus its inhabitants, could have either full Roman rights or Latin rights, and might retain some native by-laws in addition to the civil law of Rome. A town whose inhabitants were not Roman citizens would only qualify for Latin rights, although citizenship with all its privileges would be conferred on the town's magistrates and their families. *Municipia*, like *coloniae*, would have had *territoria*, that is land surrounding them over which the council would have jurisdiction and which the townspeople would farm. For some women therefore, the difference between living in a town or a village might be largely social, as their livelihoods might still be based on agriculture.

Coloniae and *municipia* were both governed by a council called the *ordo* which was made up of a hundred decurions, men over the age of thirty who satisfied the property qualifications. Peter Salway has pointed out that if one subtracts those not eligible to be decurions, such as women, slaves, children and freedmen, the numbers involved indicate that, although they were the élite, the decurions were by no means a tiny minority, and over the centuries a high proportion of free families would have been able to boast a decurion among their members, although few are known by name. An exception is Aurelius Senecio and his wife Volusia Faustina at Lincoln (23). By the second century grants conferred citizenship on all the members of the *ordo* and their families, not just the magistracy, and by the third century the intermarriage of Roman and native must have meant that the majority of decurions would have been of mixed ancestry. The honour of serving on the *ordo* was shared by the whole family and a decurion at York is presumed from the fact that his widow, Aelia Severa, described herself as *honesta femina*, 'honourable lady', a title which women of the curial class adopted unofficially.

New decurions paid an entrance fee on joining the *ordo* and the expenses of holding a magistracy could be heavy. The *ordo* was responsible for collecting local and national taxes and Diocletian made the individual decurions personally responsible for the payment of these taxes to the Treasury; if any money was outstanding the *ordo* had to make up the deficit out of their own pockets. Few wives would have encouraged their husbands to enrol as decurions, fearing reduced housekeeping money if not bankruptcy. Their rise in the social scale of the town would have brought few benefits to compensate.

There was a third class of large town called *civitas* capitals, which were based on Iron Age tribal areas and were established to act as administrative centres for these areas. Of the twenty-three known tribal areas of Britain, sixteen became self-governing *civitates peregrinae* and their capitals included the old

23. Tombstone of Volusia Faustina, a citizen of *Lindum* (Lincoln) and the wife of a decurion.

24. A town house as excavated at Verulamium.

tribal names in the new titles, for example Venta Icenorum (Caistor-by-Norwich), Noviomagus Regnensium (Chichester) and Isaurium Brigantium (Aldborough). They were set up by the provincial administration as areas were freed from military control, and were established by mutual agreement between the government and the local leaders. As a result the same level of society which had led the tribes continued to dominate the new *civitates* so, except for a few troublesome elements, the arrangements would have had little immediate effect on most people's social status. There is every possibility that the traditional native by-laws relating to female matters – marriage, inheritance and the control of children – may have continued to regulate life in the *civitas* capitals, while the stricter Roman legal code was followed in the *coloniae* and *municipia*, where the inhabitants led a more Romanised lifestyle.

The only *civitas* decurion known by name is Flavius Martius, a councillor of quaestorian rank in the *civitas* of the Carvetii, who was buried by his daughter Martiola at Old Penrith. A woman also thought to have been of same class was Flavia Victorina, wife of T. Tammonius Victor, who lived and died at Silchester.

The houses of the urban upper classes resembled rural villas in many ways. The more elaborate ground plans of both took some time to be adopted and the earliest town houses tended to be simple rectangular structures with timber frames and wattle-and-daub walls. In the mid-second century the corridor house, with a single range of rooms flanked by one or two passages, developed

25. Reconstruction of a fourth-century town house at Caerwent by Alan Sorrell.

into an L-shaped building, or into a three-range plan by the addition of two wings, and then into the courtyard house. Urban architecture, however, does not appear to have been a series of chronological developments from strip house to courtyard house, and most towns by the mid-second century will have had a mixture of all the house types. It has been suggested by Walthrew that the courtyard house was particularly favoured by veterans' families and that the peristyle in several British courtyard houses had derived from military architecture. A typical house at Caerwent, a town populated by a large number of veterans of the IInd Augusta, formed a square block looking inwards to the central courtyard or garden in the Mediterranean manner, rather than out to the street. The peristyle was supported by columns, and rainwater from the roof was collected in a drain around the edge of the courtyard and piped away to flush the latrine. Drinking water was piped by wooden and lead pipes through the main entrance: the better houses in towns were attached to the main water supply on payment of a fee. Private latrines were commonplace in town houses as well as villas, with seats of wood or stone. Latrines were usually incorporated in the house but the Gorhambury excavations have revealed a 'two-seater establishment' at the bottom of the garden. Urban latrines could be plumbed into the main sewer system or, as at Silchester and many rural sites, relied on cesspits.

We have no evidence to indicate whether the sexes shared rooms in either town houses or villas, or whether the women had separate quarters. It is difficult to identify the purpose of individual rooms in any house other than bath suites and occasionally kitchens, both of which were used by women. Bedrooms, nurseries and living rooms, other than the main reception rooms, are particularly difficult to identify. The allocation of space within the house may well have depended on the racial origins of the occupiers as well as their financial status. It is probable that slave women were expected to share their accommodation, either with each other or, in the case of nannies and maids, with their charges or their mistresses.

Many of the houses of the curial class were large and a number at Colchester and Leicester had cellars below for storage and some may also have had upper storeys to accommodate servants. So far, however, there is no evidence for the apartment blocks which were such a feature of Italian cities. Another alternative to a householder in search of more space was to move outside the town walls. A decurion was legally required to reside in a house of a specified minimum size within the town, although this could be interpreted as including the *territorium*. Some decurions would run two homes, a town house and a villa on his country estate, and his family would either commute between the two with him or make one of the houses their main base.

Roman towns were laid out in a grid pattern of streets with the official public buildings dominating the centre. The domestic buildings were democratically arranged: there appear to have been few neighbourhoods regarded as better class or as slum districts; the large curial houses shared blocks with small shops and simple strip houses, and the dwellings of craftsmen and merchants jostled together. Some of these people were Roman citizens: a man called Carinus is proudly referred to as *civi Romano* by his grieving widow Romana and his son Rufinus and two daughters, Carina and Avita, who would also have been citizens; but the majority of the urban population would have been non-citizens, with many freedmen and slaves set up in business by their masters.

According to Caesar 'nobody except traders' travelled to pre-Roman Britain 'without good cause; and even traders know nothing except the sea-coast and the districts opposite Gaul'.[4] The effect of the Claudian invasion was to open Britain up as a new market and merchants flocked to the province to take advantage of the opportunities. Some of these men married local girls, while others brought their wives and daughters with them. Flavia Ingenua was the Greek wife of a Greek trader, Flavius Helius, who died at Lincoln, while Emilia Theodora, a Greek who had married an Italian from Noventum, lived with her son Valerius Theodorianus at York until his death at the age of thirty-five. Rusonia Aventina, a tribeswoman of the Mediomatrici from Gallia Belgica, may

26. Reconstruction drawing of Caerwent by Alan Sorrell, with the forum dominating the centre of the town. The circular amphitheatre is in an unusual position inside the walls, centre right.

have been a member of the merchant class resident in Bath or simply on an unsuccessful visit to the healing shrine of Sulis Minerva, while the tombstone of Carssouna's husband may record another Gallic merchant family living in Lincoln. The cosmopolitan nature of most Romano-British towns is attested by inscriptions as at Silchester where several were set up by the 'guild of immigrants resident at Calleva'.[5]

Few of the merchants have left references as to the nature of their trade, merely describing themselves as *negotiatores* or *mercatores*. We have, therefore, no idea as to what M. Verecundus Diogenes, a tribesman of the Bituriges in central Gaul, and his Sardinian wife Julia Fortunata were shipping between Gaul or the Upper Rhineland and York. The majority of these merchants trading across the English Channel and the Irish Sea were freedmen, and as the doubtful privilege of being elected decurion was denied to them many will have become wealthy men: at York, for example, L. Viducius Placidus of the Veliocasses (Rouen) paid for an arch and a temple to be built in the city.[6]

A healthy merchant trade, confirmed by the number of harbours, the amount of imported goods available and the discovery of a number of shipwrecks, would only be possible if there were sailors to man the vessels. None of these men or their families have left any record, but the ports of Britain, both on the coast and on inland waterways, must have been teeming with the wives and children of the merchant fleet as well as those of fishermen, boat-builders, ship's chandlers and sailmakers. Warehouses at Sea Mills and Bawdrip extend the trading population to include stevedores, warehousemen and carriers.

A town's population of craftsmen included people who worked in metal, glass, wood, stone, tile, ceramics and reeds. A number of these men are known because they signed their work but less is known of their womenfolk. Domitia Saturnina may have been the wife of a mason, as her tombstone, which leaves a space for her husband, has an adze, punch, pick and plummet in relief down one edge; but the wives and daughters of L. Aebutius Thales the shoemaker,[7] Bonosius the blacksmith,[8] Vertissa the cooper,[9] or Cabriabanus the tiler[10] remain anonymous. There is also no evidence from Britain that women were engaged in trade or crafts themselves except by assisting a husband or father. Although Peacock has put forward a theory, based on anthropological parallels, that women were employed in the production of black-burnished ware, the only fragment of evidence which seemed to name a female potter, a piece of *mortarium* from Brockley Hill bearing the name Catia Maria, has been dismissed by Kay Hartley as graffiti rather than a potter's stamp. Analysis of pottery stamps has, however, revealed dynasties of potters who occasionally moved their factories to new production areas, uprooting their families and workforce in the process.

Evidence from Pompeii reveals women working as weavers, waitresses, money lenders, tavern owners, bakers and laundresses, while at Ostia female poultry sellers, vegetable sellers, shoe makers, doctors, nurses and barmaids are attested. Abudia Megiste is known to have sold grain and pulses at the Middle Stairs in Rome, Atinia Tyrannis sold seeds at the Porta Triumphalis in Praeneste, and Aurelia Nais was a wholesale fish seller at the warehouses of Galba. Sellers of purple dyes,[11] ointments,[12] beans,[13] bottles[14] and resins[15] are also recorded from Italy, and the other provinces for whom records survive paint a similar picture of female endeavour.

In Britain the complete silence about the female workforce is likely to give a completely erroneous impression of town life. The number of craftsmen who have left their names is very small compared to the thousands who must have existed, so the lack of inscriptions for female workers may not be so surprising. At the lower end of the social scale funerary inscriptions may have been more commonly of wood than stone, and it is also conceivable that the names recorded on artefacts are those of the factory owners rather than the individual workers, male or female. The only two career women in Britain who are known by name are Verecunda, the actress, and Diodora, the priestess, but between these two extremes there must have been multitudes of midwives, wet-nurses, bath attendants, agricultural workers and craftswomen. A beaker from Water Newton depicts a female acrobat, and it takes no stretch of the imagination to accept the female found murdered in the tavern at Housesteads as a barmaid.

One profession which must have been practised in Britain was prostitution. Much was written about prostitutes in the ancient world but nothing about those in Britain. Nor can any building be confidently identified as a brothel, although a building at Wroxeter might have been, judging by the suitability of its architecture and its prime position next to the baths. Brothels were often sited next to public bath-houses[16] and as a result were not allowed to open before 3 pm, so that the female clients of the baths should not be troubled on their way to their morning ablutions. Prostitutes in Italy were often of Syrian or Egyptian origin, and were identifiable by their heavy make-up, the lack of bands in their hair, and their short tunics and brightly coloured togas.[17] Some were independent operators who rented rooms in inns (most inns had a dual purpose) or a brothel, while others were employed by pimps and madams. Hadrian tried to stop the large brothels from trading by banning the sale of a male or female slave to either a pimp or a gladiatorial trainer without cause being given, but it is unlikely that he was successful.[18] Streetwalkers also plied their trade in most towns. No matter at what level they operated, all prostitutes had to be registered with the authorities and, from the reign of Caligula, had to pay a tax equal to the sum which they might expect to earn from a single client on any one day.[19] This tax continued to be payable even after retirement, and pimps and madams were also liable. Prostitution was, therefore, a financial fact of life in the Roman Empire and prostitutes likely to be found in every town or *vicus*.

Even if the women of Britain have not left any evidence for their involvement in trade or industry they would have had difficulty avoiding it, as many of the working class lived 'above the shop', or, more accurately, behind it. At Silchester the shops were rectangular buildings with their narrow frontage to the street. At least a half or two-thirds of their floor space was used for selling or manufacture, with living accommodation at the rear. Several had open fronts which could be closed by shutters or blinds after hours. More spacious shops were available at Verulamium and Wroxeter. All the shops would be limited as to stock, as each would sell only a specific type of commodity, often made on the premises; department stores were not known, although the small rented premises in the forum and the markets might have provided facilities similar to those of shopping centres. Some were owner-occupied, whilst others were erected as investments by local businessmen and rented out or run by slaves.

Evidence from Rome leads to the supposition that middle class and upper class women did not do their own shopping but relied on their husbands or servants to do the marketing. In Gaul and Germany, however, reliefs indicate that provincial women regarded shopping as part of their daily duties or entertainment.

Some of the smaller towns were established to provide housing for workers in specific industries. Mancetter, Chesterton and Water Newton, for example, were pottery towns, as was Congresbury, whilst others, such as Braughing, were metalworking centres. Mining towns were built in lead, tin and iron areas, and life in such towns might be compared with life in the nineteenth-century mining or factory towns of America or Europe, where the women were relegated to either non-skilled work such as packing or sorting, or domestic or entertainment roles. In the country districts market towns such as Godmanchester and Bourton-on-the-Water provided a focus for the surrounding countryside, holding weekly markets and seasonal fairs. Again we can look to more recent parallels to create a picture of unsophisticated small-town life. Other towns seem to have grown up around posting stations, at major river crossings and road junctions, or around temple complexes, providing services for travellers.

The impression given by most descriptions of town life in the Roman Empire is of spacious, well-organised streets, water on tap, an efficient sewerage system and well-stocked shops; but this may not be the whole picture or even an accurate one. Little is known, for example, of what effect the uprooting of agricultural communities and resettling them in towns had on the Celtic population. Modern parallels might suggest that such an upheaval might have had profound social consequences, particularly on women. If one was used to living in small family groups where one knew everyone, where life was geared to seasonal changes, where buildings were circular and where the community grew, made, hunted and cooked all that the family needed, it must have been a shock to the system to find oneself in a town full of foreigners from all parts of the Empire, with different colours of skin, different traditions and different languages, where there were enormous public buildings built of stone with lavish interior and exterior decoration but where the houses were often smaller than the native huts, and where one could not grow food or hunt but was expected to shop for one's daily needs using coinage, and could even buy bread ready baked. Towns would have been crowded, noisy, smoky and smelly: a number of trades such as fulling, tanning and dyeing were particularly unpleasant, although butchers' shops and markets may not have been much better. The streets would have been full of people and carts, and traffic accidents must have been everyday occurrences – the council at Aldborough finally built a by-pass! Women who had married away from their families, such as Regina, a St Albans woman married to a Syrian (6), Verecunda Rufilia, a woman of the Dubonni who died at Templebrough, and Ved..ic.. (4), who also died a hundred miles from home, and foreign immigrants like Rusonia Aventina from Metz in France and the Greek Flavia Ingenua, must often have felt displaced and confused: psychological illness and suicides may well have been the result.

It is also possible that the high standard of engineering has been overrated. The great civic bath-houses, unless kept scrupulously clean, would have been hotbeds of disease. Some were provided with a constant supply of running water from aqueducts but others were not and relied on regular draining and refilling in order to function. Aqueducts also supplied water to the larger houses and public fountains, but most housewives would have had to carry water from the public water tanks or draw it from a well for all the family's daily requirements. Even a housewife with the luxury of mains water would not have been able to rely on a regular supply: at Wroxeter the aqueduct provided two million gallons daily, but the system was organised so that in times of drought the supply was automatically cut off from the private subscribers.

We have seen that the houses of the curial class had their own flushing latrines, but the majority of homes did not, relying either on pots, often literally broken *amphorae*, or on public lavatories. These were often private enterprises: at Verulamium a shop ran a public lavatory as a sideline, complete with attendant and flushing system, seating ten people at a time. Most of these public facilities made separate provision for the sexes but were not divided into private cubicles: their use was a social activity. A basin was provided for washing the hands. The literary references to the use of sponges instead of paper has been confirmed recently by the discovery of spicules of marine sponges in the York sewers. Regrettably these sponges were for general use rather than individual possessions, and one can only hope that the non-recyclable moss found in sewage deposits at Bearsden was commonly preferred.

Sewerage systems have been uncovered in many Romano-British towns, and possibly the best were provided at Lincoln. However, the rough sides of the main drains at York would have been difficult to flush clean and in the summer the amount of water available may well have been inadequate. The sewers, like the aqueducts, were often open or built very close to the surface, leading to unpleasant smells and disease, while their contents invariably emptied into the nearest river or stream on which another community might rely for its water supply. Dysentry, diarrhoea and internal parasites were rife, as were the other diseases of overcrowding and pollution: London, for example, may have been decimated by plague in the second century. Without our modern knowledge about the transmission of disease, mothers would have been unable to protect their children from the dangers which a truly efficient water and sewerage system might have controlled, but even without this knowledge many women may have been aware that country living was healthier, even if it lacked the sophistication and convenience of town life. Faced with the mental and physical stresses and strains of urban life, the women who looked back longingly on their country roots may not have been in the minority.

4. At home

Most women's lives would have centred around their homes, and keeping their houses clean must have kept the houseproud fully occupied. At Cirencester the occupants of houses at the west corner of Insula XXIII must sometimes have despaired of ever having clean floors. The houses had been built with porticoes on the roadside, but the surface of the road was continually ground to dust by the passing traffic and every time it rained this dust was washed down the camber into the porticoes. This led to a continual renewal of the portico floors and, no doubt, a constant trail of muddy feet into the house. This is unlikely to have been an isolated incident. The rural housewife would have found it easier to protect her home from traffic pollution but the predominantly agricultural way of life would have brought its own cleaning problems.

Some householders considered the difficulties of cleaning at the design stage. At Colliton Park Building I had been built so that the floors of four of the rooms were progressively lowered with communicating drains so that when washing the floors one would have started at the top and worked down. The kitchen floor at Frocester Court also has a drain in one corner to enable it to be swilled down, as have several mosaic floors in other villas.

Few domestic appliances, such as brooms or scrubbing brushes, survive, nor can dusters be identified from scraps of textile. Furniture and wooden doors would have needed dusting and polishing with cedar oil, juniper oil and beeswax, and oil would also have been needed for shale furniture. The illustration of the Colliton Park leg (31) shows the splitting which occurs when Kimmeridge shale dries out; the careful housewife would have had to keep her shale furniture well oiled to keep it intact and retain its black sheen, and it would have been advisable to keep shale tables away from underfloor heating systems.

In the more elegant houses silver and pewter would have had to be cleaned with solutions of acid and polished with chalk applied on leather cloths, or simply by regular rubbing with bare hands. The high relief on some plates must have made this a laborious and complex operation. If one could afford silver tableware, however, one would also have had slaves to keep it clean. As in the Victorian era, when even quite modest establishments had a maid-of-all-work, there would be few Romano-British households without slaves to do the house-work and cooking, look after the children or mend the clothes. The female head of the house would have had her work cut out supervising her staff, unless the establishment was large enough to have a steward to keep everything running smoothly. The larger the household the more specific the task which each slave had to do, but in the smaller houses the women of the family would have had to do their share with one or two slaves for the heavy work.

One aspect of housework which we know little about is laundering clothes and household textiles. It is to be presumed that clothes were washed in rivers or lakes where possible, or alternatively in large bowls or buckets in the backyards or kitchens. Again some houses will have had a slave whose sole task was to do the washing but in most homes washing would have had to be fitted in with the other chores. Fullers, who dressed newly woven cloth, also washed clothes professionally and some town-dwellers would have been able to send their laundry out. Justinian's *Digest* refers to several cases where clothes left for washing with fullers were lost, stolen, damaged or returned to the wrong customer: all situations familiar to modern dry-cleaning establishments.[1] Washing would have been draped over bushes and from trees to dry and then the creases rubbed out by friction with a stone or a glass smoother. Several linen smoothers are known from such sites as South Shields and the method was still in use in Scotland and Ireland at the turn of this century. There is no evidence of ironing fabric by applying heat.

Windows were either glazed, shuttered or barred. The methods of producing glass resulted in panes of varying thickness which were translucent rather than transparent. Moulded glass will have been opaque if the mould was sanded or had a rough surface: one would not be able to look through these glazed windows (nor tell when they were clean!) and the light entering a room would be diffused. Most of the window glass found is the pale green of 'uncoloured' glass, although excavations at Gorhambury have recently revealed fragments of blue window glass, implying that one family at least had an elegant 'designer' bath suite.

Sliding shutters and folding shutters were used on glazed as well as unglazed windows, and elaborate window grilles of iron have survived complete at Duston, Hinton St Mary and Wall, with fragments from many other sites. The grilles were intended to deter intruders and keep out birds and animals.

Artificial lighting would be needed in most rooms and was provided by oil lamps (27), candles or torches. The lamps were made of bronze, pottery or iron and consisted of a circular well for the fuel, one or more spouts to take wicks, and a handle. They could be suspended from a wall or beam, and the more common lamps would have burnt oil, presumably olive oil, which was poured in through a small hole. The lamps, on the whole, were very small and would have had a limited efficiency in terms of light given out and the man-hours involved in their servicing. They would have required continual attention, refilling them and keeping their wicks trimmed; a tablespoon of oil would only burn for about two hours and if the flame was too high it would give off oily smuts.

The evidence from London suggests that pottery lamps were not used much later than AD 170–200, and it has been suggested that a disruption in the supply

27. Oil lamps gave a variable amount of light depending on the number of wicks they held. These examples from Great Chesters and South Shields are of copper alloy and pottery.

of fuel oil from Spain may have been responsible. An alternative was the candle, either used on its own or in groups in candelabra of pottery, bronze or iron. Pottery examples were either tubular with a wide flat base, or shallow saucers with a central ring to hold the candle, surrounded by a drip tray, as found at Verulamium. The evidence for candlesticks is by no means as great as for oil lamps, but wooden holders may also have been used, or candles may have been stuck on to table tops or potsherds with molten wax. The evidence for torches is even slimmer, as they only appear in artistic depictions (53).

A circular hut had no windows to let in light or air, so controlling the temperature was a matter of keeping the door shut and stoking the open fire. Keeping a villa or town house warm was a more complex matter. Tiled open hearths were placed in the centre of some rooms, following the native pattern; other rooms had fireplaces set into a wall. At Bignor the fireplaces were made of three large tiles set on a tiled hearth. Fire-dogs were of iron, and wood was the principal fuel, but coal may have been commonly used. The coalfields of the Forest of Dean, Redesdale and Somerset were worked in the Roman period and there is evidence that they supplied local villas and military establishments. Fire shovels and pokers have been discovered but only in industrial or religious contexts. Braziers were widely used, burning wood or charcoal. These are thought to have been made of iron although none have survived, and their existence is only surmised from scorch marks on the floors of villas and town houses.

The principal rooms in villas and the better town houses were heated by the underfloor system known as a hypocaust. By this method the floor was raised on low pillars of tile or stone, or dwarf walls, and hot air passed through from an outside stoke-hole heating the room above. Hollow tiles set in the walls carried the fumes to air vents and heated the walls at the same time. This system was efficient but also expensive in fuel and man-hours, as a slave had to be on duty full-time to keep the fire burning steadily. Like modern solid fuel heating, it was more economical if it was kept going continually so that that room did not have time to cool down, but some householders may have relied on braziers, lighting the hypocaust only when visitors were expected, as most houses only had the system installed in the dining-room.

It was in the dining-room that the most elegant interior decorations in the form of mosaics and wall-paintings were to be found and the status-conscious woman would have wanted the latest fashions in her home. Mosaics were first introduced into Britain around AD 75–80, and although it might be thought that only the most lavish establishments had mosaic floors, even timber-framed wattle-and-daub dwellings at Colchester and Verulamium and basic aisled farmhouses were provided with them.

Mosaic, made from small cubes of tile or coloured stone, makes a very hardwearing floor covering which is also decorative, and has the added advantages of adapting itself to uneven surfaces and of being resistent to the damp which will rot wooden floors. In the first century AD mosaics were more often found in urban dwellings than in villas, although early examples were installed at Eccles, Angmering and Rivenhall. In the second century mosaics became widespread, particularly those with geometric motifs, and British mosaicists set up in business: David Neal has suggested that a customer would pick a design from a pattern book and the mosaicist would adapt the general pattern to fit a particular room. Although the work of David Smith has demonstrated that different schools of mosaicists were working in Britain, and that designs changed throughout the centuries, few buildings show any indications that their floors were often replaced. Many women will have spent their lives with the mosaics laid down by their predecessors and would rarely have had the opportunity to choose a new pattern. When there was a choice this was almost bewildering, with black-and-white or red-and-white geometric motifs as well as multi-coloured patterns and figural scenes. Some of the geometric floors were very effective: a mosaic from a courtyard house at Silchester, dated to AD 140–60, has an all-over maeander design which incorporates scattered squares, each containing a different motif. Some floors were very 'busy' in effect, such as the Blackfriars mosaic at Leicester, in which nine octagonal panels separated by

28. Diana, goddess of hunting and the amphitheatre, portrayed on a mosaic at Bignor villa.

plaited borders contain multi-coloured complex patterns, the whole contained in a stylised foliage frame. Designs centred on figured panels were popular but more expensive (28): Dionysus was a favourite subject but Cupid, Venus and Orpheus were also popular, as were scenes of hunting, gladiatorial combat, marine life and mythological incidents. In the fourth century Christian symbols and busts of Christ began to appear, as for example at Hinton St Mary.

It is always possible that if one did not like the mosaic one had inherited, and could not afford to replace it, one could cover it with rugs or mats. No textile floor coverings survive but some mosaics appear to follow textile designs, and rugs and carpets may have been widely used. Rushes, either scattered loosely or woven into mats, were also a possibility, and fragments of matting have been found at Newstead and Vindolanda.

Mosaic was not the only available flooring. Wooden floors have been found in houses at Carmarthen, Colchester and Leicester, and Piddington villa had yellow and red tiles laid in a herringbone pattern. Floors could be laid in the *opus sectile* technique where stones were cut into geometric shapes. A more prosaic flooring was *opus signinum*, where broken tiles were mixed with mortar to produce a tough waterproof surface, while the most basic houses would have had no applied flooring, just beaten earth.

Marble and other stones were imported for floors and wall veneers and enough fragments survive to indicate that there was a thriving trade providing exotic stones as well as cheaper native materials. Pritchard's recent work on Roman London has produced an impressive catalogue of imported marbles of various colours used for wall veneers, but if these were beyond one's purse, 'Forest' marble from Alwalton, Purbeck marble, Rutland and Oxfordshire oolites and Collyweston slate could be used effectively. A few householders adopted the Italian method of stuccoing the walls, as at Gorhambury, where the designs include female figures, but the technique does not seem to have been widely accepted.

Almost every civilian building of any size had the walls plastered and painted inside and out. Even quite simple wattle-and-daub or wooden houses of first-century date at Colchester, London and Verulamium had plaster, which was either monochrome or painted with motifs. The most common design of wall-painting divided the wall into three horizontal bands. It was in the deeper middle zone that the principal decoration occurred, taking the form of two-dimensional panels from the first century to the fourth, with architectural schemes giving an illusion of depth appearing in the mid-second century, and large-scale scenes involving figures typifying the interior design of the third and fourth centuries.

The most popular colour scheme for flat panels was deep red with black areas forming frames, but yellow and green colour schemes were also used. Architectural illusion panels attempted to enlarge or make more impressive the basic shape of a room by providing mock niches, apses, windows and projecting columns. Most of these schemes are realistic but the grasp of the rules of perspective was sometimes shaky, as at Caerwent, where a 'niche' fails to suggest more than a pattern of geometric shapes. A motif which appears to be confined to Britain is imitation mosaic: at Sparsholt the double band of *guilloches* on the floor is repeated in paint on the wall above, blurring the edges between floor and wall and making the room seem larger. Landscape painting is rarely found in Britain, although an example, so far unique in the province and dated to about AD 75, adorned a wall at Fishbourne.

The majority of the figured scenes are mythological with later depictions of Christian significance. A female bust on the walls of the baths of Sparsholt (frontispiece) may be a mythological or religious figure or a member of the family. Still-life scenes also appear in British houses: at Verulamium one building had a painting of a lyre with a quiver and a bow against a red ground, whilst at Fishbourne a fragment shows a red plate holding yellow fruit. Bowls of fruit also appear at Brading and Dover. Animals and birds, either individually or in inhabited foliate scrolls, abound, while fish were a favourite subject in bath suites. Floral designs usually appear in a stylised form and lettering was used where it was felt necessary to label or embellish the scene.

Painted wall-plaster appears all over the province from Hadrian's Wall to Cornwall, although the greatest concentration is in the 'villa belt'. It is found on urban sites in houses, shops and public buildings, as well as in rural villas and temples. It was clearly a status symbol which reflected the civilised Roman outlook of the household and as such was often confined to the one room in which guests were entertained. The number of painted rooms might indicate the financial standing of the family – even in the fourth century the villa at Iwerne Minster had only one painted room, whilst the main house at Winterton had eleven of its sixteen rooms painted. Even in the homes of those in the upper income bracket the quality of the painting was graded, so that the more elaborate treatments were in the dining-rooms and the bath suites as well as the corridors leading to them, while the less public rooms were less impressively decorated. Again, few walls show more than one layer of paint and most homes will have looked the same for generations.

Although few ceilings survive, enough fragments have been found to indicate that some were highly decorated. Some treatments could be restrained, for example a white ground with coloured rosettes found at Fishbourne, whilst others were more overpowering. Many are painted in octagonal or square shapes to give the impression of a coffered ceiling, an architectural technique popular in Italy. Others have stylised garlands breaking up the expanse into smaller compartments. In bath-houses a random scattering of fish and marine plants on a blue-green ground continued the theme of the walls and floor to give the bather the impression of being in the sea or in an aquarium.

On the whole the ceilings and floors were lightly coloured to balance the rich colouring of the walls, but even then the general effect must have been overwhelming, not to say crowded, to modern taste. The use of deep plush reds and many clashing patterns resembles the late Victorian era of interior design, particularly as the furniture, although sparse, was also highly decorated.

Most of our information about Romano-British furniture comes from tomb-stone reliefs. Those depicting funerary banquets have as their centrepiece the figure of the deceased reclining on a couch with food laid out on a small table in front. The couches were made in a variety of materials, either with backs, like the couch on which Curatia Dinysia rests, or without, as preferred by Julia Velva (5). The finest depiction of a Romano-British couch is on the lavish tombstone of Victor, a soldier's freedman who died at South Shields,[2] but the final resting places of Aelia Aeliana (29) and Candida Barita also show a high degree of decoration.

There is no evidence that the bulk of Romano-British furniture was upholstered although it may well have been. Loose covers in textile or leather are also a possibility, with cushions and mattresses providing the padding.

Although one relief from Chester shows a child asleep on a couch,[3] it is unlikely that the couches were comfortable enough, or long enough, to be used as beds and most people will have slept on a mattress laid on a chest or platform or even the floor. A pipeclay model from Bordeaux, however, shows a couple snugly tucked up in a double bed with a high back and sides, supported on 'lathe-turned' legs. A fountain head from Bath appears to be in the form of a bed rather than a day-couch, as the high headboard has additional upholstery but not the low footboard. The reclining figure in this instance has been identified as a water god.[4]

Although both men and women are shown lying on funerary couches in Romano-British sculpture, it is rare for a man to be depicted sitting on a chair, and many chairs appear to have been solely for the use of women. One type,

29. Tombstone of Aelia Aeliana at York. She is seen reclining with her husband on a wide couch with a funerary meal laid out on a small three-legged table in front of them.

30. Relief of a lady from Neumagen, Germany, having her hair dressed by her attendants.

preferred by a mother goddess from Bewcastle, is a smaller version of a couch with undulating arms and high back (38). The more common chair, as seen on sculpture and in models, however, is the basket chair, which had its origins in Iron Age Britain. Pipeclay models of mother goddesses show them seated in such chairs (51), possibly reflecting their popularity with nursing mothers. Unlike the Lloyd Loom chairs which they resemble, these chairs have semi-circular bases rather than feet, although the elaborately woven chair used by the lady from Neumagen (30) does have feet.

Footstools were used in conjunction with chairs. The lady from Bewcastle rests her feet on a low box, as does one of the harassed mother goddesses from

Cirencester (52). A similar box stool, probably of wood, can be seen on Candida Barita's tombstone with a small boy standing on it. Proper footstools with legs do not appear on British sculpture nor do they survive in the archaeological record, although an iron leg from Mansfield Woodhouse has been tentatively identified as part of a low stool.[5]

Roman Britain has produced two folding stools from Bartlow Hills and Holborough and fittings from several other sites. Both of the complete examples have a split front bar and leather strip seats, recalling the recommendations of

31. Shale table leg from Colliton Park, showing the splitting which occurred if a housewife failed to keep her shale furniture well oiled.

Soranus for a midwife's stool. Traces of a chaff-filled leather cushion decorated with bronze ribbons found with the Holborough stool suggest that these stools were not as uncomfortable as they first appear.

Sculptural evidence from the Continent suggests that large, solidly made wooden tables with a rectangular top and four legs were common articles of furniture, particularly in the kitchen. In Britain they do not appear on tombstones nor have any fragments been recognised, although the stone uprights in the kitchen at Spoonley Wood may have had a wooden worktop. Tripods of metal or wood were used to support bowls or braziers or a flat tray forming an occasional table for use in the dining-room or bedroom. Fragments of small circular tables, similar to those seen in funerary banquet scenes, have been found in wood and marble but the majority were of shale from the Kimmeridge area in Dorset. The legs of the more elaborate are carved with a griffin's or lion's head at the top and a clawed foot or hoof at the base. A complete leg from Colliton Park, Dorchester, is typical of the type (31).

An item of furniture also peculiar to the villas in the south-west is the stone 'sideboard' or serving table. These solid rectangular slabs of stone, usually limestone, have elaborately carved geometric patterns along one or more edges which probably reflected the carving or inlay on wooden furniture. They butted against a wall or fitted into a niche as permanent additions to a room and were supported by one or two legs or brackets.

The Simpelveld sarcophagus (32) from Holland depicts more everyday furniture including a couch, a chair and two types of table, as well as shelves and cupboards, for which we have no evidence in Britain. Cupboards and wooden chests for the storage of clothes, blankets and kitchen equipment were probably to be found in every home, and cupboards under the stairs, as at Chalk, and other built-in cupboards are also likely to have been common.

We have already seen that mattresses and cushions were used and were probably of textile or leather, stuffed with wool, flax, feathers or straw. The evidence from Victor's tombstone and the Holborough barrow indicates that cushions were decorated with tassels, embroidery and appliqué, while leather from Billingsgate Buildings in London shows traces of an embossed lattice motif. A number of reliefs from other parts of the Empire show customers buying rugs, curtains and other hangings. The couple from Bordeaux are covered by a single piece of cloth, and the majority of rugs and bedclothes would have been locally made, although Lucretius refers to 'Babylonian coverlets of rich beauty'.[6] Textile hangings as decoration are seen on wall-paintings from Italy, as well as curtains hung in doorways; window curtains, however, rarely appear. Linen table clothes were used after the time of Diocletian and there are several literary references to the correct use of table napkins.[7]

Although there were some male cooks, the feeding of the population was the responsibility of the women, and most will have spent a high proportion of their

32. The inside of a sarcophagus from Simpelveld, Holland, furnished with cupboards, tables and other comforts which the deceased might need in the afterlife.

working day in their own or their employer's kitchen. This is an essential part of any house but one which is surprisingly difficult to identify through archaeological excavation. In the native huts stone hearths are usually found in the centre, suggesting that the fire was used for general heating as well as cooking, and as such formed the focal point of the dwelling. The hearth would have been kerbed and may have had a cauldron suspended over it or a spit for roasting meat. In the poorer houses pot-boilers, heated until red hot and then dropped into the mixture to be cooked, may still have been used. Small domed clay ovens have also been found.

In many Roman town houses and villas a room was set aside for preparing and cooking food. At Newport villa a tiled hearth was found built against the

33. Reconstruction of a Roman kitchen. The charcoal for cooking was stored under the stove. On the left are several *amphorae* and a storage jar for flour.

wall of a room next to the baths: a popular position which may have been intended to take advantage of the handy supply of hot water. At Folkestone two tiled hearths had been raised above floor level, one in the centre of the room and the other against the wall. This had not been a tidy kitchen, as food remains and potsherds were found all over the floor and in the small backyard. A second kitchen was found in the same building with a corner hearth of stone and a rubbish pit full of food remains behind it. There was also a large masonry platform with two upright stones to support a water tank heated by a fire placed in the space beneath. Spoonley Wood villa boasted a fitted kitchen with a stone-paved floor, a stone-lined well and two stone table supports.

Not all kitchens had a hearth. Tripods and gridirons have been found, indicating that much of the cooking was done over a charcoal fire. A reconstruction of a kitchen at the Museum of London (33) shows a gridiron supported on a tile-and-clay platform with a raised edge. Fuel was stored in the cavity underneath. In simpler houses the gridiron (34) may have stood on a single large tile or stone on the floor. Tripods were also used to hold metal washing-up bowls.

The hazards of solid-fuel cooking were ever present and at Greta Bridge a fourth-century house burnt down when a fire started in the kitchen. At Binchester a householder had taken the precaution of keeping the charcoal in a separate room to the oven. Other families preferred to have their food cooked in an outhouse or an annexe: a small building near House IV.1 at Verulamium contained a brick hearth and pottery debris and may be interpreted as a cookhouse, as may a thatched building, 20 feet (6.1 m) square, found at Lullingstone, which contained three ovens cut into the floor.

Domestic ovens have been found in other rural dwellings, such as Atworth and Bourton-on-the-Water, but are less common in town houses. This reflects the tendency for town-dwellers to buy their bread from professional bakers, while the country housewife had to provide for her family's needs by baking her own. The third-century oven at Bourton-on-the-Water was an oval structure built of the local oolite with a narrow mouth and a natural clay floor. To use it, a fire was lit inside and the ashes raked out when the required temperature was reached.

Few houses had water pumped to the kitchen and water for cooking and cleaning would have had to have been transferred from a well or cistern by wooden buckets. Most kitchens would have been hot and fuggy with the aroma

34. Iron gridiron from Icklingham, used to suport cooking vessels over heat.

of oil lamps, burning charcoal and cooking food mingling with the smell of stored food. They would also have been untidy and overcrowded by modern standards, with joints of meat, bunches of herbs, and vegetables hanging by iron hooks from the rafters, and other fresh produce stored openly on shelves or in baskets, barrels or sacks on the floor. Liquids would have been kept in their transport containers.

Amphorae are the best surviving of the storage vessels and of particular interest in the study of Roman trade, as they were usually made in the area of their contents' manufacture, and not only carry a maker's name but sometimes an indication of the quantity and quality of their contents. A full *amphora* would have been extremely heavy and the contents were probably decanted for convenience. They were used to transport small fruit, such as figs, dates and olives, as well as liquids, but were reused for a variety of purposes such as storage and even as urinals.

The housewife would have had a wide choice of cooking equipment but two basic requirements were a quern and a *mortarium*. In the early Iron Age grain was ground on a saddle quern, that is, a rounded stone rubbed backwards and forwards by hand over a flat lower stone, but in the later Iron Age the rotary quern became the more common form and continued to be so, with some slight design changes, throughout the Roman period. The native quern had a high-domed upper stone with a handle of wood fixed into a hole in the side. The Roman quern, introduced by the military, had a flatter upper and lower stone with the handle fastened on by an iron band (35). The lower stone was either bedded into the floor or fixed on to a work bench, the upper stone held in position by a spindle and the grain fed into a central hopper. Some of the larger villas may have had donkey-driven mills.

Many recipes required the ingredients to be pulverised before cooking and this was done in a *mortarium*: a pottery bowl with grits scattered over the inner surface and a pouring lip. The wide overhanging rim could be fitted over a metal frame to stop the bowl moving while the contents were pressed against the sharp grits by pestles of stone or wood. There was a wide variety of colours, forms and grits available, and one can imagine that individual cooks would have had firm views as to which were the best. Large stone mortars have also been found.

Pottery was used extensively for storage and cooking, and would have been ranged around the walls of the kitchen on shelves and in cupboards. Flagons were predominantly cream, white or buff, while jugs, jars and bowls came in a variety of wares, mostly red or grey, and varied in size from tiny examples, which may have held spices, to enormous storage bins. Lids were either of wood or flat discs cut from broken pots or stone, or specially made with lifting knobs. Flat bowls and dishes were inverted and used as lids for the larger jars and casseroles. Early pots tend to be lighter in colour and follow Continental designs,

35. Quern for grinding corn, from Chesters.

while late vessels are darker and hark back to the Iron Age tradition. The housewife would have had a wide choice as pottery which had to be transported over great distances was as readily available as local products.

Pottery vessels are easily broken and need to be replaced continually, although some Romano-British pots have been found repaired with lead rivets or clamps. The *mortaria* shops at Castleford and Lancaster and the general pottery shops at Wroxeter and Colchester will have done a brisk trade, while the many kilns scattered throughout Britain supplied both the military and civilian markets. Unglazed earthenware is difficult to keep clean and pots with large inclusions of shell or grit must have become rather unpleasant quite quickly unless there was a method of 'proving' them, such as boiling in sour milk – a method used in the Shetlands until this century.

Metal may always have been preferred to pottery for cooking purposes because, although more expensive, it was longer lasting and more easily cleaned by rubbing with sand. The majority of bronze saucepans have been found in military contexts but they were used by civilian households as well: a relief from Arlon in Belgium shows a family at dinner with a saucepan on the shelf behind them. The most common form has a deep body with thin-bellied walls, a flat rim and lathe-turned concentric rings at the base which allowed the contents to heat quickly whilst protecting them from too much direct heat. Incised lines on the inside of some examples may be level markers, those on the outside are purely decorative. It has been suggested that the saucepans were

36. A selection of pans and cauldrons from Prestwick Carr, some showing extensive repairs.

used for heating an alcoholic mixture resembling *Glühwein* but their appearance in some numbers in the camp kitchen found at Prestwick Carr (36) in association with well-used cauldrons must indicate that they were used for general cooking purposes. Many seem to have been used by several generations of cooks and Oconea, a resident of Bath, was so upset at the theft of her pan that she asked for divine intervention in an attempt to recover it, cursing the thief in the process.

Colanders found in Britain are invariably of the elegant type which echo the shape of the saucepans and are pierced by holes arranged in elaborate patterns (37). They are thought to have been used for warming or cooling wine, by filling them with ice or hot coals and pouring the wine through, a service which the mistress of the house performed for her guests. Plainer versions must have been used for straining vegetables: the wide pots with perforated flat bases found at Silchester may have served the purpose. For straining liquids a piece of cloth would have been fastened to a wooden loop, like a jelly bag. A pottery funnel with a built-in strainer, found at Richborough, would have been a particularly useful piece of equipment, as would the bronze bowl fom Aldborough which

37. Colanders and jugs were used for serving wine. The small tin cup from High Rochester is a rarer find.

has a series of holes pierced in its narrow base. Small pots with concentric ribs round perforated bases are thought to be cheese presses rather than strainers.

Large cauldrons for making stews and soups were used in both military and domestic kitchens. They were of copper alloy, either beaten from a single sheet or made in strips riveted together. The Prestwick Carr cauldrons show signs of heavy usage as they have been repaired several times with patches. Cauldrons were suspended by iron chains of some complexity.

To serve out the contents of cauldrons ladles were used. An example from Great Chesterford has a large hook at the end so that it could be hung up or used to fish large joints of meat out of hot stock. The ladles of silver are more likely to have been used for serving mulled wine.

Iron frying-pans are known which are oval or circular with a pouring lip at one end and a folding handle at the other. Copper-alloy examples seem to have been less common but were included in the metalwork hoards from Wotton and Sturmere. Other metal vessels which appear on Italian sites include fish kettles, roasting tins and moulds in the form of suckling pigs, hares or hams. A flat iron disc with a long handle found at Housesteads has been identified as a baker's peel used for moving loaves in and out of a hot oven. Peacock has suggested that the large bowls of Pompeian red ware found in London were used for making bread.

Lead was also used for cooking vessels, and analysis of human bones from Poundbury has indicated that significant amounts of lead were absorbed as a result. This cannot be accounted for purely by the use of lead water pipes, as the skeleton of one child revealed traces of lead thought to have originated in Attica. Lead pans were recommended for reducing wine, which must have added to the incidence of lead poisoning.

Glass vessels were little used in the kitchen except for rectangular or cylindrical bottles. These were mould-blown in the first and second centuries and used for transporting and storing liquids. Many have a geometric pattern or the maker's name in relief on the base. The wide strap handles do not project beyond the width of the vessel so that they could be tightly packed together in transit. Large glass jars have been found reused as cinerary urns but are likely to have been domestic storage vessels originally.

We know a great deal about cooking in Rome from the Latin writers, in particular Apicius, who wrote a cookery book in the first century AD.[8] This was not a book for beginners: there is little indication of quantities or cooking temperatures, and much is left to imagination and experience. Many of the recipes have long lists of ingredients and as such resemble modern Indian cookery. There seems to have been a dislike for the plain taste of meat, fish or vegetables, and herbs, spices and sauces were used extensively. This may have been due to the difficulty of storing fresh food, leading to a need to disguise slightly jaded produce, but could be taken to extremes: after a recipe called 'A

Patina of Anchovy without Anchovy' Apicius says 'at table no-one will know what he is eating'.

Apicius left us many recipes using both ordinary and exotic ingredients and many he listed would make a modern cook think twice: testicles of capons, sow's udder, lights of hare and entrails of fish. Modern scientific analysis of animal bones, pollen and seeds have revealed the extent to which some of the ingredients were available to the Romano-British housewife. It has often been suggested that the population of Roman Britain was practically vegetarian, with the consumption of meat confined to the wealthy, but this has been disproved by the amount and variety of meat and fish bones found in excavations. Ox (beef and veal), sheep (lamb and mutton), goat, pig (both joints and suckling pig), red deer, roe deer, boar, frog and hare bones have all been found with butchery marks (despite Caesar's assertion that the Britons would not eat hares).[9] No doubt in Scotland if one caught a bear one ate it, and at Newstead and South Shields elk bones have been identified. At Insula III at Verulamium a pile of horse bones led the excavators to surmise that horse meat had been used for making sausages. Beef bones found on several sites had been broken to extract the marrow and it could be said of all animals, not just the pig, that the only bit which was not used was the squeal.

Animal bone analysis by Tony King has indicated that unromanised civilian sites of first-century AD date have produced a much heavier representation of sheep/goat bones than military sites, while the villas, *vici* and smaller *civitas* capitals show less sheep/goat and more ox. The implication that the people who lived in Romanised houses inclined more to a Romanised diet was attributed by King to the influence of the army, its veterans and associated personnel. He also discovered that on the high-status sites in the area north of London there was a marked preference for pig or beef with sheep/goat as a third choice, but by the later period the diet across the province had changed and the proportions of ox/pig/sheep/goat were almost equal.

The variety of fowl eaten is also surprising: swan, coot, crane, raven, redwing, avocet, thrush, water-rail, golden plover, jackdaw, crow, herring gull and even stork, no longer a native bird, have been found in domestic contexts, along with the more familiar gamebirds. Ducks, geese and chickens were eaten in quantity and there is some evidence from Caerleon to suggest that birds were served with the heads cut off but their feet left on.

The list of edible fish is equally long and includes perch, dace, eel, bass, black sea-bream and grey mullet. Pike was eaten by the British but was not to Roman taste and there are no recipes recorded by Apicius for its preparation. At Waddon Hill the remains of the very bony Great Wrasse were found, possibly eaten because it resembled the Parrot Wrasse which was considered a great delicacy. Tunny-fish in oil was exported from Provence in pottery vessels and may have been available in British markets.

An essential ingredient to successful Roman cookery was *garum* or *liquamen*. This was a sauce made from the entrails of large fish and whole small fish, which were salted and then left in a warm place to ferment before the resulting liquid was drained off. It was used as a seasoning like soy sauce or Worcestershire sauce and was mostly made in factories, one of which has been identified at the Peninsular House site in London. This traded from the first to the fourth century, allowing London housewives to buy the sauce freshly made. It was also imported from Italy, Libya and Spain. An *amphora* found at Southwark is inscribed 'Lucius Tettius Africanus's finest fish sauce from Antipolis': Antipolis (Antibes in France) is known to have produced a sauce made from tunny, which Martial stated was cheaper than sauces made from mackerel.[10]

Caerleon Baths, where snacks were sold ready cooked, did a brisk trade in edible shellfish, both the common mussels and whelks, as well as the more unusual prickly cockle, otter shell, peppery furrow shell, carpet shell, razor shell and purple top shell. The edible snail (*Helix aspersa*) is known to have been eaten at Silchester and many other town and villa sites, and the escargot (*Helix pomatia*) at Shakenoak.

The earliest reference to British oysters dates from shortly after the expeditions of Julius Caesar but it was during the administration of Agricola that the gourmets of the Empire became aware of the superiority of this export: Constantine the Great in the fourth century is said to have returned from Britain having acquired a taste for Kentish oysters. The original beds were natural but as demand outstripped supply artificial beds were introduced. Oyster shells appear on sites all over the province – military and civilian, urban and rural – clearly a taste for oysters was not confined to emperors. Oysters can survive up to ten days out of water as long as they are kept shut, and can also be taken great distances by boat if continually doused with sea-water, so housewives all over the country would have been able to rely on a regular supply. They were also sold ready pickled.

Vegetables were available in a lesser array than we are used to and in a strictly seasonal capacity. Green vegetables, such as cabbage, lettuce, cornsalad and cornspurry would have had to be eaten immediately when available, while the root vegetables – radishes, turnips and parsnips – could be stored for some time. Beans, lentils, peas, vetch and other pulses could be eaten fresh or dried, as could the many native varieties of fungus. The Romano-British housewife must also have used potherbs and wild crops more intensively than is the modern habit: for example, elder, dandelions, Good King Henry and sorrel. Apicius gave a recipe for a *patina* (egg custard) based on nettles and Pliny recommended the nettle as a green vegetable, adding, 'the root, too, of the wild varieties makes more tender all meat with which it is boiled'.[11] Edible seaweeds would also have been harvested where possible.

Apicius gives few recipes for puddings but fruit was eaten either by itself, fresh or stewed, or was added to stews and stuffings. Many of the exotic fruit, such as lemons, melons, pomegranates, dates and figs, will only have been available as imported luxuries, although there is evidence from some southern sites of solitary fig trees struggling to survive. Some fruit trees were introduced by the Romans, for example, the cultivated cherry, which was an improvement on the native variety. Soft fruit, such as the black mulberry, strawberry, raspberry, currants, gooseberry and cranberry, were much appreciated in their season or were preserved in honey or pickled in vinegar: the autumn would be a busy time for the skilful housewife as she bottled fruit or picked hips and haws, blackberries, bullace and elderberries from the hedgerows. Nuts were also gathered from the wild or were imported: almonds are only known from Wiggonholt bath-house, but hazelnuts, walnuts and stone-pine nuts are common finds. The sweet chestnut is thought to have been a Roman introduction.

Mention has already been made of the use of herbs and spices in Roman cookery. British sites have revealed coriander, dill, poppy seeds (for sprinkling on bread), mustard, horseparsley, fennel and mint. Thyme, garlic and chives were also available as native species. Other herbs and spices, such as aniseed, asafoetida, cumin and ginger, would have been imported luxuries.

Bread and various forms of porridge were part of the staple diet. Spelt, emmer, barley, oats, breadwheat, clubwheat and rye were all grown in Britain during the Iron Age, but in the Roman period rye and clubwheat appear with greater frequency, while spelt became a principal crop. Apicius mentioned the use of spelt in soups, stuffings and vegetables, as well as in puddings. Oats, during the Roman era, were mostly relegated to animal fodder.

Literary sources reveal that both white and brown bread were baked, and the digestive benefits of wholemeal bread were already recognised by Petronius.[12] Some bread was unleavened but yeast and sour dough were used and Pliny mentions soaking grain in unfermented wine to make leavened bread.[13] The loaves were circular and either shaped like cottage loaves or flat discs.

Salt was required for seasoning food and pickling. This was produced in large coastal salterns and inland salt springs, and transported in jars sealed with pitch or in barrels. It has often been suggested that a common agricultural practice was to slaughter and preserve in salt a high proportion of the stock in the autumn because of difficulties in providing winter fodder. This would result in a high proportion of young animals being found in bone assemblages but this has not proved to be the case. We must presume that, although meat was salted as a regular method of preservation, few families had to survive on salted meat throughout the winter, although the seasonal limitation on supply would mean that a cook would have had to plan her meals carefully.

The other essential for cooking, medicine, lubrication, lighting and a thousand and one other uses was olive oil. Most of the oil imported into London came from southern Spain, particularly the province of Baetica, as did the oil used at Sheepen, Verulamium and Skeleton Green. Olives were also transported whole: a complete *amphora* from northern Spain was found off the Pan Sands near Kent still full of olives, and black olives preserved in wine are recorded, as are salted and unsalted olives.

The only sweetener which was available was honey and most country people would have had their own hives. Pottery hives are known from Casterley Camp (Iron Age) and Rockbourne villa, but wooden and straw hives would also have been used. Butter was rarely used for cooking, being regarded as of mainly medicinal use, but cheese was popular. Pliny mentions cheeses from Nîmes (France), the Alps, the Apennines, Umbria, and Etruria,[14] but most farms produced their own using rennet of lamb or kid. Hard and soft cheeses were made as well as smoked varieties.

The milk of cow, goat or sheep was drunk but poor hygiene must often have counteracted the food value to the extent that milk was a dangerous liquid, full of bacteria leading to dysentery and diarrhoea. The adult population regarded it as a poor substitute for wine or beer, suitable only for invalids and small children.

In Rome the day's meals would follow a regular pattern. Breakfast (*jentaculum*) would be bread and cheese or just a glass of plain water. Lunch (*prandium*) might be simply bread, cold meat, vegetables or fruit, and was, according to Seneca, an unceremonious meal which did not require the table to be set or the family to wash their hands. The serious eating was done at dinner (*cena*): a meal divided into the hors d'oeuvre (*gustatio*), the main course (*mensae primae*) and the dessert (*mensae secundae*). No doubt the upper and middle classes who followed the Roman way of life would keep to this arrangement of meal times but the ordinary household would be more likely to have just one or two meals a day. The time of the main meal varied but it might reasonably be presumed that most people would eat when their day's work was done rather than waste valuable daylight hours eating. It is also unlikely that the average family had an elaborate three-course meal with several removes, but based their diet on one course of stew, soup or joints of meat, with fruit when available. The excavation of Caerleon Baths suggests, however, that there was a tendency to nibble between meals, and shops at Cirencester and Wroxeter also supplied snacks of seafood or cooked meats.

Country dwellers would have been largely self-sufficient, growing their own vegetables, fruit and grain, and killing their own meat, with supplements from the wild. Their colleagues in the towns would have had to rely on purchasing their food in shops. Butcher's shops have been discovered at Verulamium, Vindolanda and Braintree, with a meat market at Cirencester; a seafood shop at Wroxeter and an oyster seller at Caerwent; bakers at London, Canterbury, Verulamium and Silchester; and wine merchants at York, London and Verulamium. None of these have left any indication of the price of their commodities but in AD 301 the Emperor Diocletian issued an Edict freezing prices throughout the Empire, and this gives some fascinating details. If we take an elegant three-course meal, based on recipes from Apicius, of eggs and oysters, followed by pork cooked with figs and barley, plus chicken with vegetables, and finishing with stewed plums, we can estimate the possible cost from the Edict. Eggs and oysters were 1 *denarius* each, pork 12 *denarii* per Italian pound, figs 4 *denarii* for 25 or 40 depending on the quality, barley 100 *denarii* per modius ($15\frac{1}{3}$ pints), chickens 60 *denarii* a pair, lettuces and leeks 4 *denarii* for ten, and a bunch of 25 kidney beans 4 *denarii*. Plums were 4 *denarii* for 30 or 40 depending on size. On this reckoning the meal for four would cost 114 *denarii*, excluding the sauces which would be made from ingredients already in the store cupboard: honey, wine, herbs and spices. To put this in its context the Edict also stated that a stonemason – one of the better-paid craftsmen – should be paid 50 *denarii* per day, while a linen weaver got 40 *denarii* and a sewer cleaner 25 *denarii* (all with maintenance). The housekeeping money of few wives would have stretched to 114 *denarii* per meal.

The majority of the Romanised population would drink wine with their meals. Rhodian wine was inexpensive and may have been the *vin ordinaire*, while the most expensive came from Gallia Narbonensis; other sources were Spain, Italy, Africa, the Aegean and Gaul. There is some evidence for grapes being grown in Britain and a possible vineyard has been suggested for the site at North Thoresby, but it is unlikely that the British wine industry ever offered a threat to the other producers.

As well as being drunk either neat or diluted with water, spiced or warmed, wine was also used in varying degrees of reduction for cooking. Some of these wine products, like *defrutum* and *passum*, were imported already prepared but some will have been made in the home. Wine was also mixed with honey for drinking and cooking.

The native Celts had always preferred beer to wine and continued to make and consume vast quantities. Corn driers for malting barley for home-brewed ale have been found on several villa sites and the inclusion of Celtic beer in Diocletian's Edict, at 4 *denarii* per Italian pint compared with Falernian wine at 30 *denarii* and *vin ordinaire* at 8 *denarii* suggests that beer was also brewed commercially and may have been an important British export. Athenaeus, quoting Poseidonius, referred to the Celts flavouring their drink with cumin and drinking beer made from wheat prepared with honey.[15]

The Romans had very firm views on the subject of women drinking and several writers declared that no woman should ever be seen the worse for drink.[16] This was not due to a dislike of social embarrassment but because heavy drinking was associated with loose morals. Cato was not the only one to attribute the custom of men kissing their female relatives when they met to the need to check if they smelt of drink.[17] There is every possibility that alcoholism, with all its associated social and medical consequences, was a problem for both men and women, even if many took their wine diluted. Diodorus Siculus commented on the amount drunk at Celtic feasts[18] and the size of the tankards found suggests that beer was drunk by the quart rather than by the pint. It is not known whether women shared this thirst for beer, and spirits appear to have been unknown.

The bulk of the drinking took place while entertaining friends in the dining-room, and it was in this room that the best crockery was used: red Samian ware from the workshops of Italy and Gaul, pots from Spain and Gaul dusted with shiny mica, colour-coated and glazed wares and vessels decorated with rouletting, barbotine, 'marbling' and black slip. For the first course bite-sized pieces of food would be served from an hors d'oeuvre dish; an example from Gadebridge Park is divided into four compartments by vertical walls while one from Colchester has a central circular bowl with compartments around it.

Glass was very much a material for the table, with jugs, bowls, beakers and plates of all colours imported from the Continent. Drinking beakers could be elaborate, with faceted, moulded or even painted decoration, and in the fourth century a group of vessels with engraved decoration was imported from the Cologne area. Tin, silver and gilded vessels would have been used in upper class houses or displayed on a sideboard, and many will have been given as presents. In particular pewter – a metal used solely in Britain and apparently catering to British taste – was given as wedding or betrothal gifts in the third and fourth centuries. One dish was owned by a woman called Viventia, the wife or daughter of Victoricus, who had her name scratched on the base.

A grave uncovered at Winchester contained a rectangular shale tray with a typical place setting for a meal: a Samian cup and platter, two knives and a spoon. Forks were entirely unknown, as food was first cut up and then eaten with the fingers even in the politest society. A wide variety of knives was used, mostly of iron with bone or wood handles or with looped ends. As guests were expected to bring their own, there were also elaborate folding knives with ivory handles in the form of gladiators or animals. Spoons made in metal, bone or wood had circular, oval or lute-shaped bowls varying in size from tiny 'salt' spoons to large servers. A number which have sharply tapering handles might be identified as *cochleare*, small spoons used for eating eggs and shellfish – the pointed ends being used for winkling snails or other delicacies out of their shells. Pliny referred to the superstitious habit of piercing the shells of eggs or snails with the end of the spoon immediately after eating them,[19] a practice which indicates that, however busy women were with their housework and cooking, the spiritual side of their lives played a part in their most mundane tasks.

5. Fashion

The women of the household were responsible for keeping the family clothed. Most clothes would be made at home – even the Emperor Augustus is known to have had his clothes made for him by his female relatives,[1] and it was regarded as a womanly occupation, carrying no social stigma, to spin and weave the cloth oneself. Several women appear on their tombstones carrying spindles or weaving combs, for example the wife of M. Aurelius Nepos; and Regina has balls of wool neatly stacked in a basket by her side (6). Spindles of wood, bone or jet have been found and whorls of discarded fragments of pottery, stone, bone and jet.

Some homes would have had slaves to spin and weave but most women were capable of producing plain cloth as well as fancy braids. An embroidery frame found at Pompeii has not been paralleled so far in Britain but no doubt 'fancy work' was carried out as a relaxation as well as a duty, using sets of needles of the type found at Cirencester and Vindolanda.

The basic item of women's clothing in the north-west provinces is known today as the 'Gallic coat'. This was a wide unfitted tunic with sleeves which were either sewn into place or woven in one piece with the body of the garment. Sleeveless examples are also known. The coat was a unisex garment worn knee-length by men and ankle- or calf-length by women, with the hem curved to avoid sagging at the sides. Examples of Gallic coats have been found at Les-Martres-de-Veyre in France and Reepsholt in Ostfriesland, but in Britain we are dependent on tombstone evidence for proof that the coat was worn (see 6, 11, 39, 42).

Alternative dresses were available but appear to have been indicators of tribal origins rather than fashion changes. A costume, now named after a woman called Menimane from Mainz-Weisenau, was worn in the northern provinces in the pre-Roman Iron Age and the Roman period up to the end of the first century AD and then reappeared in the fourth century when German mercenaries on active service were accompanied to Britain by their womenfolk. The ensemble involved a closely fitting bodice with long tight sleeves ending in turned-back cuffs. The front of the bodice was fastened by a brooch. Over this a loose tunic was worn, in the form of a simple tube of cloth with the back and front held together at the shoulders by a pair of brooches and, occasionally, at the breast by a third. Menimane's tunic is shown slipping from her left shoulder. Around the waist a girdle took some of the weight but the garment is literally pinned together and the many finds of chained pairs of brooches in Britain may suggest that this was a common form of dress (18).

Tunics had regional variations across the Empire and may have been worn in the tradition of their homelands by foreign women in Britain, such as Javolena Monime (a Greek), Titullinia Pussitta (a Raetian) and Ursa (a German). The dress of the women of the Ubii from Germania consisted of a series of tunics worn one over the other, and John Peter Wild has suggested that this dress, with its enveloping cloak and accompanying large bonnet, was common throughout Lower Germany. Altars at Domburg dedicated to Nehalennia show the goddess in a tunic and cloak similar to that of the Ubii but with a smaller bonnet and shoulder cape. One of the inscriptions names a merchant from York trading between the Walcheran and Britain,[2] so this costume may have been familiar to the inhabitants of York.

Tunics were also indicators of class and age: the small figures seen hovering in funerary banquet scenes are often dressed in tunics and it is difficult to say if some of these are the children of the household or servants. The three-year-old Vacia from Carlisle is shown in a girdled long tunic with three-quarter-length sleeves, either covered by a shorter tunic or caught at the waist in a heavy overfold – all the better to grow into! The young Pervica, in a shapeless calf-length tunic with long sleeves, is clad similarly to the four-year-old Ertola in her sleeved tunic with a tuck at the waist, while Mantinia Maerica's tunic is worn very short. Clothing appears to have been the same for boys and girls, any differences in appearance on tombstones being possibly the difference between winter and summer clothing. Such evidence for children's dress, however, should not be taken too literally, as they are often shown far older than their age at death. Flavia Augustina's children, for example, at the age of one year and three days, and one year, nine months and five days, stand sturdily in front of their parents fully dressed in Gallic coats and ankle boots (11). Gypsum burials at York have revealed that small babies were swaddled as recommended by Soranus.[3]

Deities were also shown in tunics with girdles tied below the bust, particularly mother goddesses, and many of these costumes appear to have been based on copy-book representations of the dress of the Italian matron. Women such as Julia Pacata and Julia Lucilla may well have continued to wear the sleeveless or short-sleeved tunic known as the *stola* in which they would have been comfortable in Rome.

Over both the coat and the tunic a cloak was worn, usually rectangular in shape although the Ubian costume included one of semicircular shape with the straight edges rolled back on the shoulders and fastened at the waist by a brooch. The rectangular cloaks were worn in various ways: either over the head, or across the shoulders, or folded lengthwise and wound around the neck and shoulders like a scarf with the ends thrown back over each shoulder. Aurelia Aureliana's cloak has fringed ends (39). Cloaks are the only form of female outer garment shown in British sculpture, but a curse tablet has revealed that at Bath

38. Seated mother goddess from Bewcastle showing details of furniture and dress.

Lovernisca lost a *mafortium*,[4] which has been identified as a short cape covering the neck and shoulders and resembling the *pallium simplex*, described by Varro as worn by women, particularly those in mourning. We cannot be confident that in rough weather women did not wear the hooded cape seen on men's tombstones or even the *byrrus britannicus*, the long wet-weather garment of heavy wool or skin which was one of Britain's more famous exports. Severus Alexander, when banning the use of a type of cloak known as the *paenula* in Rome, did concede to its use by both men and women when travelling 'since that sort of clothing has always been for journeys and wet weather'.[5]

Small shawls were also worn and examples can be seen on the relief of the three mother goddesses from Midlothian, drawn tightly across the shoulders and pinned centrally by large circular brooches. The figure in a funerary banquet scene from York (York 1) preferred to fasten her mantle at the left shoulder with the other end drawn forward. Another woman from Bewcastle has her shawl crossed over in front and fastened by invisible means. Scarves were worn either crossed at the neck with the ends tucked into the top of the coat or folded like cravats.

Under the coat was worn an undertunic: Regina has a long full shift which is invisible at the neck except for the fastening brooch (6). The close-fitting sleeves end just above her bracelets; fragments of material adhering to a bracelet worn by a female skeleton of fourth-century date at Castor indicate that shifts were made of linen. Regina's shift hangs below the hem of her outer garment and, as so many respectable ladies are portrayed with their undertunics visible, we must presume that they were intended to be seen, Marcus Aurelius Nepos' wife going so far as to hold up the front of her dress in her left hand.

Joan Liversidge has suggested that next to the skin a linen band was worn around the bust as a brassière, although no examples have been found. Briefs, when worn, are also likely to have been of linen, although three pairs made of leather are known from London. The pair from Queen Street (7) had been cut to an hour-glass pattern from a single piece of leather and hemmed at the edges. The garment was worn with the grain outwards for comfort with reinforcing pieces at each corner of the original shape to take the laces which were tied in a 'granny' knot. The briefs were described by Tony Wilmott as 'well worn, with deeply defined stretch marks across the front, the pattern of which would appear to preclude a male wearer'. Allowing for leather shrinkage he estimated that they had been worn by a woman with a hip measurement of 31 inches (78.74 cm). The date of the deposit was Flavian (AD 69–96) or earlier, while a similar pair of briefs from Shadwell came from a third-century context. These are more ornate with openwork decoration at the front and frilling around the legs, fastened with three integral laces at each corner. Figures wearing such garments are known from a mosaic at Piazza Armerina in Sicily and statuettes from Rennes, Hamburg, Dougga and Pompeii, identified variously as acrobats,

39. Tombstone of Aurelia Aureliana who died at Carlisle, showing her wearing a Gallic coat with a cloak thrown over her shoulder, and holding a bunch of flowers.

athletes and dancers. It is possible that leather briefs, which must have been uncomfortable for day-to-day wear, were worn only for energetic pursuits. Alternatively it has been postulated that they may have been connected with monthly protection. The discovery of the lacy briefs in the water storage tank of a military watch tower at Shadwell, some distance from the town of London, with broken laces suggesting violent removal, does not assist in identifying their precise function although it does exercise the imagination.

Corsets (*capitus*) were worn at Rome but a leather article found at London, which was initially identified as a corset, is now no longer thought to be an article of clothing. Excavations at Micklegate, York, have produced a stocking made in the sprang technique, whereby woollen threads are stretched between fixed rods and interlaced. This (if Roman) is the only known example of sprangwork from Roman Britain although fragments are known elsewhere in the Empire. The stocking is fringed at the top and stops short of the knee so could be more accurately described as a sock. The foot is missing. A pair of stockings found at Les-Martres-de-Veyre were of heavy woollen twill with a back seam and the feet attached at the ankle. Again, the tops were fringed and help up by a string garter which passed through the holes in the fabric.

Head-dresses are not commonly seen in sculpture of provincial women, possibly because having spent time arranging their hair they may have seen no reason to cover the result. However, enough representations survive to suggest that there were many types of bonnet, snood or hat available which may have varied according to fashion or tribal origin. There is no evidence to indicate whether the wearing of a head-dress was related to a particular period of a woman's life, for example marriage or widowhood, although Garbsch identified life-stage variations in the costumes of the women of Noricum and Pannonia in central Europe. The women of the Treveri in Gaul sometimes appear in a close-fitting bonnet like a bathing cap, fine enough for the contours of the hairstyle underneath to be discerned, which resembles that worn by Mantinia Maerica. The mother goddesses of the Ubii are depicted in enormous, almost spherical, bonnets, an example of which might be seen worn by the woman seated in a basket chair on Julia Velva's tombstone (5). A remarkable cap is worn by a head from Birrens which completely covers the hair and is drawn into two 'wings' on either side of the head by two bands or 'fillets', like a Dutch bonnet (40). The form of the silk head-dress on the skeleton of a small child from Holborough is not known but the weave was a simple geometric damask of different colours giving a tiny check pattern.

A stylised mother goddess from Caerwent has a hood which fits snugly around the head with a raised edge framing the face, and tied under the chin, and Macdonald has suggested that the mother goddesses from Midlothian are also wearing hoods which cover the neck. A *capitularem* lost at Bath[6] may have been a garment of this type.

40. Bonneted head from Birrens.

It has been suggested that gloves were not worn but that long sleeves were used to cover the hands in cold weather. Excerpts from Palladius and Ionas indicate that leather gloves were worn for rough work,[7] and a curse tablet from Bath seems to bemoan the loss of a pair of men's gloves.[8] It would seem odd, considering the British climate, if some sort of mitten was not worn by men and women alike.

The most popular material for clothing was wool and the fragments of woollen cloth found in Britain indicate a surprising variety of weaves: herringbone twill, two-over-two weave with weft chevron pattern, two-over-two diamond twill (the most compact weave and suitable for outer clothing) and half basket, as well as plain weaves. Linen was of secondary importance but was used for tunics and undergarments, in plain weave or basket weave. Fragments of silk are rare but are known, for example at Holborough, and silk and linen tunics with tapestry woven decoration may have been worn in the later period. A piece of silk cloth from Colchester was made from cultivated silk, not the wild variety, and both silk thread and woven fragments were exported from China or India. The only identifiable piece of cotton in Roman Britain, so far, is a piece of thread from an early fourth-century well near Chew Stoke, although cotton is known to have been exported to the Roman world from India and Sudan. It is always likely to have been an expensive rarity.

Very few of the sculptural representations of clothing from Britain retain traces of colours but there is no reason to doubt the bright colours seen on the Lullingstone wall-paintings. Evidence of fabric samples from excavations has revealed black cloth with a single tapestry woven band in a lighter colour inserted into the weft, from London; a band of red ribbed or purple cloth from Clementhorpe, York; wool dyed russet brown from Caerwent; and fragments of a tartan cloth of light yellowish brown and dark chocolate brown from Falkirk. Dyestuffs available would have created blue,[9] black,[10] yellow,[11] green,[12] brown,[13] and scarlet red,[14] red-purple,[15] and red-purple-brown.[16] The use of madder is well attested as a dye but recent work on the Vindolanda textiles has revealed the use of the local bedstraw to achieve a similar red colour. Lichen in the Vindolanda area also produces a purple dye similar to that of orchil.

Literary evidence also gives us an idea of the colours used throughout the Empire, from Tacitus' reference to the black-robed women on Anglesey[17] and Ovid's many references to 'wool that blushes with Tyrian dye' as well as sky-blue, golden, green, grey, saffron, amethyst, white, chestnut brown, pink and yellow.[18] He advised women to 'choose those that are sure to please, for not every one suits every woman. Snowy white skins like dark grey colours ... those of dark hue like white'.[19] The dyes could also be controlled to create designs: Tacitus, when describing the Germans, says 'women often wear outer garments of linen ornamented with a purple pattern'.[20] Tertullian, the early Christian writer, was against display and this included dyeing cloth, his attitude being that if God had wanted people to wear purple and sky-blue clothes He would have created purple and sky-blue sheep.[21] It was possible to create attractive designs in white, cream and shades of brown using the natural hues of the full fleece, but the majority of women preferred bright clashing colours. A female figure in a Claudian family group at Ingelheim (Germany), for example, wears a light-green undertunic, a red overtunic and a cloak and scarf of dark grey, while a female figure on the Lullingstone wall-paintings is more tastefully attired in mauve with purple bands.

Where these garments are confined it always seems to have been by a fabric band. Metal buckles have been found in numbers in Britain but mostly in military contexts and it is unlikely that women wore buckled belts. Vacia tied her girdle at the back, while a woman from Castlesteads has hers neatly tied in a bow at the front. A woman from Bowness-on-Solway has her girdle slung loosely round her hips and a *maenad* at Corbridge wears a band with a chequered design. Such decorative belts could have been produced by tablet-weaving and the number of bone and bronze tablets found throughout the province shows this to have been a common technique. By using different coloured threads and turning the tablets individually or in groups, complicated patterns could be achieved. Another method was to use a rigid heddle, only one example of which

41. Bone weaving heddle from South Shields, used for making hair ribbons or braids for decorating clothing.

is known from Britain at South Shields (41). This could take eleven threads and would produce a fine braid 10 mm wide for use as decorative edging or hair ribbons. Gold thread was also incorporated as decoration on clothing and soft furnishings.

Fastenings for clothing other than brooches and girdles were known but not common. At Caerleon Baths small hooks were discovered which resembled modern hook-and-eye fastenings and may have been used to secure cuffs. More ambiguous are the button-and-loop fasteners found throughout Britain. These are of bone or metal and consist of a head (the button), which can be of various shapes and is occasionally enamelled, and a triangular loop set back from the reverse of the button and intended to be sewn on to leather or cloth. It has been suggested that these were used to fasten capes but those seen on sculpture seem to be fastened on the inside, while the *byrrus* was fastened by clasps and the military cape by thongs. Two button-and-loop fasteners were found in toilet boxes at York but Wild has expressed an opinion that they were used to fasten horse blankets rather than human clothing.

Pockets of leather and textile have been found but not as yet in circumstances which make it clear whether they were attached to male or female garments. Women are known to have carried coins and personal belongings in purses of various types. On her tombstone one woman from Ilkley is shown carrying a wedge-shaped purse which may have been formed by two pieces of leather sewn together and held at the top by a metal ring or a gathered cord; another (Chester 2) appears to carry a 'Dorothy bag', while her neighbour (Chester 5) holds a semicircular object like a clutch bag. In a barrow at Holborough a purse made of leather with a linen lining was found in a child's grave but unfortunately no details survive of its form, while the bag found 'quite decayed' with a small coin hoard at Husthwaite was entirely of linen. The bronze arm-purses found in the north are thought to have been a military accessory only worn by men.

The use of fans is known from sculpture; the woman from Murrell Hill, Carlisle (42), holds her fan unfurled and shows it to be circular with spokes radiating from the sticks. One of the women from Chester (Chester 2) holds what may be a folded fan in her right hand, as it resembles the ivory sticks of a fan found in a grave at York. No trace of the material has survived on the York fan but it was probably of textile or fine leather. An ivory catch held the sticks together when not in use. York has also produced the ivory ribs of a parasol with the ends protected by silver sheathing. Comparison with examples from Italy suggest that this was covered with light green material.

Shoes in the Iron Age were simple pieces of hide tied by thongs: not always very attractive nor particularly serviceable, but with a surprising number of variations, so that the *carbatina* found at London and Bar Hill differ in style from those from southern Germany and the Lower Rhine. So marked are these differences that the variations may be seen as reflecting regional costume. They

42. Tombstone of a lady from Murrell Hill, Carlisle. She fans herself whilst watching her child play with a bird seated on her lap.

were worn by all age groups and sexes in early Roman London. Examples survive which retain their uppers, many of which had openwork designs, and the effect must have been very attractive with coloured stockings showing through the gaps.

Single-piece shoes found at London and Vindolanda show Roman features at a very early date and suggest that, whatever the populace thought of the invasion in general, they were ready to welcome Roman footwear with enthusiasm, particularly the nailed sole, which was specifically Roman and whose spread across the known world was in direct relation to Rome's political expansion.

Sandals, initially, had naturally shaped soles and were only worn by women and children but became acceptable male footwear after AD 180 when male and female modes were developed. Women's sandals became narrower and more pointed through the third century, while men's sandals became rounder and blunter until they were triangular in shape. Women's sandals often had a single notch to indicate the big toe, although some had extra notches for other toes. It has been suggested that sandal shapes were made by tracing round the customer's feet so that each pair was bespoke. Rhodes has commented that, if this was so, then the female owner of one sandal from Billingsgate, London, suffered from bunions, as the first three toes are displaced.

The soles of early sandals consisted of several layers of leather held by stitching with a line of nails round the edge. At London it would appear that only sandals have this stitching, which makes even small fragments easily recognisable. Towards the end of the second century the stitching became more closely spaced and set further in from the edge, and this appears to have been seen as a decorative feature, as by the third century stamped or incised lines imitate the pattern of slits originally left in the sole by stitching. The sole of a woman's shoe from the Bank of England excavations in London was decorated with flowers and the figure of a bird. Wooden soles are also known.

Few sandals retain their uppers but the principal thong invariably started between the big toe and the second toe. One sandal from London has traces of an upper margin, suggesting that only the toes were left exposed, whilst another appears to have had a wide band of leather over the instep, as have sandals found at Vindolanda. Sandals were regarded as *de rigueur* for women in Rome but were probably only worn out of doors in the summer in Britain. Men wore them as house shoes, politely removing them when reclining to dinner. In London sandals were less common than one-piece shoes and rare in comparison with more solid nailed shoes.

Calcei covering the entire foot were worn out of doors by men and women and could be brightly coloured. At London the nailed shoes with closed uppers fall into two types: those with intricate openwork decoration which would not have been suitable for manual labour, and plain ankle boots seamed at the front, with a series of holes for thongs at the instep. The largest range of nailed shoes found in Britain are *caligae* and from their size appear to have been worn by men only, although some of the adolescent sizes may have been worn by women doing active work.

A form of ankle boot with an elaborate lacy openwork upper was popular and has been found in military and civilian contexts of the late first century. It was an expensive item of footwear and examples from a burial at Southfleet are of purple leather with gilded decoration (43). After the AD 130s it was largely replaced by the latchet shoe which was worn by men, women and children throughout the Western Empire. These were shaped like children's shoes in Mabel Lucie Attwell illustrations: round at the toe with sensible straps fastened across the instep and with occasional openwork decoration on the uppers.

Another type of boot, worn in the third century, had a front fastening and integrally cut laces. Examples are known from London and Usk. The nailing on this type was often arranged in a tendril motif, although nailing became sparser in the third century and had all but died out by the end of the fourth century. At Lankhills the women and children gave up nailed shoes before the men, although the native population in general continued to affect the nailed shoe for longer than the possibly Germanic immigrant population. A woman's shoe which incorporates most of the features of late Roman footwear – a low vamp with an openwork top and an ankle strap made from an asymmetrical pattern – has been found at Low Ham.

Slippers were worn by women only and an example from St Magnus House, London, has gold leaf decoration which would have been familiar to ladies all over the Empire. These slippers have a raised cork sole. From Vindolanda a 'Persian' slipper has a single strap emerging from between the toes to fasten to the decorated instep strap. Other slippers found at Vindolanda have thick wooden soles and wide leather straps across the instep, and appear to have been

43. Openwork purple leather shoe from Southfleet.

intended for use in the bath-house, where thick soles were needed to protect the feet from hot concrete floors.

Joan Liversidge suggested that women's shoes were generally of softer leather and brighter colours than men's but the recent discoveries appear to contradict this. Indeed, Carol van Driel-Murray has commented that the richest decoration on shoes from Saalburg, Cologne and Vechten is on the men's shoes. Naked footprints on tiles from Leicester and Silchester, however, show that some people, at least in the summer, went barefoot.

From the amount of jewellery found in excavations it is clear that Romano-British women, whatever their station in life, were fond of bedecking their necks, wrists and ears with precious metals and semi-precious stones. Solid neckrings, known as torcs, had been seen as symbols of power and status in pre-Roman Britain and as such had magico-religious significance (3). Dio Cassius tells us that Boudica 'wore a great twisted golden necklace'[22] when she led the Iceni into battle and, as torcs were not normally worn at this time by women, it is to be presumed that in donning a torc Boudica was symbolically investing herself with the authority of a Celtic warrior chieftain. During the early Roman period torcs were awarded to soldiers for acts of bravery but later came to be regarded merely as good luck symbols. It is in this guise that Regina (6) and another Celtic lady (Chester 3) appear to be wearing their torcs; the woman from Chester adds a crescentic pendant, another lucky amulet.

Necklaces worn for purely decorative purposes were lighter and more delicately constructed. Thin gold chains set with emerald crystals, or green glass copies, are known from Wincle, Canterbury, London and Thetford, while a similar chain with double links from Richborough incorporates small sapphires. Amulets and religious symbols were hung from some necklaces, as at Backworth, where two chain necklaces and a matching bracelet all have wheel pendants thought to have been associated with a sun cult such as that of the Celtic god Taranis (44).

A necklace from the Aesica Hoard at Great Chesters comprises three silver chains of double loops held in a rectangular box at each end and supporting, in the centre, an oval cornelian set in a cable-edged mounting. The fastening and back section is missing. A similar necklace in gold with a central crosspiece instead of a mounted stone is known from Newtown in Cumberland.

Necklaces were more commonly made from beads, particularly of glass, strung on leather thongs, copper alloy wire or fibre string. The relief of Volusia Faustina (23) shows that beaded necklaces were worn around the base of the neck rather than hanging on the chest, although some necklaces from graves at York and Lankhills seem to have been longer. Some examples were made from matching beads but at Lankhills the majority were of mixed beads: Grave 199, for example, had a rope consisting of 108 beads of cylindrical, biconical, globular and hexagonal shape, and green, blue, reddish amber and yellow

44. A gold bracelet and two necklaces from Backworth decorated with wheel and crescent symbols: these are amulets to ensure good luck.

coloured glass, as well as double-segmented beads of clear white glass enclosing gold foil. This necklace includes examples of nearly all the glass bead types common in the late Roman period, the gold foil segmented beads being the most exotic, as they are thought to have been manufactured in Egypt and imported into Britain from the second century AD. Beaded necklaces had either hooked fastenings or were continuous strands.

As far as is known bracelets were only worn by women in Britain, although there is some evidence for gold armlets being male accessories in the early Celtic

45. Bracelets and finger-rings of copper alloy, silver and jet, from sites on Hadrian's Wall. Semi-precious stones were set into the costlier pieces, such as the wide hinged bracelet from Aesica (Great Chesters) at the top.

world. Two massive gold armlets in the form of serpents from Dolaucothi may have been worn as symbols of the warrior class in the same manner as torcs. The two silver bracelets in the form of snakes from Castlethorpe, however, and the many copper-alloy bracelets with snake's head terminals are more delicate.

Bracelets could be very elaborate, such as a first-century hinged gold strip bracelet from Rhayader, which has plaited designs of applied beaded wire, with Celtic motifs on the end plates filled with green and blue enamel; and some were simple, such as a broad silver strip bracelet from Great Chesters which has a single cornelian as decoration (45). The majority of bracelets found in excavation are of copper alloy and are based on narrow strips, either decorated by incised or stamped motifs or twisted together to give a cable effect.

Three main types of annular glass bracelet have been recognised, the earliest having bands of chrome yellow, dark crimson or dark blue over translucent glass, while the other two types are based on opaque white, yellow or translucent coloured glass with blue-and-white cable mouldings or inlaid scrolls. It has been suggested that Roman vessel glass was recycled to provide the raw materials for the bracelets, which appear most commonly on the military sites and civilian settlements of the north.

The evidence from graves suggests that women wore several bracelets at the same time, although sculpture suggests rather that one bracelet on each forearm was the preferred fashion, as shown by Regina (6). The Rudston Venus also has a single bracelet pushed well up on each forearm (53).

Balsdon considered anklets to have been worn by less respectable women only and the few examples from Britain do not provide enough evidence for this to be proved or disproved. A decapitated female skeleton from Wroxton St Mary wore a twisted wire circlet on the left ankle and a skeleton from York wore two jet anklets as well as a jet bracelet and a bone and silver bracelet, but the only evidence in the western provinces for anklets being 'respectable' comes from Neumagen, where the hairdresser on a relief is seen wearing an anklet on her right ankle (30).

Finger-rings were worn by both men and women as decoration and as a convenient way of carrying seals. Some rings are very small and may have been worn on the top joint, although children are known to have worn finger-rings at a very early age. In some families rings were exchanged on betrothal and the late fourth-century gold rings from Richborough and Thetford (12), which show pairs of clasped hands, could have been made for this purpose. A custom, thought to have come from the east and popular in aristocratic circles in Rome, was the placing of an iron ring on the third finger of the woman's left hand by her fiancé at the betrothal ceremony. This was based on the belief, explained by Aulus Gellius,[23] that this finger was directly connected to the heart by the nervous system. In Britain the majority of iron finger-rings are solidly made, of large size and mostly hold intaglios, and are usually considered to have been worn by men. Skeletal evidence, also, does not reveal a bias for a particular finger for the wearing of rings, so it would appear that the custom was not widespread in Britain. Nevertheless, the frequent mention of rings on curse tablets suggests that many finger-rings were of sentimental value to their owners.

Finger-rings came in various forms from simple annular strips to the elaborately decorated, inlaid with semi-precious stones, applied wire or granulation. A narrow band with a small circular cup holding a bun-shaped inset of green glass was a popular trinket ring in the second and third centuries, while in the fourth century an openwork design running around a wide gold band might include a name or a motto. A gold ring set with a cornelian from Vindolanda inscribed *Anima Mea* ('my life') is one of many inscribed rings which were probably presents from husbands to wives or between lovers.

Ear-rings are now known to have been worn by many women in various forms, all designed for a pierced ear. There is no evidence as to how the ear was pierced nor if there was any significance in the operation, bar a passing comment by Tertullian which implies that a girl had her ears pierced when still a baby.[24] Roman writers made derisive comments about the eastern habit of men wearing ear-rings and in Britain it appears to have been a form of adornment confined to women. The most common type is a plain penannular ring of gold, silver or copper alloy, sometimes with pendants of glass or stone. A form found in third- and fourth-century coffins has the ends overlapped and inter-twined so would have been permanent or semi-permanent, with pendants ringing the changes. Elaborate gold ear-rings with semi-precious stones in box settings with rilled flanged borders are known, as well as the pendant type known as 'Hercules' club' ear-rings, which Jack Ogden has suggested may have been love tokens alluding to the legend of the love-lorn Hercules, who gave Omphale, Queen of India, the trophies of his labours. This type has a wide distribution in Britain from Birdoswald to London and a wide date range from AD 50–150 at Ashstead to the fourth or fifth century at Thetford. It is possible that some of the many studs found on Romano-British sites were worn in the ear as was the fashion in Egypt, but proof is sadly lacking.

Many of the simpler ear-rings are of similar manufacture to some of the bracelets and finger-rings, being based on decorated single strips of metal or several strands twisted together. This similarity suggests that women wore matching sets of jewellery. It is clear from some of the Egyptian panel paintings that parures were being worn in other parts of the Empire at the same period, although some women clearly preferred to wear a great deal of jewellery whether it matched or not. The individual from Rome who was praised because 'she wore her jewellery without drawing attention to herself' may have been the exception rather than the rule.[25]

Brooches do not appear to have been included in parures but this may have been because brooches were largely utilitarian, and their aesthetic qualities may have been regarded as secondary to their usefulness in holding garments together. The majority of brooches were made of copper alloys: brasses, bronzes and 'gunmetals' with a number tinned or silvered to give a silvery finish. A lack of native sculpture and early grave-goods makes it difficult to envisage how the early brooches were worn by the British and if they were worn by both men and women. Even later in the Roman period it is difficult to assign specific types to male or female wear. It has been suggested that the use of brooches had become less popular by the end of the second century, particularly in female fashions, and at Lankhills it is noticeable that the brooches – all massive crossbow brooches – are confined to male graves. Pairs of brooches linked by a thread or chain appear to have been exclusively female, worn to fasten dresses of the Menimane type. A pair of chain-linked simple silver brooches is known from Great Chesterford in a very early context and a pair of bronze bow brooches from Red House, Corbridge, found complete with a length of bronze chain, may well have belonged to the wife of the Commanding Officer of the Agricolan supply base. Two copper-alloy brooches from the River Tyne at Newcastle are linked by a typically complex chain even though the brooches are not matched (18). The chain would be fastened to a head loop, which is a feature found rarely on the Continent but a common element of first- and second-century British brooches. There has been some argument as to which way up Roman women wore their bow brooches and much evidence has been put forward to suggest that they were worn 'head' down in a way which looks very odd to modern eyes. However, there is also evidence for the brooches being worn horizontally and it may have been a matter of personal taste.

So far we have concentrated on jewellery of gold, silver, copper alloy and glass but many other materials were used. Iron, for example, does not always survive but is known to have been employed for the manufacture of brooches until about AD 55. The fourth-century Lankhills cemetery has produced nine iron bracelets, all from female graves, and there is an expanding iron armlet from Thamesside, London, dated to the first century AD. The Colchester iron armlets are plain, except for one which seems to have been bound at regular intervals with plated copper alloy and carries an annular bead.

More exotically, ivory was also used for bracelets. Lankhills, again, has yielded eighteen, two of which are annular and made from transverse sections cut across the tusk. The rest have bronze or silver sleeves joining two semicircles. Armlets of bone were cheaper and the forty-two from Lankhills are mostly plain with only a few aping the incised decoration of the copper-alloy bracelets. Plain bone bracelets have also been found, but finger-rings and beads of bone are rare finds compared to those of other materials.

Coral may have ceased to reach Britain in any quantity as early as the third century BC, but some necklaces have been found at Heslington Field, Cirencester and Walmgate, York. The necklaces found at Lankhills are either made solely from coral or from both coral and glass beads. They were only found in rich graves and coral is likely to have been an expensive commodity. The Romans regarded it as having magical properties and, when fashioned in the form of a phallus, as a powerful charm to ward off the Evil Eye. The British coral objects, by comparison, seem to have been purely decorative.

Amber, also, was more popular in prehistoric Britain than during the first to fourth centuries AD, and it did not enter the Empire from the Baltic in any great quantity after the late second century. The few pieces of amber jewellery which have been found can all be associated with Pliny's comment that amber was very expensive and of special appeal to women.[26] Both Pliny and Artemidorus in the second century noted that for women to dream of amber rings signified benefits to come:[27] it has even been suggested that amber was only worn by women when asleep. Amulets from Fordington Hill, Dorset, and Butt Road, Colchester, have been identified as fertility symbols. Plain amber beads have been discovered at Walbrook in London, South Shields, Lankhills and Icklingham. A grave group from Walmgate, York, has produced a bracelet of amber and pearl beads.

Pearls were valued for their exactly spherical shape, as well as for their size and white colour; consequently Tacitus thought little of British pearls, regarding them as undersized and of poor colour but this was probably because the majority were fresh-water pearls rather than by-products of the Richborough oyster beds.[28] They were worn in groups hanging from ear-rings to make a clacking noise like castanets but as pearls dissolve in acid soils they rarely appear in the archaeological record. Only one British ear-ring, from Gloucester, retains its four pearls. As beads they were normally mixed with other materials to make necklaces or bracelets, as at Fordington Hill, where a necklace was made of beads of glass, bone, and both seed and blister pearls.

Apart from pearls, emerald crystals, jasper, sapphires, chalcedony, amethyst and garnets were used in decorating jewellery, but not in the quantity found elsewhere in the Empire. Cornelian beads, in particular, were rare in the later period and Margaret Guido has suggested that a cornelian necklace from Lankhills was imported from Hungary. The use of jasper was confined to intaglios in finger-rings, while sapphires and emeralds tend to appear as beads well separated by lengths of chain. Garnets are more common and a notable example of a pear-shaped garnet dominates a gold ear-ring from Bath. Many semi-precious stones only appear cut as intaglios, but the Thetford hoard contains amethysts, chalcedonies, garnets and emeralds used purely for their colour. Rare stones include the use of variscite for a finger-ring from Gadebridge Park and a few beads from York, and chrysoprase beads on a necklace fragment from Colchester. Alternatives to these luxury stones were glass, often used in place of emeralds, and enamel, which was particularly favoured by the northern craftsmen in the second century.

An important group of jewellery in the third and fourth centuries was made of jet and shale. The best-known centre for Roman jet-working was at the Railway Station site at York, where pins and bracelets are known to have been made, but other workshops in the city made beads, finger-rings and pendants. The pendants are either in the form of animals such as bears, or flat ovals with relief decoration of Medusa heads, portrait busts of betrothed couples (8) and family groups. Necklaces and bracelets were made of beads, or were solid and annular, either plain or decorated with chevrons, continuous spirals or faceting. Finger-rings of jet are found in the same shapes as metal rings, but one type, with a sinuous s-motif running across the centre panel, seems to have been made in jet only. Hairpins adopted the decorative motifs of bone pins with faceted cubes, urn shapes, spheres and male and female heads.

As well as jewellery, spindle whorls, spindles, knife handles and a few fragments of inlay were also made of jet, and it is noticeable that the majority of items are for female use. Even when one includes the jet artefacts found in Germany only one exclusively male artefact, a scabbard chape from Bonn, is known. The reason for this bias may be religious, as the British finds have mostly been from religious contexts, or because jet, like amber, had a particular significance for women. Pliny related that 'the kindling of jet drives off snakes and relieves suffocation of the uterus. Its fumes detect attempts to simulate a disabling illness or a state of virginity. Moreover, when thoroughly boiled with wine it cures toothache, and if combined with wax, scrofulous tumours'.[29] These comments do not fully explain why jet should only be worn or used by women and there is a noticeable lack of fertility amulets among the finds. In Britain the distribution of jet artefacts is largely confined to the east, although there was a major sales outlet at Silchester. This distribution appears to be related to transport constraints rather than tribal preference.

Shale had been worked in Dorset, and in particular at Kimmeridge, without a break since the fourth century BC and continued to be popular even when jet was not in demand. The Kimmeridge factories were very productive, with an emphasis on tables, trays and lathe-turned armlets, the latter following the shapes and motifs of their jet counterparts. At some time in the third century AD a rival factory was established at South Shields using a local shale, again aping the products of the York factories. This was on a smaller scale and catered to the needs of the women of the military along Hadrian's Wall who wanted armlets, spindles, spindle whorls, pins, gaming counters and figurines. Shale was not a suitable material for the manufacture of finger-rings but a few were successfully produced, as were some beads.

Jet must always have been more expensive than shale by reason of its limited accessibility, and it is possible that shale, well oiled to give it a good rich polish, was passed off as jet and sold at inflated prices. Yet the Roman shale-working tradition in Britain was older than that of jet and required different techniques to avoid the splitting which occurs when shale dries too rapidly. Shale is only known to have been used for jewellery in Britain and was never popular on the Continent. It is thought to have been referred to by its Celtic name as no Latin term or description has been discovered.

To keep all this jewellery safe a casket was needed. Regina is shown holding open the lid of a solid box with binding at the corners (6), a decorative crescent motif and hefty lock, and at York a wooden trinket box was found in a grave, bound with copper alloy, with a lock, leaf-shaped mountings and studs, and containing jet armlets and glass perfume flasks. Strips of ivory and bone inlay were used to decorate wooden jewellery caskets. An unusual lathe-turned circular shale box with a raised lid seating and a turned ridged lid was found with the Thetford Hoard. A fragment of a similar lid comes from Verulamium. Boxes of shale could not have been locked but the wooden and bone examples usually have lock plates. It is probable that the keys worn as finger-rings were used to secure caskets and document cases, as well as the toiletry boxes holding the array of cosmetics and perfumes which the well-dressed woman applied before facing the day.

According to Lucian: 'a woman does not just wash away her sleepiness with cold water, and proceed to a serious day's work. No, innumerable concoctions in the way of salves are used to brighten an unpleasing complexion ... a multitude of boxes, enough to stock a chemist's shop, jars full of mischief, tooth powders, or stuff for blackening the eyelids'.[30] Ovid offered advice to young women on how to improve their appearance in order to attract men.[31] In his poem *On Painting the Face*, he started with the basics in the form of a face pack which included ten eggs with an equal measure of vetch to two pounds of skinned barley added to twelve ground narcissus bulbs, gum, $\frac{1}{6}$ pound of Tuscan seed and $1\frac{1}{2}$ pounds of honey. To get rid of spots he recommended 'a remedy taken from the querulous nest of birds: halcyon cream they call it, mixed with Attic honey'.[32] For a toner he mentioned that he had 'seen one who pounded poppies moistened with cool water and rubbed them on the tender cheeks'.[33] Oyster shells mixed with water were recommended by Pliny to improve the complexion. Lomentus, or bean flower, was widely used to smooth out wrinkles and there were many imitations on the market. Juvenal complained, from the husband's point of view, about the use of highly scented night creams and bread face-packs.[34]

Once the skin was improved one could apply foundation. The most popular was called *oesyspum* – a preparation of the sweat and dirt extracted from sheep's wool and available throughout the Empire, although the product of Attica was acknowledged as being superior. Rouge made from ochre or the lees of red wine was then applied, according to Plautus, Tertullian and Ovid:[35] 'art gives complexion if real blood gives it not'. If blemishes were still visible Ovid advised covering them up with small patches. The face could then be powdered with one of the many face powders available: Ovid recommended those which contained ground roast lupin seeds, white lead, foam of red nitre or Illyrian irises.[36]

From a number of references it is clear that it was the eyes which received the most attention. Tertullian referred to 'that black powder itself wherewith the eyelids and eyelashes are made prominent'.[37] Pliny gave a recipe for mascara consisting of bear's fat and lampblack, but also mentioned ants' eggs and squashed flies.[38] Ovid suggested the use of 'powdery ash' and saffron as eye-shadow, and also mentioned that 'by art you fill up the bare confines of the brow'.[39] Juvenal recommended the use of soot to darken the eyebrows.[40]

The literature refers only to the use of cosmetics by aristocratic women or their less respectable sisters, and it is difficult to judge whether the ordinary women of the Roman Empire used cosmetics. Evidence of make-up in Egypt and the eastern provinces is well known, and there are hints that the use of cosmetics was widespread among the Celts. As early as 20 BC Propertius was commenting: 'even now, mad girl, dost [thou] ape the painted Briton and wanton with foreign dyes upon thy cheek? Beauty is ever best as nature made it; foul shows the Belgian rouge on Roman cheeks'.[41] In Britain a number of artefacts suggest that the use of cosmetics was common, although it is not always possible to say which instruments were used for medical purposes and which for toiletry. The contents of both ointment pots and make-up flasks would have been extracted by long-handled bronze or silver implements known as *ligulae*, hundreds of which have been found with long narrow spoon terminals, bulbous probes for mixing and applying ointments and tiny angled disc heads for extracting small amounts of powder.

Ralph Jackson has recently identified the boat-shaped pestle-and-mortar sets found throughout the south of Britain as cosmetic utensils used to grind the powders for mineral-based applications, and suggests that their size and shape make them particularly suitable for eye make-up such as mascara and eye-liner. Unfortunately analysis of the substances left in some of the mortars has not yielded any clear proof. A fragment of a glass vessel shaped like a bird, found at Silchester, has been identified as a flask of the type used in the first century AD for exporting face powders from North Italy.

Scents were used extensively, particularly those made at Capua, and Nero's wife, the Empress Poppaea, is known to have introduced a very strong perfume which was named after her. Phials of perfume were also put into tombs and perfumed oils used to anoint corpses, using an ancient recipe of salt, cedar oil, honey, myrrh and balsam. Analysis of basketwork found in a barrow at Bartlow Hills has revealed myrrh or frankincense, while a white substance found in a mid-second-century barrow at Weston Turville proved to be frankincense.

It is believed that the perfumes used at the dressing table, in the baths and in funerary rites were imported in individual glass flasks known as *unguentaria*, also used for face powders and medical ointments. A squat vessel with a tulip-shaped neck and wide flat base from York has PATRIMONI on the base, which is considered to be the name of the manufacturer of the contents rather than the maker of the vessel. Late first- to second-century *unguentaria* tend to have long necks and conical or globular bodies, while some resemble waisted test tubes. Rarer forms include a ring-shaped bottle found in a grave at York with a bronze mounted casket and jet bracelets.

Glass *unguentaria* were mostly of 'uncoloured' glass which is light green in appearance, but tubular examples are known at Gloucester in yellow/green and blue/green, and globular forms are found in bright colours with white opaque spiral trails. Flasks were also made in pottery and metal: a very beautiful bronze example from Catterick is decorated with blue and red enamel and has an internal clip to keep the small knobbed top in position.

Chatelaines with ointment scoops, nail-cleaners and tweezers are found throughout the province (46). Tweezers were used by both men and women for removing unwanted hair and Ovid took it for granted that women would remove underarm hair as well as hair from the legs: 'how nearly did I warn you that no rude goat find his way beneath your arms and that your legs be not rough with bristling hairs'.[42] It is from his advice to men that we learn that hair was removed from the legs by the use of a pumice stone.[43] Pliny discussed depilatory creams made from various noxious substances, such as the blood of a wild she-goat mixed with sea-palm, and powdered viper or she-goat's gall.[44] Hares' blood was used to prevent plucked hairs from growing again.

Ovid, despite his encouragement of the use of make-up and depilatories, felt that their application should be a private act carried out behind locked doors.[45] Lucian also saw cleaning the teeth as a cosmetic practice rather than a matter of oral hygiene.[46] Ovid suggested that a man should make himself attractive to women by ensuring that his teeth 'be clear of rust' and took it for granted that women would clean their teeth: 'why should I enjoin that no laziness leave the teeth to darken'.[47] Powdered horn was the main ingredient of tooth powders, although oyster shell ash was also used, as were the ashes of dogs' teeth mixed

46. Chatelaine from London which includes all the tools required by a woman at her toilet: nail cleaners, tweezers and cosmetic scoops.

with honey, which must have defeated the object. The use of toothpicks was acceptable in public.

False teeth were available, made of gold or ivory, although these have only been found singly and it is not known whether a dentist could supply a full set. The false teeth were wired into place with gold wire which was also used to anchor loose teeth to their neighbours.

Some cosmetic surgery was carried out, mostly removing slave brands from freed men and women. However, the raising of slack eyelids and patching of mutilated ears, lips and noses are recorded, although the lack of efficient anaesthetics must have limited such surgery to cases of dire need.

There was a great deal of interest throughout the Empire in new ways of dressing the hair, to the extent that Ovid commented that it would be easier to count the acorns on an oak tree than to list the number of different hairstyles in fashion in the first century.[48] That British women were just as fashion-conscious as their Mediterranean counterparts is clearly shown by finds of hair in gypsum burials and by sculpture. To keep up to date women will have studied the portraits of empresses on coins and sculpture, travellers will have been questioned closely on their return from Rome and the wives of newly posted officers and civil servants relied upon to bring the latest ideas. Even so, it is likely that Britain would often be several years behind the times, and some hair-dos would continue to be popular despite the dictates of fashion. Ovid advised women to stick to styles which suited their faces: 'an oval face prefers a parting upon the head left unadorned ... Round faces would fain have a small knot left on top of the head so that the ears show'.[49]

During the Republic it had been considered improper for women to resort to artificial aids to improve their looks, and most females wore their hair gathered into a simple loose knot at the back of the head. This style continued to be popular among the less fashion-conscious, even when very complex modes were in favour, and Tertullian considered it to be a suitable style for a Christian woman.[50] On a tombstone of the late second or early third century (Bath 2) the woman has her hair parted in the centre, framing the high forehead, and drawn back behind the ears in a homely bun, whilst a tombstone from High Rochester shows the bust of a woman wearing her long straight hair drawn back into the nape of her neck. A young woman or goddess portrayed in stone from Aldborough wears her hair in a Greek version of the bun: very wavy with a centre parting and a raised braid over her forehead held in place by a piece of ribbon. Julia Velva and her daughter also wear their hair parted in the centre but fixed into a roll framing the face before being tied back at the nape of the neck (5). It is possible that the rolls were arranged over padding in order to achieve a fuller effect.

The head of hair discovered in a fourth-century burial at the Railway cemetery at York had been twisted into a loose bun which would have covered the whole

47. Auburn hair wound into a bun and secured by jet pins, from a woman's grave at York.

of the back of the head (47). It was held in place by a couple of jet pins with cantharus-shaped heads. Mantinia Maerica preferred to wear her bun on the top of the head and cover it with a bonnet, but the mother and daughter on a tombstone from Halton Chesters leave their topknots uncovered (Halton Chesters 1).

Women with social pretensions will have followed the lead of the empresses as closely as possible, so we cannot tell if a head from Bath (Bath 3) is a portrait of a member of the imperial family or an aristocratic citizen. The hair is parted in the middle and wound into a roll around the head, with the back hair plaited and looped into a clubbed ponytail of the type which Lady Evans called a 'catogan'. This particular catogan was carved separately and is now missing. Other strands of hair are wound over the head and a ringlet hangs down the side of the neck. The fashion is similar to that favoured by Agrippina I, the wife of Germanicus, and the two-piece hairstyle may confirm that this is an imperial portrait, as the statues of empresses often had some of the hair carved in different stones so that alterations could be made to keep pace with changing fashions.

The visit of Julia Domna (15) to Britain in AD 208–11 led many British women to adopt the Syrian style of hairdressing, with the hair hanging in crimped waves on either side of the face and taken in a large roll up the back of the head. The roll may have been interlaced with ribbons. Candida Barita wore her hair in this style, as did the figure behind Volusia Faustina on a tombstone from Lincoln (23), while Faustina herself wore the slightly later style which retained the crimped waves but rolled her back hair into a small tight knot at the nape of her neck.

In the mid-third century a variation on the Syrian tradition appeared, where the waves left the ears free but the back hair was carried in a single strip or a band of small plaits straight up the back of the head from the nape to the crown. This has been called the 'helmet' style, as it recalls a crested helmet. A good example of this fashion can be seen on the woman's head from Fishergate, York (York 2), and it was also affected by Aelia Aeliana and her daughter (29).

Only one sculptural example of the complex hairdressing of the Flavian court is known from Britain, although a number of bone pins have been found decorated with elaborately coiffured busts, and a tiny gold bust from Richborough has curls across the forehead with the rest of the hair piled up under a net. The head of a woman from Walcot (Bath 4) is carved to twice life-size and may portray an empress. The hair is divided into lots of thin plaits coiled into a heavy chignon at the back of the head. At the front a high diadem of bubbly curls, probably of false hair arranged over a frame, towers above the face. This was certainly not a style to be attempted without the aid of an accomplished hairdresser armed with curling tongs. Such a hair-do would have had to have been slept in overnight, as it would have taken a great deal of time to achieve, and if the style was copied in Britain it must only have been by those of the highest rank. A Celtic version may be seen on a wooden head from Llanio, where the hair has been divided into a series of plaits from the forehead and pinned into a flat bun at the back of the head. The effect is smoother and less fussy than the head from Walcot but would also have required the assistance of a hairdresser to be successful. Another example from York (York 3) shows a woman wearing her hair in a series of braids wrapped around the head with one wide plait starting from the forehead and running back over the crown, but unfortunately this may be a nineteenth-century import. The discovery of two six-strand plaits of brown hair at Poundbury may indicate a Celtic fashion or, alternatively, may reflect the Roman custom of dividing a bride's hair into six parts fastened at the back of the crown.

Several of the styles known in Britain bear no resemblance to the styles of the empresses and may reflect an independent Celtic tradition or local fashions. Decimina, from York, has her wavy hair parted in the centre and arranged in two long braids hanging loose down her back, and partly covering her ears. 'Ved...ic..', a tribeswoman of the Cornovii, has very thick hair which falls forward on either side of her face in two braids which reach to her lap (4). Sepronia Martina wears her long hair loose, but at the age of six she may not have been old enough to wear her hair up. Her mother, Julia Brica, has her hair combed back without a parting and tied at the nape of the neck. Shoulder-length hair is worn by Aurelia Aureliana from Carlisle (39), as well as by the mother on a family tombstone from York (York 4), while another woman (Bewcastle 2) appears to wear her shoulder-length hair curled up at the ends. Short hair was preferred by the daughter of Blescius Diovicus and an anonymous woman (Halton Chesters 1). Ringlets appear to have been largely the prerogative of goddesses: Venus is often portrayed with her hair in a chignon with ringlets falling to both shoulders, although a bunch of auburn ringlets has been found in a York burial.

A head from Lansdown, Bath (Bath 1), is dressed in a most peculiar way, although it is possible that the hair is shown covered by a cap. The hair seems to have been tied in a bun at the back from which strands have been brushed forward into a roll framing the face. However, the carving bears a resemblance to an object of woven hair-moss recently discovered at Vindolanda, which has been identified tentatively as a wig or head-dress. A similar object is known from Newstead.

False hair was often resorted to, either in the form of complete wigs or as extra tresses, particularly in the Flavian period when, as we have seen, the hairstyles were elaborate and required bolstering. Black hair from India was so popular that the government in Rome included *capilla Indici* among the commodities on which customs dues had to be paid. The blonde locks of the Germans were also popular, so some women may have sold their hair to supplement their income, while Ovid mentioned female prisoners-of-war having their hair cut off to supply the wig-makers.[51] A chestnut wig has been discovered in the catacombs of Rome and a coil of false hair attached to a piece of leather is known from Les Martres-de-Veyre in France, but the hair found so far in British graves appears to have belonged naturally to the deceased. An exception may be some long brown hair which, according to the excavator, was found 'plaited and coiled around' in a cremation urn at Rainham Creek and could have been a hairpiece.

If one's hair was not the requisite colour it was always possible to dye it. Tertullian objected to women dyeing their hair with saffron,[52] whilst Ovid referred to women dyeing their 'whitening locks with German juices'.[53] Pliny and Martial described a dye invented in Gaul and used in Germany, called 'Mainz soap'.[54] This was a mixture of goat-fat and beechwood ash, which probably worked like a tinting shampoo. There are also references to 'Batavian foam' and 'Wiesbaden soap-tablets'. Propertius denounced those who dyed their hair with 'lying hue', but henna is known to have been extensively used.[55] Diodorus Siculus commented that the Celts washed their hair in lime water, which would have lightened the colour as well as stiffening the hair.[56] Tertullian, however, was against even washing the hair, as he warned that 'the force of the cosmetics burns ruin into the hair; and the constant application of even any undrugged moisture, lays up a store of harm for the head'.[57]

British women seem to have had an advantage over the women of Rome, as the coveted red hair was commonplace: Tacitus commented on the red hair of the Caledonians[58] and Dio recorded that Boudica had ' a great mass of bright red hair ... to her knees',[59] but brown and blonde hair has also been found in the Poundbury cemetery. There has been some discussion as to whether the predominance of red hair from graves is simply the result of melanin oxidation, but the work on hair from Poundbury would seem to suggest that such 'oxidation' effects rely on the hair being red to start with. A head of hair and its associated plait from the same cemetery may give archaeological evidence for hair dye. The burial is likely to have been that of a man who wore his hair in a plait 18 inches (45 cm) long. Under the microscope the surface of the strands is pitted as bleached or heat-curled hair would be. Unfortunately, when the hair was submitted for analysis the results were ambiguous – the only hint of artificial dye being an unexpected trace of nickel, a substance used in modern chestnut hair dyes. The pitted surface of the hair strands could also suggest that curling tongs had been used. Several of the styles mentioned above would have required the hair to be artificially curled, particularly the crimped waves of the Julia Domna style. Iron curling tongs (*calamistrum*) heated in braziers are known to have been used, as well as animal fats to keep the hair in place. These would also have had an adverse effect on the hair and many fashionable women would have lost their hair at an early age because of overheated curling tongs.

Hairpins provide the best evidence that hair was worn piled up. Hilary Cool has recently described how pins became popular very rapidly in the first century AD, suggesting that hair was worn loose or braided before the invasion, although some Iron Age graves at Danes Graves, Driffield and Garton Slack have produced pins which could have been worn in the hair. They also reflect changes in style: the complicated towering fashions of the first and second centuries required long pins, while the simpler styles of the third and fourth centuries only needed short pins. The longer pins may have protruded a distance from the hair so that their decorated heads could add to the effect: some of the more elaborate have glass insets, beads fitted over the shanks, or pendants. Others have heads in the form of human busts, hands, vases, animals and birds as well as religious symbols. One from London has the full figure of Venus standing on a Corinthian capital (48). In the later period pins were made in coloured materials: York, for example, has produced pins in gold, crystal, glass,

48. Silver and bone hairpins. The more expensive pins could be very elaborate and depictions of deities and empresses were popular: the bone pin on the right depicts Fortuna, while the silver pin to its left shows Venus.

silver, jet and copper alloy as well as bone, and several sites have revealed bone pins stained red with madder or green with copper salts, which would have produced an attractive effect of dots of colour in the hair.

Bone and bronze are the most common materials for hairpins found today but it is likely that there were large numbers made in wood, either in the elaborate forms seen in bone or, at the bottom of the social scale, whittled from twigs. Metal pins tend to have straight shanks but those of bone, jet and shale, and presumably wood also, often expand in the middle to counter-act the weakness of the shank. Bone, shale and jet pins have been found with reshaped ends – clearly if one snapped a hairpin it was worth re-sharpening.

Pins are found wherever women passed – road surfaces, domestic buildings and public buildings – as it is easy for such pins to slide out, particularly if they fix buns low at the nape of the neck. Large numbers are found in bath-houses, either because women pinned their hair on the top of the head whilst bathing or lost them when rearranging their hair afterwards.

Few other hair decorations are known. Some jet and shale rings have been identified as ponytail restraints and illustrations from the Eastern Empire suggest that some coils of bronze were used to hold small tufts of hair on top of the head or at the sides. At Lankhills a pin was found on a child's brow where it may have secured an ornamental band. A pin found in a similar position in a grave at Butt Road, Colchester, recalls the hairstyle of the bust from Aldborough. Alice bands and ribbons of braid are presumed but traces are elusive, except for a decorated headband found in Grave 323 at Lankhills. The band itself was of leather with six bronze-gilt scallop-shaped mounts sewn into position on either side of four yellow glass discs held in bronze frames. Comparable headbands have been found in Hungary, southern Bavaria and Gaul. A bone strip from Dunstable, thought to have been a hairband, is now considered to have been a necklace. At the upper end of the market a complex object from a child's grave from Southfleet has been identified tentatively as a hair ornament on the evidence of parallels from Palmyra.

Early combs were single bone or antler plates with rounded backs and teeth cut along one edge. This type is not well represented in Britain, although there is a late Iron Age example from Ghegan Rock, Lothian. A preferred type was a rectangular sheet of boxwood with teeth cut into two opposing edges, those of one side often being coarser than the other, like a toothcomb. In the late first or second century, in an attempt to make a longer type of comb, plates of bone or antler were positioned side by side and fixed by a riveted bar along one edge. These were more popular in the eastern parts of the Empire, only appearing in any numbers in the west at Richborough in the fourth century, where triangular-backed combs were preferred and many were decorated with stamped dot-and-ring motifs and incised borders. In the late fourth century rectangular combs

49. The Wroxeter mirror, the largest and most ornate silver mirror from Roman Britain, would have had to have been held by an attendant, as can be seen on the relief from Neumagen (30).

with a central 'handle', outswept ends and zoomorphic terminals appear in the south-east of Britain, with a few examples from York.

From the third century double-sided composite combs became common in Britain. These had rectangular strips holding the plates in the centre, the teeth being sawn after the plates were fixed. In the fourth century the decorative endplates became increasingly zoomorphic in appearance, as can be seen in the examples from Lankhills, twelve of which can be dated to after AD 365. The majority of combs were made of wood, bone or antler but a few survive in horn and bronze; iron combs seem to have been used only for dressing hides or weaving.

In order to dress the hair neatly or apply make-up an essential piece of equipment is a mirror and these were available in various shapes and sizes. The most common were small rectangular or circular sheets of polished metal held in wooden frames or set into toilet-box lids. Circular mirrors with handles attached at one point of the circumference are known from Iron Age Britain, with magnificent examples from Desborough and Birdlip. These Celtic mirrors are noted for the elaborately incised or enamelled decoration on the backs and the handles. Roman examples can be seen on a tombstone from Chester (Chester 4) and falling from the hand of Venus on the Rudston mosaic (53). A complete hand mirror was found in 1973 at Whitchurch and proved to be of an alloy of copper and tin called speculum. It is circular with a series of holes around the edge and concentric rings on the reverse. The handle, which was originally soldered at the joint, is tapered with elegant moulded decoration. Traces of wood suggest that it was buried with its case.

Lid mirrors are rare in Britain but a circular example is known from the St Pancras cemetery at Chichester. A more complicated lid mirror, the only one of its type in Britain, was discovered at Coddenham. This is decorated with the head of Nero on the cover and a scene showing the emperor addressing the troops on the underside of the mirror. The largest surviving mirror from Roman Britain comes from Wroxeter (49): it is a circular mirror of silver with two rosette-decorated rod handles straddling the back with a central reef-knot. This is a particularly ornate example, dated to the late first or early second century, and simpler versions are known from Verulamium and Chester of silvered bronze. Glenys Lloyd-Morgan has commented that this must have belonged to a very wealthy woman who, like the aristocrat on a relief from Neumagen (30), had attendants to hold the mirror, which gives a better image if held at a distance.

Pliny referred to the use of glass mirrors, examples of which are known from Reculver and York as well as Ospringe (Kent), where one was found on the hip of a female skeleton and another showed traces of lead 'silvering' on the back. Square frames of decorated lead for glass mirrors are also known from Ospringe, Verulamium and Chester. Despite the paucity of surviving examples, glass mirrors must have been the most common type during the period and were cheaply mass-produced in the Balkans and Cologne.

Whether women dress for the men in their lives or to retain their standing among other women is a debate which has raged through the centuries. Ovid suggests that the former was the case in Rome, although he was directing his comments at courtesans rather than respectable matrons. It could be presumed from the evidence of sculpture and artefacts that many women in Britain tried to make the best of their appearance, although the very elaborate dresses and hairstyles and the excessive use of cosmetics and perfumes would be confined to the middle and upper class women, particularly those with time on their hands. Among the slaves, freedwomen and country women the style of dress and use of cosmetics may have reflected their origins rather than their status.

6. Religion

It would be impossible to discuss any inhabitants of Roman Britain without reference to their religious beliefs, as these dominated the lives of Romans and Celts alike on both a personal and political level. This has been described by many writers on the period but the importance of their spiritual life to the female population, and the way in which religion emphasised the gulf between the sexes, has not received the attention it deserves.

Roman religion in the provinces was divided into the official state religions, classical cults, native cults and the exotic mystery religions of the east. The part which women played in these different cults varied between complete exclusion to full participation. To be sure which cults practised in Britain were open to women one has to rely on the sparse evidence afforded by inscriptions and there are difficulties in judging the extent to which they participated. The cult of the Deified Emperors is a case in point.

It was recognised at an early stage that there was a need to weld together the provinces with their multitude of religious convictions in a way which bolstered the State. This was not achieved by establishing a single state religion and banning all other professions of devotion, but by adding another tier: the cult of the Deified Emperor. As we will see later, this caused difficulties with some people whose religion, such as Christianity, recognised only one god, but was easily absorbed by the majority of the emperor's subjects, who had been brought up to believe in a multiplicity of gods. Even if an individual might have personal difficulties in according the Deified Emperor his full veneration as a god, it would not have offended most religious sensibilities and no doubt many went through the ceremonies in a spirit of civic duty rather than religious fervour.

One of the earliest public buildings to be built in Britain was the massive temple at Colchester, mentioned by Tacitus[1] as being dedicated to the Deified Claudius. The Britons saw this as a symbol of Roman dominance and it suffered accordingly at the hands of Boudica's tribesmen. As part of the drive to Romanise the population several leading citizens had been appointed as priests of the Imperial Cult but at their own expense. Although they were in the post for only one year this proved to be a very costly honour, as Tacitus related: 'those who had been chosen as its priests found themselves obliged to pour out their whole fortune in its service'.[2] The *seviri* were wealthy men but this responsibility must have been a drain on their resources which will inevitably have taken a toll on the domestic budget. Even if women had little active involvement in the ceremonies the knock-on effect in financial terms will have effected them deeply, and the regulation that the *sevir* was expected to reside near the temple during his year of office must also have brought its own problems. Despite the enhanced social standing it brought with it, the post must have been seen as a mixed blessing.

Colchester was not the only town to have a temple erected to the Deified Emperors, although it seems to have remained as the cult centre. Several inscriptions suggest that there was another substantial temple at London, where the governor resided. One of these is the tombstone of the nineteen-year-old Claudia Martina, whose husband Anencletus is referred to as 'slave of the province'. Anthony Birley has interpreted this as meaning that he belonged to the *concilium provinciae*, the council to which each community sent representatives every year, and whose principal task was to conduct the annual ceremony of devotion to the Deified Emperors.

In the towns ceremonies to the Deified Emperors in temples and fora may have been open to women but it would be unlikely that female participation was allowed in ceremonies in the shrine of the headquarters buildings in forts, where the statue of the reigning emperor and the standards of the unit were kept. Outdoor ceremonies involving the whole unit and the local populace, at which the Commanding Officer officiated, may have been regular occurrences, as part of the programme of Romanisation. No doubt the officers' wives and daughters were expected to turn out on these occasions to set a good example.

The worship of the personified virtues extended the worship of the Deified Emperors into more philosophical areas, and here we have evidence for the direct involvement of women. For example, at Maryport Diana Hermione dedicated an altar to the Emperor's Virtue and at Risingham Aelia Proculina erected an altar to the Emperor's Fortune. Both of these altars come from forts, and the worship of the Emperor's Virtue, Fortune, Discipline and Victory may have appealed more to the wives and daughters of military men than to civilians.

The Roman invaders also brought with them the official state gods such as Jupiter, Juno and Minerva: the Capitoline Triad. These cults in Britain were largely supported by the army and dedications to the Triad by women are rarely found. An exception is an altar dedicated to Juno by Diana Hermione at Maryport. More dedications to Juno might have been expected, as she was the classical goddess who oversaw the lives of women and offered protection during major life events such as marriage and childbirth. A few statues have been tentatively identified as being of Juno but may be more accurately described as depicting empresses in the guise of Juno – a popular conceit. It may be that the women of Britain preferred to rely on their native deities in moments of stress and that Juno was only worshipped by women who had been born in Rome. Minerva, who was patroness of spinning and weaving among other crafts, had several altars erected in her name, although none by women, and a number of statuettes have been found, in both temples and domestic shrines. Jupiter's only dedications by women equate him with the eastern god Dolichenus and bear little relation to his role as a member of the Capitoline Triad.

Other deities brought from Rome include Fortuna, Mars and Diana. Sosia Juncina, wife of Quintus Antonius Isauricus, imperial legate at York, set up an altar to the goddess Fortuna, while at the other end of the social scale Antonia, the slave or daughter of Strato, dedicated to Fortune the Preserver. No temples to Fortuna have survived in the province but altars and statuettes were often set up in bath-houses where extra protection was felt to be needed whilst one was in a state of undress. Fortuna was a particular favourite in Britain, where she personified Good Luck – appealing to the Celts' love of gambling and their general superstitious nature. Mars was primarily a soldier's god, but temples for his worship have been tentatively identified at the civilian sites of Barkway, Kingscote, Kings Stanley, Lower Slaughter and Stony Stratford. He was also invoked in his role of Peace-bringer at Ribchester by a woman whose name is now lost, and as Mars Corotiacus by Simplicia at Martlesham. No shrines have survived for the worship of Diana, the divine huntress, but as she was worshipped, traditionally, in a grove, this may not be surprising. A statue of her was found in a late temple at Maiden Castle and she also appears on a relief at Housesteads, but for evidence that she appealed to women we have to turn to an altar dedicated by Aelia Timo at Risingham. This altar was the result of the fulfilment of a vow and it may have been Diana's role as huntress which was invoked – Aelia Timo having taken to hunting in an attempt to while away the time at a remote outpost fort – or a more basic role as a fertility goddess.[3]

On a day-to-day level a woman's religious life was centred on the rituals carried out in the home. The household god was known as the *lar familiaris*, while the *penates* were the spirits of the store-cupboard. *Lararia* could come in many forms, either as niches set into the wall of the house or as miniature temples. The shrines in a shop and house at Verulamium, both destroyed by a fire in AD 55, were cupboards made of tile or stone, while a household shrine at Silchester consisted of a small room with a mosaic floor and a plinth to support the statuettes. *Lararia* were probably a feature of almost every home, although the majority may have been glorified wooden cupboards or shelves on which statuettes could be arranged, rather than architectural elements. One of a woman's daily tasks was to tend the domestic shrine and provide flowers to decorate it on special occasions. She also prepared the food for rituals, such as the purification of a new-born girl on the eighth day and the rites of puberty. A death in the family would also have meant complex rituals involving the whole family.

The cult of the ancestor was shared by Roman and Celt alike. The Romans kept alive the spirit of their ancestors by displaying busts of the deceased in the *lararium*, or elsewhere in the house, and they were also carried at funeral ceremonies. There were traditional festivals which linked the living and the dead, such as the Parentalia in February and the Rosalia in May, when the tombs were decorated with flowers and the whole family participated in a solemn picnic.

Orthodox Roman religion involved numerous rites and festivals for set days of the year when presents were given – Ovid mentions 1 April (the feast of Venus) and 1 March (the feast of the Matronalia) as days when presents should be given, as well as birthdays:[4] any one of these might account for the flagon from Ilchester given to 'little Vrilucolus' by Verina. In Britain only the army is likely to have followed the full calendar, with the civilian population confining themselves to the birthday of Rome[5] and other officially designated days, unless the Roman festival could be linked with the old Celtic feasts which divided the agricultural year: Imbolc (lambing), Beltine (spring), Lugnasand (late summer) and Samain (harvest). Henig has described the scene at a sanctuary on a festival day of sacrifices, theatrical performances, bear-baiting, acrobats, gladiatorial combat and an enormous consumption of food and drink.

Many of the classical religious rites would have been followed by army families and civil servants in the early years but as fewer and fewer Roman citizens of recent Italian descent were domiciled in Britain so these rites would have become less important and replaced or adapted by native Celtic rites.

At the end of the Republic and in the early days of the Empire, the citizens of Rome had a profound disbelief that anything existed after life on earth. By the Antonine period (AD 138–92), however, this mood seems to have changed and the rites of inhumation and more attention to the needs of the deceased indicate a more hopeful attitude. Henig has indicated that the Lullingstone temple-tomb, the Holborough sarcophagus and the fashion for surrounding the corpse with gypsum are indications of this trend. The Celts, on the other hand, had always considered that the soul was immortal and that the afterlife was superior to the bodily life. Iron Age graves were often lavishly equipped with food and drink and other necessities, and this native belief in another world also appears in the early Romano-British graves, although manifested in the provision of Roman artefacts.

After a death the women would have prepared the feasts which were held before and after the ceremony and on set days in the ensuing months. The anniversary of the death would also be marked by a feast, and some cremations at Caerleon were provided with a pipe through which wine could be poured, suggesting that the deceased was expected to participate fully in these meals. There were no markedly different funerary rituals for the sexes, although Lankhills cemetery gives the impression that at some periods there were seg-regated burial areas, and in Britain, unlike the Rhineland, it was more common for the tombstones of women to show the deceased reclining at the funerary feast (29). There were large family tombs, but an anonymous body buried at York (50) had a formal stone-and-tile mausoleum to herself, with a vaulted roof

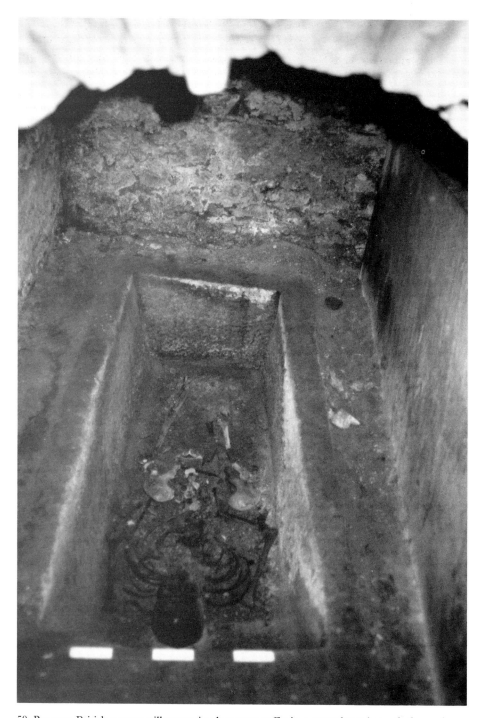

50. Romano–British woman still occupying her stone coffin in a mausoleum beneath the modern streets of York.

and a stone coffin, although few grave-goods. Some of her colleagues at York were accompanied by boxes of jewellery, phials of oil or perfume and other items of personal significance. Female graves elsewhere had spindles and spindle whorls and a high proportion had oil lamps; others had kitchen pots and tableware.

Despite the home comforts provided in the tomb, and the carvings which provide domestic architectural details, Martin Henig has expressed his doubts that many Roman Britons expected to last out eternity camped in a hole in the ground even though many memorials, such as that to Aurelia Lupula, end with 'may the earth lie lightly upon you'. The images of the next world, however, might make the confines of the tomb pleasant by comparison: Flaminius Pansa's gravestone at Risingham portrays the afterlife as a place where the ground is always frozen[6] and the general impression of Corellia Optata's memorial is of a world of dark and gloom. The worst fate which could be imagined was to wander forever haunting the living, and as a precaution many cemeteries were provided with perimeter fences or deep ditches. As the money found in graves may be to pay Charon to ferry the deceased across the River Styx, so the food may be seen as rations for the journey and the provision of shoes and boots in cremations and inhumations, reduced to a symbolic handful of hobnails at Cirencester, may reflect the thought that one needed a stout pair of walking shoes for the journey to the Underworld. Some people preferred to position this shadowy place above the earth or across the Ocean: the birds shown on Curatia Dinysia's tombstone have been interpreted as representing the flight of the soul, while symbols such as tridents, wind gods, shells and dolphins, as on Aelia Aeliana's tombstone, may also indicate the soul's voyage to the Islands of the Blessed.

The burial rites and beliefs of Roman Britain reveal an enormous variety of religious convictions. Fashions in rituals changed with time but there were also local traditions which meant that the rites followed and methods of burial at Dunstable would bear little similarity to those at Petty Knowes in Northumberland, or those at Lankhills, Winchester, to those at Guilden Morden in Cambridgeshire. In the face of death men and women may have felt that they had more chance in the afterlife by following the rituals of their own ancestors, and many foreigners will have been concerned to leave instructions so that even though they were far from home their bodies would receive the correct ceremonies. This responsibility was usually left in the hands of the husbands or wives or heirs of the deceased, and many tombstones reflect these last requests: Placida, at Wroxeter, for example, set up her late husband's tombstone by his instructions. Others took no chances and, like Julia Velva's heir (5), had tombs made for themselves and their families during their lifetime. Some unmarried women, like Pervinca, may have joined burial clubs in order to ensure a decent burial. In mixed marriages the beliefs of the surviving partner could occasionally override those of the deceased; Regina's husband, Barates, put a phrase in his native Palmyrene language on his wife's tombstone (6) although she herself was British born and bred, and her tombstone in general bears more resemblance to those of Palmyrene women than of her fellow Catuvellaunians.

It is rare, as Joan Alcock has pointed out, to find a burial linked to a specific deity. Exceptions are pipeclay statuettes of Venus found in graves in the south-east. It has been suggested that these burials were of women who had died in childbirth, and a similar explanation has been given for the statuettes, also of pipeclay, of the Dea Nutrix (nursing mother goddess) found at Canterbury and Welwyn (51). The Canterbury Dea Nutrix, and a number of Venus figurines from Kent, had been deliberately broken before being added to the tomb in the belief that in doing so the spirit of the object would also die and so accompany the deceased. A figure of Cupid found in a woman's coffin at London is another deity associated with death, but female figurines found with cremations near Brighton, and from the cemetery outside London's north wall, are more likely to represent the deceased.

The gods, on the whole, were seen as being more useful during life than after death, providing assistance in times of trouble and protecting their worshippers. It was in this role that many native deities were invoked. The policy of the Roman state on conquering a province involved no missionary zeal to convert the population to their gods; as long as the inhabitants gave due reverence to the cult of the Deified Emperors and any other officially designated Roman deities, they were free to worship whom they pleased. Exceptions were those cults which involved human sacrifice or denied the existence of multiple gods: both because they could be seen as undermining the fabric of the Empire. Druidism was already an ancient religion in Gaul and Britain when it was discussed by Julius Caesar, and its priests held a great deal of political and social power. The ancient authors depicted the Druids variously as philosophers, magicians, law-enforcers, theologians, bards and poets, but invariably give the impression that the Druids were men. Who then were the 'black-robed women with dishevelled hair like Furies, brandishing torches' on the shores of Anglesey, whose gibbering so terrified the troops of Suetonius Paulinus?[7] Were these priestesses, or did they belong to the families of Druids? Or were they servants or devotees? It is not clear but it is possible that they were priestesses: Strabo referred to a group of Druidic priestesses on an island at the mouth of the Loire,[8] and the prophecies to Severus Alexander, Aurelian and Diocletian were all made by female Druids, although by the third century the term 'Druid' may have just indicated someone with magical powers. Pomponia Graecina, wife of the first governor of Britain, Aulus Plautius, was accused by her enemies of practising a foreign religion and there is a suggestion, albeit unlikely, that this was Druidism picked up in Britain.

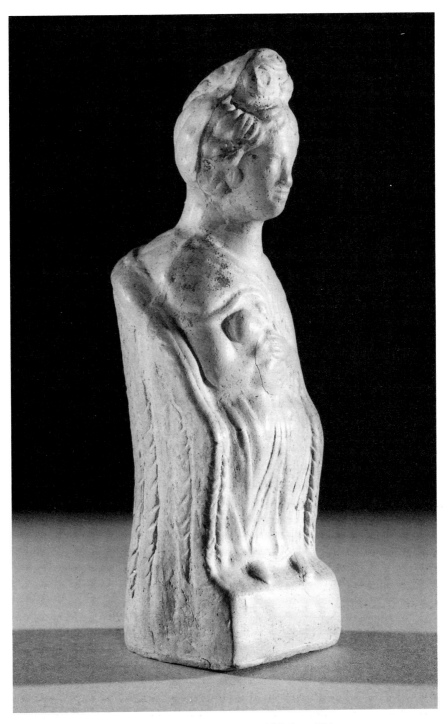

51. Pipeclay statuette of a mother goddess suckling a child, from Welwyn.

Claudius is said by Suetonius[9] to have abolished Druidism on the grounds that its followers practised human sacrifice. There is no evidence that this was so and possibly was merely an excuse to mask a shrewd political move which removed a potential focus of rebellion. The cult may not have been totally destroyed but driven underground, and there is evidence that human sacrifice as part of other cults continued in some rural areas, resulting in the crouched infant burials found under the foundations of the corners of Temple IV at Springhead in the second century and the young woman buried under a threshold at Piddington villa. There was also a long history of venerating the human head, which the Celts saw as the essence of the being and the repository of the soul. This belief survived into the Roman period in the representations of heads on metalwork and pottery, as well as on altars, and as simple stone carvings which are referred to as 'Celtic heads'. The discovery of one of these heads in the domestic shrine at Caerwent shows that the significance of the human head continued to be fundamental to some families' religious beliefs.

Under this heading may also come post-mortem decapitation, evidence for which has appeared on over thirty sites. The heads, when found, are normally placed between the knees. It has been suggested that beheading was the cause of death – capital punishment for some crime – but there is little conclusive proof for this and it is hard to imagine what horrendous crime the baby of six months at Dunstable or the three-year-old at Lankhills could have committed. Furthermore, Matthews has indicated that one in ten of the population in the Dunstable cemetery was decapitated; if all these were the result of capital punishment the crimewave in the area must have given cause for alarm. Throughout the country more females than males were decapitated, according to present figures, although at Dunstable the ratios were equal. This has been compared with the male/female ratios at medieval gallows sites where men tend to outnumber women five to one. Matthews also mentioned that, although the methods of inhumation varied, all the bodies could be described as having had a decent burial.

Decapitation has been interpreted as the result of witchcraft and the severed head and neck of a woman deliberately placed behind the wicker lining of a well at Odell might support this theory. Martin Henig has theorised that the practice was to stop ghosts walking, and Lethbridge commented that the rheumatoid arthritis suffered by one decapitated female at Guilden Morden had made her bad-tempered and therefore likely to return to haunt the living. It was a predominantly rural tradition and as such may reflect less sophisticated beliefs, only adopted in towns after about AD 350.

Other than the belief in the importance of the human head, the pre-Roman religious practices of Britain and the women's participation in them have left few traces. Except for a few timber shrines of the late Iron Age, there was no tradition of temple building or of imbuing gods with a recognisable human form. Centres for religious ceremonial were often groves in the forest or sacred enclosures delimited by a boundary ditch and surrounding a focus for ritual such as a tree, a spring or a rock. This belief in the sacred nature of natural phenomena continued in a Roman form in the worship of the *genii loci* – the spirits of the place. Occasionally the location was specified, but was more often left vague. The altar at Lincoln dedicated by a woman in fulfilment of her vow to the *genius loci* shows that, although the majority of such dedications were made by military men, women were also devotees.[10]

Other Celtic gods were named, although their precise function is unknown, as is their appeal to women. John Mann has suggested that it was due to the Roman invasion that Celtic gods developed into individual personalities and that what seem to be different deities may be merely local names for more widespread divine powers. We know that Boudica sacrificed to the goddess Andraste[11] and Anne Ross has suggested that this goddess might be analogous with Andarte, worshipped by the Vocontii of Gaul. Romana at Great Chesters dedicated to the mysterious Vitiris, whose name is variously spelt and may be a group of deities rather than an individual god. Mocuxsoma and Ivixa are also thought to have been female worshippers of Vitiris. The small size of the altars and the crudeness of the inscriptions has led to the theory that this religion appealed to people of low social scale, and was based on a pre-Roman cult whose deity's name could not be expressed in the Latin alphabet.

Nymphs may also have had a pre-Roman ancestry, personifying the hazier Celtic spirits of spring and wood. Specifically named nymphs, such as Coventina, have left no indications of female worshippers, although dedications have survived to anonymous nymphs: one at Risingham reads 'Forewarned by a dream the soldier bade her who is married to Fabius set up this altar to the Nymphs who are to be worshipped', while an altar at Carvoran was erected by Vettia Mansueta and Claudia Turianilla to 'the Goddesses the Nymphs'. A dedication by another mother and daughter, Brica and Januaria, at Greta Bridge seems to conceal the name of the local nymph in the letters NEINE. *Nymphaea* have been discovered in the grounds of villas, for example at Chedworth, where it resembles a garden pavilion, or at Lullingstone, where one room in the house was dedicated as a *nymphaeum*.

Nymphs were often worshipped in groups of three, a trend shared by mother goddesses. Anne Ross has argued that the mother goddesses (*matres*) were introduced 'representationally' into Britain during the Roman period but that the depictions expressed a concept which was already entrenched in Celtic belief: that of a threefold goddess concerned with fertility and childbirth. Such a triad can be seen in a relief from Cirencester (52) where one mother is suckling a child while the others play with their offspring. Other mother goddesses are more stately and sit firmly on couches or chairs holding baskets of fruit or other fertility symbols (38).

52. Mother goddesses are often depicted in groups of three, although their offspring are not usually as unruly as these infants on a relief from Cirencester.

The majority of dedications which survive to the mother goddesses were made by men. This may mean that men were more likely or in a better position to spend money on expensive dedications rather than that the women were not interested. This, of course, must hold true with all the other altars and religious dedications from the province, as female dedicators are considerably outnumbered by male. It is also possible that religion was largely a family affair, so women relied on the head of the family to make dedications on their behalf. One dedication to the mother goddesses Ollototae ('of other peoples'), however, was erected by Julius Secundus and Aelia Augustina, and there is no reason to suppose that they were related in any way; a bronze statuette base reads 'To Mars Corotiacus, Simplicia for herself, willingly and deservedly set up this offering', while at Carrawburgh Tranquila Severa took the responsibility of dedicating an altar on her family's behalf: women clearly could, if they had the funds, dedicate on their own and other people's behalves.

The surviving evidence for women worshipping in Roman Britain is unlikely to give a full picture. Noticeable by its absence is the devotion of women to female deities, although Ross has commented that 'the function of the goddess must, to a certain extent, reflect the function of the woman, and her most potent and striking characteristics'. There is also a surprising lack of a recognisable Celtic goddess of love; even Venus appears as a fertility goddess (53) rather than the last resort of the lovelorn. John Clayton suggested that the rings and brooches found in Coventina's Well were thrown there 'by love-sick damsels

53. The goddess Venus as depicted by a native mosaicist at Rudston is surrounded by huntsmen and exotic animals and birds. She appears to have been startled into dropping her mirror by a triton holding a torch.

... in the hope of obtaining the countenance of the goddess in their views', but it is more likely that such offerings were seen as being appropriate gifts for a goddess, rather than revealing the sex of the worshipper.

Recent finds of curse tablets at Bath and other sites have revealed a rich spiritual life in which women were fully involved, running alongside the formal rituals. The tablets are sheets of lead on which was scratched a demand for action from the gods. These could be used to ensure ill luck for someone or to correct one's own misfortune and have been called by Roger Tomlin 'the loser's last resort'. Of those so far interpreted, about seventy are concerned with theft: a 'memorandum' from Uley asks Mercury to retrieve a stolen piece of linen for Saturnina, for example (54). The god, sometimes named, but occasionally left unspecified, is expected to perform like a celestial hybrid of Sherlock Holmes and Gilbert and Sullivan's Lord High Executioner, not only discovering the perpetrator of the crime but also exacting a fitting punishment. In order not

54. The curse tablet commissioned by Saturnina at Uley in an attempt to engage the assistance of the god Mercury in recovering her linen cloth.

to influence the deity by unjust suspicions many use the formula 'whether man or woman, whether boy or girl, whether slave or free', but some name names, such as Anniola and her accomplices, who are accused of taking six silver coins. The deity could also be offered suggestions as to a suitable punishment, and these give a splendid picture of frustrated fury: Basilia asked that her silver ring be returned and that the thief and accessories before and after the fact 'be cursed in [his] blood and eyes [and] every limb, or even have all [his] intestines eaten away'.

Some tablets do not explain the cause of the curse but still express themselves with choleric spleen: 'I curse Tretia Maria and her life and mind and memory and liver and lungs mixed up together, and her words, thoughts and memory: thus may she be unable to speak what things are concealed'. Unfortunately the rest of the curse is missing so we do not know how long the invective continued, nor what Tretia Maria had done to deserve it. This particular *defixio* shows the shadowy line between religion and magic, as no deity is named and the names Tretia and Maria may be reversed – a powerful curse. Some are simpler, such as 'Tacita, hereby accursed, is labelled old like putrid gore', which has a flavour of pure vindictiveness.

Not all the tablets are curses. Examples from Bath are more in the nature of swearing a sacred oath; for example, 'Uricalus, Docilosa his wife, Docilis his son, and Docilina, Decentinus his brother, Alogiosa; the names of those who have sworn at the spring of the goddess Sulis on the 12th of April. Whosoever there has perjured himself you are to make him pay for it to the goddess Sulis in his own blood'. Others ask favours, such as a gentleman at Old Harlow who petitions 'To the god Mercury, I entrust to you my affair with Etterna, and her own self, and may Timotneus feel no jealousy of me at the risk of his own life blood'. The author of this touching revelation of a love triangle, however, loses some sympathy as on the other side he takes the opportunity to ask Mercury to look after a business transaction!

These tablets reveal not only fascinating personal details of a level of society which rarely leaves any record, but also the business-like relationship between mankind and gods. If the god plays his part he will be rewarded. A striking example of this is set out in a tablet from Caistor-St Edmund, where the theft of 15 *denarii*, a wreath, bracelets, clothes, a mirror and two pewter vessels is recorded and Neptune told firmly: 'if you want the pair of leggings they shall become yours at the price of his [the thief's] blood'.[12] What Neptune was expected to do with the leggings is left to our imagination but they no doubt joined the rings, cloaks, bathing costumes and other impedimenta which he had also recovered.

Superstition played a major part in everyday life. Tacitus[13] recorded that prior to Boudica's rebellion the statue of Victory fell at Camulodunum and 'women, converted into maniacs by excitement, cried that destruction was at hand'. Seeing visions and interpreting signs was common and we have already seen that Fabius' wife at Risingham and Antonia at Kirkby Thore paid due attention to visions and dreams. Sorcery as an act was illegal because magic could be used to destabilise the settled pattern of society, but the confused thinking behind the curse tablets shows that the situation was not black-and-white and even if the State banned witchcraft a large proportion of the population believed in it and carried amulets as a protection against evil. The phallus, in particular, was a powerful symbol against evil and as such appears on buildings, on pottery and on jewellery: small gold rings found at London and Faversham decorated with phalli may have been worn by the children of the wealthy to ensure their protection. Bells were also used to ward off evil.

The evils against which these amulets were directed were usually nameless and unspecified, but to the living a fear of disease was an ever-present worry. Physicians and surgeons, mostly of Greek origin, are known to have practised in Britain although the only ones known by name were attached to the army.[14] One can only presume that women attached to the army had access to these military medical men for their own ailments and those of their children. The civilian situation is less clear, as no inscriptions have survived naming civilian doctors, nor have any buildings been identified as civilian hospitals. In other parts of the Empire physicians were employed by the town councils to provide treatment for any citizen who might require it and there seems no reason to doubt that this system was followed in Britain.

Roman doctors were highly trained and remarkably competent, given their limited scientific knowledge. The treatment of wounds, the repair of broken limbs and many complex operations were carried out with confidence, even if a lack of anaesthetics other than opium, henbane and mandrake, made them ghastly experiences for the patients. Many doctors, such as Soranus, Galen and Celsus, wrote treatises on medical practice which would have been read widely, so patients in Britain could have expected as up-to-date treatment as those in Rome or Athens. However, doctors were not expected to act alone: the gods were required to play their part and many people put more faith in divine treatment than in practical remedies; going to see the doctor might be seen as a last resort rather than a first call. This was recognised by the doctors themselves, who did not scorn divine intervention: Abrocomas at Binchester[15] is known to us because he dedicated an inscription to Aesculapius and Salus, both deities with an acknowledged role in healing. The sick would either make offerings to a god of healing – there were plenty to choose from, both Roman and Celtic – in the hope of receiving a cure in return, or could visit a shrine famous as a centre of healing such as the temple of Sulis Minerva at Bath. There are indications that the native goddess Sulis was worshipped at Bath before the Roman invasion, but the magnificent temple erected over the spring was firmly in the classical manner and must have been an overwhelming sight to the sick and lame who visited it. The water at Bath has medicinal properties and is still used for this purpose, but in the Roman period visitors were prepared to make sacrifices to the goddess as part of their cure as well as immersing themselves in the water or imbibing it. Sulis Minerva was expected to cure a multitude of complaints and may have done so in cases of gout, arthritis and rheumatism. In other cases her skill was supplemented by various physicians of differing levels of competence. The stamp for an eye-salve found in the baths suggests that Titus Janianus, for example, may have had a permanent surgery on the site.[16]

The number of women visiting the shrine is hinted at by the names mentioned on the curse tablets, but some models of parts of the anatomy, known as *ex votos*, such as ivory or bronze breasts (55) also suggest that Sulis Minerva assisted in female ailments. Fewer *ex votos* have been found in Britain than in Italy or Gaul, but at Wroxeter thirty-five eyes carved from wall-plaster and two from sheet gold indicate a shrine which specialised in eye troubles.

The visitors to Bath or Wroxeter relied on a mixture of practical relief and faith to heal them, but another method in which Greek and Celtic traditions came together could be found at the temple of Nodens at Lydney. This was a temple with an adjacent bath suite and a guest house for visitors, as well as a long narrow building which has been identified as an *abaton* in which the patient slept overnight in the hope of being visited by the god and healed, or at least given a prescription in the form of a dream message which could be interpreted by the priests. Among the offerings to Nodens were statuettes of dogs and *ex votos* of a miniature bronze arm and a bone plaque of a naked woman clutching her stomach. This temple complex has been dated to the fourth century and might indicate that the emergence of Christianity had not diminished the appeal of the healing gods.

It was in the eastern religions, of which Christianity was one, that women seem to have shown most interest. The only priestess known by name is Diodora at Corbridge, who dedicated an altar in Greek to Herakles of Tyre. Other priestesses must have had full-time employment or officiated on a voluntary basis, as a number of statuettes of women with veils drawn over their heads in preparation for sacrifice have been found (56). Some eastern cults had a strong appeal for women. The worship of Isis, for example, had its origins in Egypt and was introduced into Rome as a mystery cult in the second century BC. Its

55. Ivory *ex voto* from Bath. The two breasts carved on the front indicate that the petitioner suffered from a breast complaint such as mastitis.

secret foreign nature led to its suppression by Augustus but it was supported by Gaius Caligula, who erected an Iseum in the Campus Martius. Isis was a mother goddess, described by Apuleius as 'the natural mother of all things, mistress and governess of all the elements' who could dispose of 'the planets of the sky, the wholesome winds of the seas, and the lamentable silences of hell'.[17] The cult's appeal lay not in its doctrines, which differed little from those of other mother goddesses, but in the fact that worshippers of both sexes took part in the ceremonies, supervised by professional priests, instead of watching others performing the rituals.

Although the cult demanded abstinence from the pleasures of the flesh at

56. Bronze statuette of a priestess with her head veiled for sacrifice, from South Shields.

certain times, it was seen in the first century in Rome to be an unsavoury religion which appealed to courtesans, and Ovid offers the excuse of a visit to the Iseum as a suitable cover for an assignation with a lover.[18] However, by the time it reached Britain the cult had become respectable: an altar from London records the restoration of the Temple to Isis by a third-century governor of Britannia Superior, Marcus Martiannius Pulcher.[19] This may be the same temple referred to on a buffware jug of first-century date found at Tooley Street, London, which has *Londinii ad Fanum Isidis* (London at the Temple of Isis) scratched on the shoulder (57).

Devotees of the cult may have been scattered throughout the province and may not have been able to participate regularly in the rites. There is evidence of followers of Isis at Wroxeter, Silchester, Exeter and Dorchester, and there may have been temples in these towns. An oval amulet of haematite found at Dicket Mead shows Isis with a lion and the god Bes within a frame formed by the Ouroboros, the Serpent devouring its tail. Below the goddess there is a stylised representation of a womb, and around the edge there is an invocation in Greek to Typhon, the elemental force. On the reverse there is a scarab and a second Greek legend which invokes Ororiouth, the spirit which gives protection against women's diseases, and Iao, the Jewish Jahweh. Haematite amulets were carried in pockets or strapped to the thigh to relieve labour pains and this example may have belonged to a woman of eastern descent, although there is no evidence to indicate that she was a slave as has been suggested.

A particularly interesting religious dedication by a woman is that to the Silvanae and to the Quadruviae (the goddesses who presided over crossroads) by Vibia Pacata at Westerwood. This association of deities is characteristic of Upper Pannonia (modern Hungary), but the epithet *Caelestis* which is attached to the deities is of African origin. Eric Birley has suggested that Vibia Pacata had been influenced by the African cult of the Punic Tanit, either as a result of her husband, the centurion Flavius Verecundus, having had a posting in Africa, or because she herself was of African origin.

The dedication to 'The Goddess Mother of the Gods' by Tranquila Severa at Carrawburgh, may point to another eastern cult, that of Cybele; a theogeny claims that she is the 'Mother of the Gods, Peace, Virtue, Ceres, the Syrian Goddess, weighing life and laws in her balance'. The worship of Cybele was a complex cult which also involved worship of Atys, her lover who castrated himself in her service, in memory of which priests of Cybele castrated themselves during initiation rites. A temple to Cybele and Atys is thought to have existed in London on the grounds of sculptural evidence and others were built outside the forts on Hadrian's Wall.

Some eastern religions, like Mithraism, were specifically barred to women, although they would be well aware of the importance of the cult to their menfolk – Julia Similina carefully included Mithraic figures on her husband's

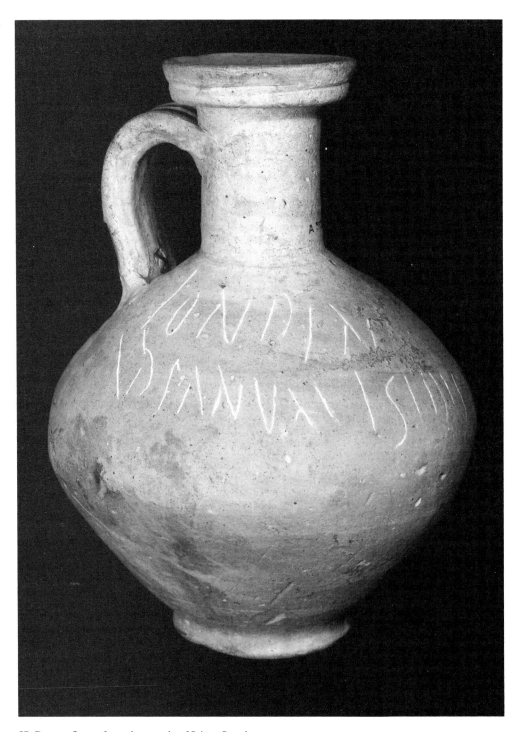

57. Pottery flagon from the temple of Isis at London.

tombstone as the widow of a Freemason today might include Masonic symbols. Other cults were open to both sexes: a case in point is the worship of Jupiter Dolichenus. Dolichenus was an ancient Hittite sky-god who was assimilated with the Roman sky-god, Jupiter. This habit of pairing off Roman gods with those of other lands, known as syncretism, was common and seems to have been an attempt to render the exotic more familiar or to draw foreign elements into the standard Roman framework. Jupiter Dolichenus largely appealed to army officers, who linked his worship with the health and safety of the emperor. The cult never achieved official status but became closely connected with the Severan emperors, and the third century saw an increase in dedications, with temples built at Cirencester, Customs Shrubs and most of the Wall forts. Why the cult should have appealed to women is not clear; possibly the element of emperor veneration was responsible, as neither Magunna at Birrens nor the daughter of Sabinus at Great Chesters appear to have had an eastern origin.

The eastern cult which appealed most to women was Christianity, but despite later claims that it was brought to Britain by the mother of Constantine the Great, St Paul or Joseph of Arimathea, it is more likely that its origins lay in the visits of traders and merchants. British Christians start to be mentioned in the works of Tertullian and Origen in the third century but the church does not seem to have really become established until the fourth century. Possibly individual Christians lived in the province as early as the late first century but anti-Christian sentiment, which lasted until the late third century, will have kept the Church underground. This lack of sympathy may have been a reaction to what Charles Thomas has called 'the stubborn exclusivity of the Christians', which cannot have endeared them to their neighbours, some of whom may have seen the cult as a threat to the delicate balance between man and the gods, to disturb which might result in major natural disasters. It was only after AD 313 that Christians could feel confident enough to build churches, and even martyria, to those like Albinus, Aaron and Julius, who had suffered under the persecutions of Decius and Valerian (250–9).

There is not the space to give a detailed history of Christianity in Roman Britain: interested readers can do no better than read Thomas's masterly and very readable account. However, it is worth noting the effect it had on the women of the province to whom several aspects of the new religion appealed. First, and most important, it offered a more optimistic view of the afterlife than any other religion. This hope of a better world must have attracted people whose lives were often hard and restricted, particularly as this better life was available to everyone, rich and poor, slave and free, male and female. Membership of many of the eastern cults and classical Roman religions had been denied to the poor because worshippers were expected to donate large sums of money to support a priesthood or stage festivals. Christianity relied on its richer members for practical support: silver vessels used in ceremonies were donated by the wealthy such as Innocentia and Viventia at Water Newton (58), but the religion did not close its doors to the poor.

The development of Christianity had a more basic effect on women than just fulfilling a spiritual need. The belief that it was necessary to preserve the body so that it could be resurrected on the Day of Judgement led to cremation being replaced by inhumation, often with the bodies preserved in gypsum. Even Christian women, despite the strictures of Tertullian, insisted on being accompanied to the grave by their jewellery and personal items in caskets: a grave at York, for example, contained *unguentaria* and jewellery as well as an openwork bone plaque which contains the Christian message 'Hail sister, may you live in God'. Christian symbols and imagery also began to appear on mosaics

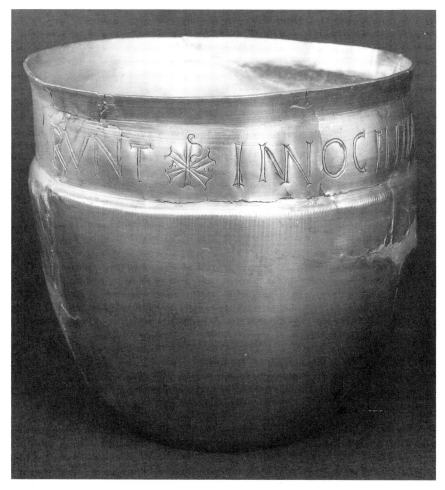

58. Silver vessel from Water Newton inscribed with the Christian *chi-rho* symbol and the names of the donors, Innocentia and Viventia.

and wall-paintings as well as on domestic items, such as spoons and bowls, and jewellery.

Christianity had an effect on the appearance and manners of women. Tertullian gave specific instructions as to how a Christian woman should conduct herself: he deprecated the use of make-up, allowed only the plainest of hairstyles, and directed that only the simplest garments of uncoloured cloth should be worn.[20] The increase of infant burials in the fourth century may also be the result of the spread of Christianity, as the early Christian writers disapproved of contraception, abortion and infanticide, which may have led to a sharp increase in the birth rate. Lactantius preached that a Christian couple who were too poor to have a family should remain celibate, and that abortion and infanticide were against Christian principles.[21] However, as Valentinian I made infanticide illegal in the Western Empire as late as 370, it would appear that the practice continued.

The number of eastern cults known to have thrived in Britain highlights the difficulties of following one's religion in a foreign country. Many of the cults were brought into the province by the army, and shrines and temples proliferated around forts, so women attached to the army had a chance of finding a shrine to their favourite deity close at hand or at least other adherents with whom to share their devotions. However, with the number of mixed marriages and the trade in foreign slaves there may have been many women who were cut off from the comfort of familiar ritual, particularly if they were devotees of a cult which involved elaborate ceremonial. The aristocratic lady from Rome, Julia Lucilla, for example, may well have missed worshipping at the Temple of Vesta or the excitement of the Lupercalia, when young men dressed in the skins of sacrificed goats ran through the streets of Rome striking at bystanders with thongs. Even Britons moving around the country might find themselves among strangers who had different festivals and ceremonies, as Celtic deities, by their very nature, were limited to a small locality.

It is, therefore, likely that it would be her religious beliefs which would emphasise to a woman how far she was from home if she married outside her tribe or followed her male relatives to a different area or province. It would be important for these women to meet like-minded people with whom to attend religious services or carry out simple rituals. Even within the family a wife might follow a different religion to her husband, and as family ritual was led by the *pater familias* any children of a marriage would be brought up with the religious beliefs of their father taking precedent over those of their mother. Mothers would have introduced their daughters to those cults which allowed them access or which were confined to female worshippers, but they would have been isolated from their sons when it came to religions which were totally or partially closed to women. Unfortunately, it was these latter groups which had the greatest influence on the social and political life of the province.

7. Entertainment and recreation

A woman's day would not necessarily be a round of toil from dawn to dusk. Various entertainments were available to her, both inside and outside the home: time would be spent playing with her children, the household might include numerous pets, the family might enjoy listening to music or playing board games, and there would be other occupations in which she could participate for pleasure and relaxation.

In the cradle babies played with rattles and bells until they were old enough for more sophisticated toys. Dolls, in particular, were popular; a jointed doll of wood found at Hitchin resembles others found elsewhere in the Empire in bone, wood or clay (59). It was customary in Rome for brides to dedicate their dolls to Venus, or the *lares* and *penates*, before their marriage as a sign that their childhood was over. Examples found in Egyptian tombs of the period demonstrate that even the rag doll has a very respectable lineage. Other cuddly toys may have been common but have left no trace unless some of the 'pets' seen on tombstones come into this category.

Wall-paintings from Pompeii and Herculaneum show cupids playing games such as leap-frog, blindman's buff and hide-and-seek, which of course leave no evidence for archaeologists to find. A bone spinning top from South Shields and balls, seen clutched in the hands of the young Ertola at Corbridge and Flavia Augustina's offspring (11), indicate that simple games were enjoyed. Balls may also not have been purely for children: a mosaic at Piazza Armerina, in Sicily, shows two bikini-clad females playing handball with a ball which has clear seams like a cricket ball, presumably of leather stitched in gussets.

Board games have left evidence in the form of the boards themselves and gaming pieces. Many of these have been found in military contexts, as might be expected, but there is enough evidence to suggest that women were also keen players; Ovid was of the opinion that all women should include games of chance among their skills of seduction.[1]

Four games involving the movement of counters on a board are known. *Duodecim scripta* was played on the same principles as backgammon, with two players moving fifteen counters each in opposite directions around a board of twenty-four squares. The moves were controlled by throwing three dice and the object was to move one's own counters to safe squares while knocking off the opposition's isolated pieces. The first player to move her counters around the board won. A pottery board decorated with rows of incised ivy leaves found at Holt is thought to have been a sophisticated *duodecim scripta* board.

A second game, which may simply have been a version of *duodecim scripta*, was played on a board with six six-letter words arranged into columns of three. Unfortunately, although fragments of boards survive, we have no clear idea of how the game was played. *Terni lapilli* was the Roman version of noughts and crosses played on a square board with nine squares, each with incised diagonals. Boards for this game are known from a number of sites.

The best known of the Roman board games is undoubtedly *ludus latrunculorum* (60), also known as 'soldiers' as it was a battle game requiring great skill. The pieces were used like the rook in chess and the player's aim was to capture the counters of her opponent by surrounding an opposing piece with

59. Wood puppet from Hitchin, its hinged arms now missing. The hair is dressed in the elaborate style of the Flavian empresses.

60. Stone gaming board from Corbridge. Ovid was of the opinion that every woman should include board games among her social skills. Counters of glass were used at Corbridge, with dice and shakers of bone and pottery.

two of her own. This game was extremely popular and boards made of stone, pottery, wood and even marble (at Richborough) have been found, with exotic boards in precious metals referred to in literature. *Ludus latrunculorum* was exempt from the ban on gambling because the moves depended on the players' skill and foresight, and it may well have been regarded as a spectator sport as well as a private battle.

Dice were required to play *duodecim scripta* and the word game, and no doubt throwing dice was regarded as a game in itself. Dice were made in bone and pottery; some of the bone dice found at South Shields and Corbridge were loaded, suggesting that cheating was commonplace. The game for the long bone dice found in Iron Age contexts, mostly north of Hadrian's Wall, is puzzling as their shape would seem to preclude normal methods of dice throwing. However, their use seems to have continued well into the Roman period.

Simple guessing games were played at home. The Emperor Augustus enjoyed playing *par impar* or 'odds and evens' with his family, allotting them 250 *denarii* a piece to make it more fun. The game appears to have needed all the help it could get as one merely betted on the odd or even number of pebbles hidden in the player's hands. In *inicatio* two players each raised the fingers of the right hand, varying the number raised and calling out the total number of fingers raised by both, until one or other guessed correctly. This game still survives in Italy today as *morra*.

Nine men's morris is commonly regarded as a medieval game but stone boards for nine- and three-men's morris have been found at Corbridge and other sites in Britain in Roman contexts. In three-men's morris the squared board has nine points and each player has four counters which are placed alternately on points. The first player to place three counters in a straight line wins. In six-men's morris each player has six pieces and in nine-men's morris they have nine, with the rules and the board becoming correspondingly more complicated.

Literary references suggest that Roman women at all levels of society kept pets for companionship and protection, and coped with the demands for exercise and feeding, as well as the extra housework involved. Animal bones reveal the presence of a large number of cats and dogs in domestic contexts. These may have been kept as guard dogs and vermin catchers but some will have been regarded purely as pets. The evidence of animals found in burials or depicted on gravestones is ambiguous as they could have had a funerary significance, but a tiny dog, like a chihuahua, found in a coffin at Stanwick villa must have been the pet of the deceased. In an early fifth-century family burial at Canterbury, where the parents had been buried seated, one child was on the mother's lap while the family dog had pride of place on the father's lap. Dog pawprints of various sizes are common on tiles and a small dog must have incurred wrath at Lullingstone when he trotted over the wet cement of a low barn wall. A dog jumping up for titbits on a woman's tombstone from Bowness appears to have been a favoured animal. Cats regularly occur on tombstones in Gaul although not so far in Britain, where evidence for their place in the home relies on bones found on such sites as Lullingstone and Vindolanda, and the pawprints of full-grown cats as well as kittens on tiles. A small boy from Lincoln appears on his tombstone with a hare on his knee and another hare is carved on the tombstone of Anicius Ingenuus from Housesteads – both could have had religious significance but it is not difficult to see them as pets. No doubt children also kept beetles, mice and orphan ducklings as they do today and it is tempting to see a dormouse found in the hypocaust of the South Shields granary as the Roman equivalent of the modern family hamster disappearing behind the central heating pipes.

Birds were particularly popular as pets for women. Pliny referred to those which could be taught to talk, such as starlings and magpies,[2] and Indian parrots were imported into Rome. Nightingales and other birds were kept for their song. The child on the Murrell Hill, Carlisle, grave relief (42) is shown playing with a bird on the mother's knee, and Julia Velva's daughter (5) and Sepronia Martina both hold birds. The woman on the Bowness tombstone holds a dove in one hand.

Wild animals were captured alive for displays and combat in the arena. Not every town was provided with an amphitheatre – so far only eight in Britain have produced clear evidence of an amphitheatre, although there are possible examples at York and Leicester. It is unlikely that British spectators were often treated to the sight of gladiators in combat with lions, tigers, panthers or rhinoceroses, nor does the *venatio*, or wild beast hunt, appear on British mosaics, which may suggest that it was not to British taste or that there were practical or economic difficulties in producing exotic beasts for popular edification. Bear-baiting and bullfights were a different matter, as there were ready supplies of both animals, bears being a regular export from Scotland. A scene on a beaker from Colchester may show a scene of bear-baiting although no dogs are shown.

Hand-to-hand fighting between both male and female gladiators also took place in the amphitheatre and the evidence for regular bouts being held in Britain includes a fragment of graffiti from Leicester which refers to 'Lucius a gladiator' as well as a gladiatorial helmet from Hawkedon. Various representations on pottery, glass, mosaics and wall-paintings show gladiators in training or in combat, so whether or not women were allowed to witness such displays, they would have accepted the amphitheatre as a part of everyday urban life. Their possible exclusion from the audience may be suspected from various rules and regulations in force in other parts of the Empire: in Rome women had to sit at the back at gladiatorial shows by decree of Augustus,[3] and were barred from watching athletic contests. This was an attempt to prevent disorderly behaviour and may not have been in force in Britain. The amphitheatres were also used to mete out various punishments, including the death penalty, and there is no reason to believe that women were not as keen to witness these treats as their menfolk.

Celtic women are known to have been enthusiastic race-goers, and in the Roman Empire race tracks called circuses were often built in association with amphitheatres. None have so far been identified in Britain, although a pair of parallel walls below Knightrider Street in London has been tentatively suggested as a circus. Again, circuses appear often enough in artistic impressions for it to be concluded that racing was known in Roman Britain. Many of the products of the Nene Valley and Colchester pottery factories show chariot and horse races, which may reflect the long tradition of Celtic interest in racing even before the Roman conquest.

Women would also have attended theatrical performances. Theatres are known at Canterbury, Verulamium, Colchester, and Gosbecks Farm, although the latter may have been intended primarily for religious performances. Tacitus also mentions the theatre at Colchester at the time of the Boudican revolt,[4] and there is an inscription referring to a theatre at Petuaria (Brough-on-Humber) although no structures are known.[5] The only completely exposed theatre in Britain is at Verulamium, first built in the mid-first century (61). It was

61. The theatre at Verulamium. The stage is to the left with the column marking the scenery.

built in conjunction with a temple and originally served the needs of priestly ceremonial. The earliest building had a central orchestra surrounded on all sides, bar the north-east, by an earthen bank supporting wooden seating. In the north-east section there was a small stage building which was built with a raised wooden floor and a small dressing-room behind. Three aisles led under the stands to the orchestra and wooden staircases against the outer walls allowed the public access to their seats. It was more common in Roman theatre architecture for the orchestra to be semicircular in shape and at Verulamium many members of the audience would have had a poor view of the stage although a performance taking place in the orchestra would have been visible. This may support the theory that the theatre had a dual purpose, with religious or state ceremonies being enacted in the orchestra and theatrical performances on the stage.

Most of the plays performed in British theatres are likely to have been the same old favourites which had first been played in Rome during the Republic, and there is little evidence for new plays being produced in quantity. Tragic and comic masks were used by actors to identify their characters; an ivory tragic mask from Caerleon and pottery masks from Baldock and Catterick used as decorative appliqué may suggest that bands of travelling players brought popular productions to rural areas. The owners of a house at Leicester may have been theatre buffs, as they chose to decorate a room with a painting of tragic masks. A rare figurine from Colchester shows an actor in the guise of Priapus and hints at the Rabelaisian character of the comedies.

The status of actor was not high and persons of quality who appeared on the stage did so at the risk of losing their standing in society. Actresses were even less highly thought of, and Augustus decreed that no-one of senatorial rank could marry an actress. In Italy the behaviour of actresses had become a byword as early as the time of Cicero and full-frontal nudity was a commonplace on the Roman stage. In Britain there is a fragment of pottery graffiti which links Verecunda, an actress, with Lucius, a gladiator. Unfortunately pots are transportable and we cannot assume that Verecunda or Lucius ever appeared nightly or 'for a short season only' at Leicester. However, it is likely that actresses regularly formed part of the company at Canterbury, Verulamium and Colchester as well as the smaller travelling groups.

We have little evidence for the proportion of women making up the audience at these performances. If the theatre at Canterbury could hold seven thousand we must assume that it was open to men, women and children, otherwise there would rarely have been a full house. Nor do we know if the sexes were segregated; Ovid's advice to predatory men to 'do your hunting in the round theatre' suggests that they were not.[6] One wonders, however, whether the British theatre bore much resemblance to the Italian in the quality and regularity of the performances, which may often have resembled pantomime rather than high drama, with both tragedies and comedies accompanied by singing and dancing and the audience joining in with favourite verses. In some plays the music got the upper hand and the performance approached modern opera in character, while on other occasions there would be just solo or harmony singing. Soranus referred to the medical fates, such as failure to menstruate, which could befall professional female singers, particularly those who took part in competitions,[7] and there is little reason to suppose that female singers received any more respect than actresses.

Remarkably little is known about music in the Roman period even though it played an important part in religious and civic ceremony as well as public and private entertainment. Ovid, among others, considered it essential for an educated woman to be able to sing and play both the lyre and Phoenician harp,[8] but very few pieces of manuscript have survived to indicate the level of skill required. In Britain we have to rely on rare finds of instrument fragments and representations in art for any impression of the musical life of the inhabitants. Some of the latter are rather fanciful and show deities or nymphs at play: a mosaic at Sherborne, for example, shows Apollo playing the lyre in competition with Marsyas on the double pipes. Orpheus is depicted on several mosaics

62. The Mildenhall silver platter showing a maenad playing the double pipes whilst dancing.

playing an instrument which could be either a lyre or a *cithara*. The Mildenhall plates show several instruments being played by frolicking bacchanalian revellers: cymbals, tambourines, double pipes (62) and panpipes, all used in the worship of Bacchus.

Religious ritual in general would have involved the use of the larger brass section, such as the *tuba*, the *litmus*, the *cornu* or the *carnyx*, all of which also had a military role. The *sistrum*, a rattle with loose discs strung along metal bars within a small frame, was mostly associated with the worship of Isis, a sect which particularly appealed to women, and is occasionally found decorating the heads of hairpins. Women would therefore have been familiar with the appearance and sound of many instruments even if they were not competent musicians themselves.

Fragments of musical instruments have been found which might indicate that music was also played in the home. A set of bone mounts from the yoke of a lyre was found in a fifth-century context at Abingdon and a similar piece of antler from Dinorben suggests that the lyre had been played in Britain from the late Iron Age. A fragment of ivory from Cirencester has been identified as part of a *cithara*, an instrument like a lyre but with more strings and a broader sound box. Both instruments had their strings attached to bone tuning pegs and were either plucked with both hands or with a plectrum.

A small figurine of a young woman from Silchester (63) holds a *tibia*, a reed pipe which was played either singly or in pairs. Bellicia is known to have owned a *syrinx* at Shakenoak, although her skill is unrecorded. Small pipes have been found in ivory and bone on several sites in London but, unfortunately, none comes from an unequivocally Roman context. One has a single note and might be more accurately described as a whistle. The pipe found in a well at Ashton, however, was provided with a reed.

Some instruments, such as the lute and the harp, both considered by classical writers to be female instruments, have left no record in Britain, so their use has to be assumed from Continental evidence and literary references. More exotic instruments such as the bagpipes – tentatively identified as being played by an Atys figure from Gloucester – might not bear much relationship to everyday life, but there is some evidence that the *hydraulis* might have been quite commonly played by women. This was a form of organ invented by Ctesibios of Alexandria at the end of the third century BC, in which air was pumped by hand into a chamber containing a bronze bell surrounded by water. Notes were played by opening and closing vents by means of a keyboard, which forced air through pipes by altering the balance of pressure between the water and the air coming from the bellows. This instrument is known from clay models as well as remains found at Pompeii and Aquincum in Hungary, and its use in Britain is attested by its appearance, standing on a pedestal, as decoration on Castorware vessels made in the Nene Valley.

Some householders would hire musicians and singers to entertain their guests at dinner whilst others relied on their womenfolk performing traditional melodies. No doubt there were some airs which had never been written down but passed through the generations from prehistoric origins, and women from other provinces will have brought with them the melodies of their native areas. Traditional dances are also likely to have been performed, particularly on festival days, although nothing is known of their form. The motif of three female figures dancing in a ring has a very long ancestry and may reflect one of these old dances. In Rome dancing was regarded as respectable only if it took place in the home, professional dancing being regarded as immoral unless it formed part of a religious ritual.

Singing, dancing and playing musical instruments would have been taught initially by mothers, with music teachers hired if affordable or if the children

63. Bronze statuette of a young woman playing a *tibia*, from Silchester.

showed aptitude. Mothers were also responsible for teaching their children the elementary skills of reading and writing before both boys and girls were sent to school or had home tutors. In Rome formal education began at the age of seven and this practice may have been followed in Britain.

It is possible that formal education was confined to the middle and upper classes who could afford to pay for schooling or the upkeep of an educated slave. Some children went on to secondary education which was in the hands of Greek *grammatici* who taught in rooms in fora or in private houses. Agricola made it a priority during his governorship of Britain to ensure that the sons of leading Britons received a thorough grounding in the Latin language, rhetoric and literature, and was of the opinion that the Britons were naturally more able than the hardworking Gauls at learning Latin once they set their minds to it.[9] Whether this opportunity was extended to daughters is not mentioned. The only teacher known by name in the province is Demetrius of Tarsus, who took part in the reconnaissance of the western islands in AD 82 and is known to have resided in York for a time.[10] He may not have been actively involved in teaching whilst in Britain, but the results of his many anonymous colleagues' efforts is visible in the number of inscriptions, graffiti and lettered pottery stamps which appeared from the first century AD onwards.

The majority of the native rural population will have continued to speak Celtic dialects as their first language, with enough dog-Latin to get by in trading and in any brushes they might have with officialdom. Survivals in the Welsh language, for example, suggest that in some areas Latin was, at best, only a second language and it is possible that some women in the rural backwaters never bothered, or needed, to know more than a few basic words. Contact with merchants and the army helped to spread the Latin language, while those who had had some education or close contacts with officials would have been fluent. Kenneth Jackson has shown that the Latin spoken in Britain remained purer and of a more archaic form than that spoken in other provinces simply because it was a second language, learnt with all its grammatical subtleties at school rather than in a looser form at mother's knee. The well-educated minority, and those of eastern origin, would also have been familiar with Greek. By the end of the first century AD the increasingly cosmopolitan flavour of the urban population will have resulted in many languages being heard in Britain with the consequence that a knowledge of Latin would have been essential for efficient communication between people who could have originated as far afield as Scotland, Africa or Turkey. Native Britons will have continued to speak Celtic at home but the increasing number of mixed marriages will have added to the number of families speaking Latin.

The many finds of graffiti indicate that most people could not only speak Latin but also write it down. The cultured pre-Roman Briton, often educated in Gaul, may have been able to write, but the Celtic language had no script –

any written Celtic words, as on Belgic coins, were in Latin characters. The concept of ordinary people being able to write was new, therefore, and shows how successful Agricola's policy of education had been. Writing was employed to keep tallies, make lists, ask favours of the gods – the number of inscriptions to native deities indicates that the population presumed that the gods, too, had taken part in this education programme – as well as to send letters and make bizarre comments, such as 'Austalis has been wandering off on his own every day for a fortnight' which is scratched on a tile from London.[11] The new-found skill was also used to write obscenities on wall-plaster at Leicester, showing familiarity with slightly more than mere text-book Latin. Graffiti, however, tends to be confined to urban sites and rarely appears in the country, which may reflect social factors or the limits of education.

A number of letters have survived, mostly from military men, but three examples from Vindolanda show that women also sent and received letters. These letters are all that survive of what seems to have been a regular correspondence between Claudia Severa, wife of Aelius Brocchus, and Sulpicia Lepidina, wife of Flavius Cerialis, prefect of the 8th (or 9th) Cohort of Batavians. One letter invites Sulpicia Lepidina to Claudia Severa's birthday party and is written by a scribe but with a postscript added by Claudia Severa herself: 'I shall expect you, sister. Farewell, sister, my dearest soul, as I hope to prosper, and hail'. This has been described by Bowman and Thomas as the earliest known example of a woman's handwriting in Latin, as even the literate regularly used scribes.

The Vindolanda writing tablets, in general, indicate that letter-writing for purely personal reasons was common and that families kept in touch over great distances by this method. Sons in the army wrote home asking for food parcels or extra socks and a fascinating, if largely illegible, letter from a man called Vinicius at Wroxeter, to a married woman called Nigra, warns her of the imminent arrival of one Bilonicus, whom he describes as 'a dog of Arius'! So far no love letters have come to light although, no doubt, they were also common, and the love of a woman called Armea apparently moved one lovesick youth at Binchester to express himself in hexameters on a tile he was making. Ovid referred to confidantes carrying letters concealed in their bosoms, stocking tops or shoes, and even goes so far as to recommend the use of new milk and 'stalks of moistened flax' for secret writing.[12] Most letters, luckily, were inscribed in wax or written in ink on wooden tablets or papyrus. A number of styli have been found but only a few bronze pens, and quills or brushes may have been used. Inkwells of pottery, metal and glass are also regular, if not common finds, using ink of carbon black mixed with gum and water.

Writing tablets which have survived intact consist of rectangular leaves hinged together in pairs or in sets opening out like a concertina. One letter from Vindolanda is unusual in that the text is written on both sides of a single piece of wood, like a postcard. The letters were tied shut with string and sealed with wax or lead, stamped with a personal seal, so that they could travel without anyone but the recipient being able to read the contents. The name of the recipient was written on the outside and occasionally that of the sender was added. Sending the letter relied on finding someone who was travelling in the right direction, possibly an easier task for the wives of the military than civilians.

Letters were not the only reading matter available. Books were written on papyrus and stored in cylindrical boxes (the lid of one has been found at Housesteads) and some wealthy families may have had small libraries. Through these books Britons would have been introduced to the classical writers. Barrett has recently catalogued allusions to the *Aeneid* of Vergil found in the province. These include a wall-painting from Otford showing Turnus riding out to battle, and mosaics from Lullingstone and Keynsham, which both relate the tale of Europa's abduction by Jupiter in the guise of a bull. Barrett considered that, whereas many of the depictions of the *Aeneid* might be explained away as the result of pattern books or the use of well-known phrases or sayings, the Lullingstone mosaic indicates a personal knowledge of the story on the part of the owner of the villa as it is accompanied by a couplet commenting on the scene. He also concluded that the composition of this couplet indicates that the author had had a thorough grounding in the works of Ovid. The works of Vergil appear to have been a popular source of writing exercises and as such would have been more familiar than those of other authors. Certainly as a theme in interior design its influence would have extended beyond the literate, as would a quote from *Aeneid* II on coins of Carausius.

After Vergil the works of Ovid were the most popular in the Empire as a whole and there was a revival of interest in his writings in the fourth century. It is less easy to pinpoint his influence on life in Britain than Vergil's, but the birth of Dionysus on a mosaic at East Coker, the Labours of Hercules at Bramdean and the life of Cyparissus at Leicester may all have originated in a knowledge of Ovid. There is no reason to believe that reading these classical authors was a male privilege and women must also have read for pleasure and instruction.

The depths to which education had penetrated into society might be seen in references on tombstones such as one from Lincoln where a parent's grief at the loss of a daughter is compared with the grief which accompanied the Rape of Proserpine.[13] Eumenius, writing about Constantine's victory in Britain, took it for granted that his audience would have read both Caesar and Tacitus and one wonders what the Britons of the third and fourth centuries thought of these descriptions of their forbears and the invasion of Britain.

For those who could not read, and probably many who could, stories would be related verbally, some giving the British version of history and others continuing a long story-telling tradition of heroes and heroines, gods and battles.

No doubt mothers told their children simplified versions of the old tales. Little is known of the sagas of prehistoric Britain except what can be distilled from surviving Welsh and Irish stories. The importance of these stories in keeping alive a tribal identity should not be disregarded even if, in Roman Britain, the tradition of telling the old stories may have survived into the fourth century only in the more remote rural areas. In towns tales told by travellers from distant lands may have taken the place of the native sagas and enlarged the gulf between the sophisticated town dwellers and the simpler rural inhabitants.

One form of entertainment which would be familiar in both town and country, appealing to aristocrat and slave alike, was gossip. Women from settlements and villas would have looked forward to trips to market to catch up on the latest gossip and those in towns foregathered in the forum or the shops to discuss their neighbours, events and scandals. The best place for a good gossip was the baths, and it was here that women of different racial origins, ages and status would have been most likely to meet and exchange opinions, as well as beauty tips and recipes.

Bathing to the Romans was not just a matter of hygiene; it was a relaxation, a social activity in which one met one's friends, ate and drank, took exercise and transacted business. The authorities saw bathing as such a civilising activity that the provision of public bath-houses was made a priority and substantial civic baths were built as soon as towns were established. Villas, too, had bath suites or separate bath-houses erected as soon as the inhabitants could afford them and the lavish decoration expended on these indicates that it was a matter of etiquette to offer one's guests a bath.

A bath-house consisted of a series of rooms graded in temperature (64). The

64. The baths at Halton Chesters show the sequence of heated rooms in a Roman bath-house. It is likely that the officers' families and the local residents were allowed to use these facilities.

bather, once divested of clothing and wrapped in a linen towel, moved from room to room getting progressively hotter until reaching a steamy room like a Turkish bath, where dirt was sweated out and scraped away with a metal blade called a *strigil*. Scented bath oils were used but not soap, and after immersion in a hot bath the pores were closed by a quick plunge into cold water. Women might bathe naked or wear a two-piece bathing costume, like a bikini, although the more sedate matrons preferred a shift or a capacious towel.

Hadrian and other emperors issued edicts forbidding mixed bathing, possibly in vain. Modesty was otherwise catered for in the larger establishments, such as Huggin Hill in London, by separate suites for men and women, children usually bathing with their mothers. In the smaller baths arrangements were made for specific opening hours for the sexes. In Rome the sixth to eighth/ninth hours were reserved for women, with the rest of the day for men. At Vipasca, a mining district in Portugal, the terms of the lease stipulated that the baths were to be open for use by women from daybreak to the seventh hour at a charge of one *as* each.[14] Balsdon has indicated that the charge for women was often more than for men, which seems a little unfair as women's bathing establishments were rarely as well appointed and were usually kept at a lower temperature. This matter of temperature, however, may be explained by the popular theory that bathing in very hot water was not good for women or for the more prosaic reason that steam makes the hair go frizzy. Subsidies from public benefactors meant that only a nominal charge needed to be made at the main public baths, and children, soldiers and slaves were usually admitted free.

The legionary fortress baths at Caerleon were clearly open to women and children. Some of these may have been the dependants of the garrison but it is likely that the local residents were also allowed, even encouraged, to use the facilities. A lead bath ticket found at Caerleon indicates that some control was kept over the comings and goings of the civilian customers. All the forts along Hadrian's Wall were provided with baths for the use of the military and it has been suggested that some were enlarged in the third century to accommodate the increased numbers of wives and children. Certainly provision must have been made at an early stage for the wives and families of the commanding officers to have a bath; women such as Julia Lucilla are unlikely to have given up the pleasures of bathing without a fight even if, as Pliny mentioned, 'sitting baths' were used for day-to-day washing.[15]

Private bath-houses in villas would have been for the use of the whole household, not just the landowner and his immediate family: possibly mixed bathing was more usual *en famille* than in public baths. At some sites there is a bath suite in the main building and a separate bath-house but whether this catered for a division of sexes or a division of class is not clear. It may be that the bath-houses were intended for the farm-workers and their families with access also allowed to local villagers.

The social aspect of bathing is particularly notable in villas as it formed part of the entertainment offered to an honoured guest, but some baths appear never to have been fired, remaining as status symbols rather than useful fixtures. Firing private baths may have involved considerable expense but experiments have shown that, like hypocausts, once the furnaces were lit it was more economical to keep them going. It follows, therefore, that villa inhabitants may have been in the habit of bathing every day rather than having the baths heated once a week, or alternatively the baths were fired only rarely, on special occasions.

Private baths are known in town houses but are comparatively rare. Such was the multiplicity of public baths that private suites may have been regarded as unnecessary luxuries, or possibly the population preferred the sociability of mass bathing. Baths would have been very crowded: Wacher has estimated that in a town like Leicester with a population of between three and four thousand even a weekly bath per person would result in nearly five hundred people a day using the baths, that is fifty or sixty an hour. With such numbers of clients it is hardly surprising that various traders converged on the baths. Seneca referred to the sale of ready-made snacks[16] and at Caerleon the remains indicate food which would be eaten in small portions with the fingers, such as chicken legs, chops and shellfish. The other services available included massage, hair-plucking, dentistry, medical advice and the repair of clothes, while bath oils and the other accessories of bathing would also have been on sale. At Caerleon there is even evidence of a goldsmith working on the premises, possibly selling or repairing jewellery.

The large number of clients also led to crime and 'bath-house thieves' were a recognised problem, as bathers had to leave their belongings unguarded if they were not accompanied by a slave or could not afford to pay an attendant. The curse tablets at Bath refer to several thefts of clothing or jewellery. One could also lose one's shirt through gambling: gaming counters, dice and boards have been found in profusion in bath-houses and there is evidence at Caerleon and Exeter that cock-fighting bouts were laid on by the management. These extra facilities may have been confined to male bathers, the women indulging in more sedate activities. The picture painted by the number of handicraft tools found at Caerleon is of the women sitting sewing or making braid while they gossiped and sweated, although many will have taken the opportunity to shave their legs and cream their faces. Martial describes the particularly unlovely sight of a female called Thais who, 'in order craftily to substitute for such a reek another odour, whenever she strips and enters the bath she is green with depilatory, or is hidden behind a plaster of chalk and vinegar, or is covered with three or four layers of sticky bean flower'.[17]

The entertainments discussed so far have been rather sedentary and there is little evidence of women participating in more energetic pursuits for pleasure.

There are no sculptural representations or other indications of women hunting or fishing for sport, although they may have done both as part of their food-gathering role. Skating may have been a winter pastime as well as a means of transport: skates made from the *metapodia* or *radii* of horses have a long history stretching back into the Bronze Age, with examples known from Iron Age contexts. Sledges made from *radii* and *metapodia* of cattle, unfortunately, come from undated contexts but examples have been found from the late Hallstatt period on the Continent and it is possible that they were used in Britain.

In Italy much attention was given to gardens and gardening, and many leisure hours were spent out of doors. Unfortunately, excavation in Britain has tended to concentrate on buildings and has largely ignored the ground in between, so archaeological evidence for horticultural enthusiasm is limited. The most extensively excavated garden, and the most impressive, is at the first-century palace at Fishbourne. To build the residence a rectangular platform of land had to be levelled, which involved filling in part of the harbour and diverting two streams. This impressive engineering feat meant that extensive gardens could be laid out on level ground but it left large areas of stripped, ill-drained clay which had to be prepared very carefully before planting, particularly in the formal garden in the central court. As a result the bedding trenches show black against the orangey clay in excavation, revealing a formal pattern down both sides of the central path as well as edging the lawns or gravelled areas. These trenches probably held low box hedges (65).

The bedding trenches form regularly spaced niches, either to avoid uninter-esting straight lines or to frame statuary or ornamental shrubs in the manner illustrated in Italian wall-paintings (66). In the north-west corner of the garden a large pit filled with topsoil was found, probably the bedding trench for a tree screening the awkward junction of the two building wings as well as providing visual interest. The eastern side of the garden was more elegantly laid out than the northern or western, possibly because it formed the backdrop to the principal view from the terrace in front of the west wing. Close to the east path a row of post-holes packed with stones alternating with loam-filled pits was found, which may hint at a trellis supporting climbing plants designed to screen the entrance hall until the final approach – a dramatic visual device much appreciated by the Romans. It is this formal planning which gives the gardens at Fishbourne their typically Roman atmosphere and implies that they must have been designed by an immigrant landscape architect, well-trained in contemporary gardening techniques.

The south garden may have been designed as a 'natural' landscape to merge with the countryside on the opposite side of the salt-water inlet. This is the only garden in Britain to suggest that some of the larger villas might have had great parks in the eighteenth-century English manner. In Italy landowners such as P. Cornelius Scipio Aemilianus Africanus Minor and Decimus Brutus Augur

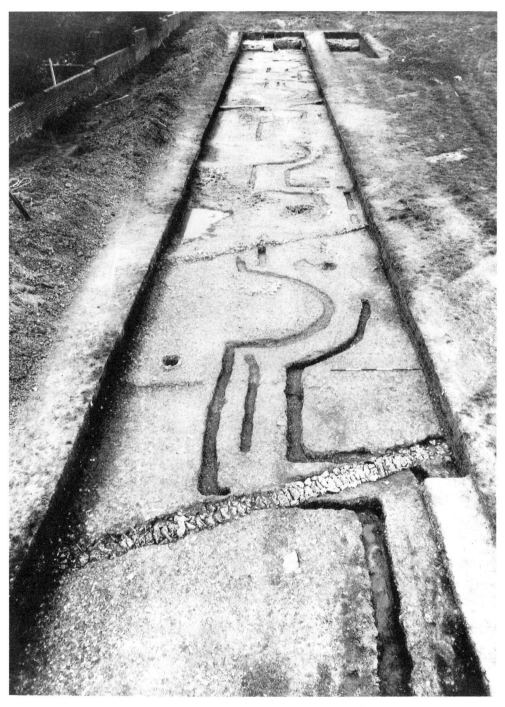

65. The bedding trenches in the Fishbourne palace garden showed up clearly against the natural clay and gravel in excavation.

66. Wall-painting from the Villa of Livia at Prima Porta, Italy. It shows a garden of similar design to that uncovered at Fishbourne.

had had pleasure grounds as early as the late second century BC, modelled on the eastern *paradeisoi* and Hellenistic public gardens.

The arrangement of the wings at Fishbourne villa creates five small internal courtyards or peristyles. In Italy these were seen as extensions to the house; areas for dining or lounging in fine weather. Diodorus referred to such gardens as 'a useful device for avoiding confusion when crowds are present',[18] and they were filled with flower beds, statuary and fountains which the owner could show off to guests. Unfortunately, little is known of the five peristyle gardens at Fishbourne; on the evidence of gardens in Pompeii and Herculaneum, however, it is likely that they were laid out rather formally in smaller versions of the great courtyard garden.

At Frocester villa the gardens were not laid out until the fourth century and consisted of two formal flower beds near the house, a hedge and two long beds on either side of the approach road. Again the bedding trenches had been dug into the stone and gravel of the courtyard and filled with topsoil which contained sherds of pottery, bits of animal bone and small items of jewellery, suggesting to the excavators that the gardeners had used composted kitchen refuse and that the women of the villa had taken an interest in the garden. It is not clear whether the area of the courtyard was laid out to lawn or was gravelled, although there were grass verges between the flower beds and the drive.

Mention has been made of box hedging, but for an indication of the other plants grown in Romano-British gardens we have to rely on pollen analysis. Silchester has revealed mallow, rose, violet, ox-eye daisy and white campion as well as various types of buttercup, speedwell and other plants which may have been regarded, then as now, as weeds. At York there is evidence of heather and red campion as well as such horrors as stinking mayweed, deadly nightshade, hairy buttercup, stinging nettle and the lesser nettle. Alcester has produced columbine, London corncockle and corn marigold, which must have been imported from the eastern Mediterranean, and tradition has it that the *Erinus alpinus* growing in the ruins of the Commanding Officer's house at Chesters was brought to Britain by the Romans. Even without exotic imported species a garden could have had a very impressive display, particularly in the spring, with native plants such as irises, honeysuckle, snowdrops, violets, daffodils, primroses and bluebells; later in the year windflowers, bellflowers, cowslips, forget-me-nots, foxgloves, globeflowers, marguerites, pasque flowers, pinks and scabious would be in flower.

There are also several species of rose native to Britain, but none were listed by Pliny as being worthy of note. He preferred the roses of Praeneste and Campania, although he allowed that the Milesian rose had a good fiery red colour even if it was not a prolific bloomer.[19] Pliny and Varro[20] both gave advice for taking cuttings and recommended the correct soil for the best results, so it is possible that some immigrants to Britain may have brought cuttings of their favourite roses for their gardens.

Whilst many plants will have been grown for display in the garden and particularly for their pleasant smell, a number will have been intended for cutting. A pottery vessel from London has been identified tentatively as a flower vase and simple flower arrangements can be seen on wall-paintings from Rome, suggesting that flowers were used for domestic decoration. Aurelia Aureliana is shown holding a bouquet on her tombstone (39), which may be an allusion to the custom of decorating the tombs of the recently deceased with flowers at the festival of the Rosalia. Cut flowers were also in demand for other festivals, banquets and weddings, either loose or wound into garlands. These would have been grown commercially as well as domestically, although no plant nurseries of the Pompeian type with rows of broken *amphorae* used as seed trays have so far been found in Britain.

At Fishbourne there was a kitchen garden in the north-west corner, immediately adjacent to the ovens. Every villa would have had a large kitchen garden to supply the kitchen with its needs and, according to Pliny, 'it was immediately concluded ... that a woman was a poor housewife when the kitchen garden – for this was considered to be the woman's department – was badly cultivated.'[21] At Latimer a formally arranged garden with an orchard and vegetable garden beyond shows the blend of formal aesthetics and practicality typical of Roman taste.

In towns the atrium houses will have incorporated peristyle gardens of the Italian type with vegetable gardens and orchards in vacant building plots. Houses iiis, iis, and viis at Caerwent, for example, had peristyle gardens, iiis having a statue base opposite the main entrance to the east wing. In the larger towns, where there was less space, the Italian habit of growing kitchen herbs and flowers in window boxes may have been introduced, and roof gardens may also have been popular.

The planting of flower gardens indicates that the householders had reached a certain social level where there was no economic need for all their land to be utilised for growing food. It also suggests time to design the arrangement, supervise the gardeners and wander about, appreciating the sights, smells and sounds. How was this leisure time available? In the more extensive establishments enough slaves will have been kept to ensure that the day-to-day tasks were undertaken and a few lucky women will have had little to occupy their hours except the pursuit of pleasure. In other homes the womenfolk will have been run off their feet trying to cope with the kitchen garden, the cooking, the children and helping their husbands in their work. Yet even they would have had occasions when they could relax. There was no concept of a regular weekend off or annual holidays, but certain days were set aside for religious festivals and once the formal ceremonies of the day were over the rest may have been free. These days seem to have occurred on average about every ten days. To many women, particularly slaves, these days may have made little difference to the amount of work which needed to be done, but some festivals will have attracted travelling traders and entertainers like a medieval fair, and these would have provided diversion.

Some of the wealthier families may have adopted the Roman habit of moving to a second home in the country or at the seaside in the warmer months but the majority of women will only have travelled any distance when following their husbands or masters in career moves. Another reason for travel might have been to visit a famous temple or shrine of healing such as Bath or Lydney for a cure. Evidence is beginning to emerge, however, that women travelled for social reasons, such as a visit to the theatre or amphitheatre or a party. The invitation from Claudia Severa presumes that Sulpicia Lepidina will travel some distance to be at her birthday celebrations. Around AD 100–5 the possible places within easy travelling distance of Vindolanda were limited and all are at least half a day's march away, so we might assume that Sulpicia Lepidina was not expected to walk. Some women will have travelled on horseback; a skeleton of a woman from Bradley Hill seems to suggest that she was a rider, but most of the sculptural depictions of women on horseback are of the goddess Epona sitting either astride or sideways and cannot be taken as evidence that riding was a regular means of female transport. The best saddle horses would inevitably be reserved for cavalrymen, hunters or dispatch riders, and if women did ride

67. Relief from the Church of Maria Saal, Austria, showing a covered waggon. Fitted with beds like a modern caravan, these were used by families and merchants travelling about the Empire.

it was more likely to have been on a mule or donkey. Another method of travel was the carriage, of which several types are known to have been used in the Empire. The wheels were made of wood with iron tyres and as none of the carriages were sprung, travelling in them must have been an uncomfortable business, even on the excellent surfaces of the Roman road system. The subsequent jolting might explain why Soranus recommended horse-riding and light carriage exercise as useful aids to convalescence and helpful during pregnancy.[22] Litters, carried by men or mules, were a common sight in Rome but it is not known if they were ever popular in Britain.

A relief from Shirva in Scotland has been interpreted as showing a woman reclining in a canopied carriage drawn by a mule, but could equally show a high-backed couch with the animal and wheel present in a symbolic role. Gaul and Italy have produced some delightful reliefs showing couples or families driving along in carriages (67) but none so far have been discovered in Britain. The ordinary person who did not have access to a carriage or a mule would have had to walk or hitch a lift, or series of lifts, from traders' waggons.

Anyone wishing to indulge in foreign travel would have found it a relatively simple business, as there were no customs barriers for private travellers to cross. From Britain to Turkey, northern Germany to North Africa one could use the same language, the same currency and be expected to abide by the same laws. An elaborate network of roads with inns and posting stations linked the towns and cities, and merchant vessels would usually take passengers if the price was right. How many women availed themselves of these facilities is unknown but many will have only done so when accompanying their husbands or joining them on a foreign posting, as did Claudia Rufina, a British woman living in Rome in the first century AD whose charm and manners were applauded in an epigram by Martial. There is a theory that Egeria, a nun in the fourth century who travelled to the Holy Land, was by birth a Briton and, although her birthplace is doubtful, her urge to travel may not have been unique. Certainly British women are known all over the Empire: for example, Lollia Bodicca at Lambaesis in Algeria, and foreign women from Sardinia, Greece, Raetia, Gallia Narbonensis, Aquitania and Italy are attested in Britain. This gives a picture of continual movement but this is likely to have been confined to a minority of the population with the majority of women never travelling further than their nearest market town.

The way they could spend their leisure hours emphasises the difference between the urban women and the women of the country districts, as well as between civilians and army wives. In the large towns women will have been able to attend theatrical and musical performances, as well as contests in the amphitheatre or circus. They would also have been able to spend time at the large public bath-houses with all the added side attractions, and no doubt street life, markets and fairs would have had considerable entertainment value. It is unlikely that an urban woman in Roman Britain ran the risk of being bored, whatever her class. In the smaller towns, villages and villas there was less opportunity for formal entertainment and women will have had to entertain themselves and their families at home with music, story-telling and dancing, with occasional trips to larger centres. There may, of course, have been com- pensations in country life, such as gardening and walking, hunting and hare- coursing.

It was the women of the military who ran the risk of boredom. Although *vici* housed jugglers and other entertainers, these may have appealed more to male tastes than to those of the wives and daughters of prefects or centurions. In the frontier zones there would not even have been the compensations of a garden or activities outside the fort unless accompanied by guards. Entertainment for these women would have been limited to board games, music, reading, playing with their children and conversation with their household servants or other wives, as well as corresponding with other women in similar situations.

8. Finale

The end of the Roman occupation of Britain is traditionally dated to AD 410, when the Emperor Honorius wrote to the city fathers telling them that in future they would have to provide for their own protection.[1] Britain had already been at risk of invasion from several directions for some years and few women living on the coast can have slept soundly in their beds. Most towns had been provided with fortifications as early as the late second century, but initially these had been intended to protect people and property from brigands and outlaws, and did not prove their real usefulness until the fourth- and fifth-century raids by Saxons, Jutes, Franks and Picts. Some coin hoards deposited in the late 260s and 270s may reflect the fears brought about by the Saxon raids – fears which led families to hide their valuables and treasured possessions. The destruction suffered by some towns (Colchester, Chelmsford), villages (Park Brow) and villas (Preston) show that these precautions were justified. In the fourth century even small settlements such as Margidunum were provided with walls, and an inscription from Dorchester-on-Thames records that some housed police posts for *beneficiarii*.[2] Towns which already had defences improved them at this time and there is some evidence for the strengthening of town garrisons.

The general sense of insecurity at this time must have caused distress to many women and might be compared to the tensions felt in Britain during the Napoleonic era or during the Second World War, when again there were constant fears of invasion. Women living in the towns may have derived some comfort from the increased defences but otherwise would have been fearful for their husbands, who faced the possibility of having to defend their homes and families. Britain was also racked by internal dissensions caused by localised peasant revolts, and was occasionally caught in the cross-fire of the power struggles ambitious generals and would-be emperors, as for example when Constantius wrested London back from the troops of Carausius and Allectus.

In the country women will have had less protection from invaders. The villa at North Wraxall, on the evidence of bodies and architectural fragments flung down a well, seems to have been destroyed by enemy action in the early fifth century, and country folk will have lived in daily fear of having their homes attacked and burned (a fate suffered by the villa at Great Casterton), their food crops and stock captured, and themselves or their families raped, killed or carried off into slavery. In these circumstances most women will have preferred to have kept their families under their eye all the time.

Between AD 378 and 388 the number of new coins being minted was drastically reduced and the use of coins for daily transactions appears to have been increasingly rare. This may have been due to the difficulties in transporting the cash but was more likely the result of the periodic inflation which affected the Empire as a whole. The modern reader needs no description of the effect of economic inflation on daily life. The rise in prices and the difficulties in obtaining basic essentials must have been exacerbated by the destruction of stock and crops by raiders and a barter system may have developed. It could have been the lack of cash with which to effect repairs which led to the abandonment of the majority of villas or the evacuation of the owners, who sought safety in the towns, the old hillforts or even Gaul. Some villas such as Bignor fell into decay, while the ruins of Great Casterton were taken over by squatters, possibly dispossessed refugees from other villas or settlements.

The insecurity of the times and the rate of inflation also affected the merchant classes and craftsmen, particularly the potters. Many factory owners will have had to pay off their work-force and housewives will have had to replace their broken pots with wooden or leather vessels. Unemployment will have taken its toll in many families and having to 'make do and mend' will have become a way of life even for women of some pretension.

In the military north the situation was even more complex. We have already seen (chapter 2) that there is some difficulty in identifying the accommodation of the women and children of the military in the late third and fourth centuries. The activities of various emperors in Gaul and Germany had depleted the garrison of Britain considerably and the *Notitia Dignitatum* records several British units serving in the Continental provinces as well as in Egypt and the East. The wives of centurions and the other ranks will once again have had to pack their belongings and move to a new land. They were replaced to some extent by German troops and their families, such as the group led by Hnau-difridus at Housesteads, leading to a change in the make-up of the population along the frontier. This population faced innumerable dangers brought about by the uniting of the Pictish tribes from Scotland with the Scotti from Ireland and the Attacotti. People in Wales had already suffered several invasions from Irish tribes and matters were brought to a head in AD 367, with the barbarian conspiracy recorded by Ammianus Marcellinus.[3] Some military men may have thought it wise to evacuate their families to the southern fortified towns or back to their homelands.

There may have been few soldiers left to hold the northern frontier by the time the troops' pay failed to arrive in AD 410. There was no formal withdrawal of the army from Britain and the fate of the soldiers and their dependants after 410 is open to speculation. Some will have made their way to the Continent to join up with other units. Some may have become mercenaries with the local tribes or joined the defending forces of the towns. These courses of action may have appealed more to bachelors than to married men with responsibilities. It

68. Bronze head from Otterbourne depicting a young woman. The features are typical of Celtic
sculpture during the Roman period.

is possible that the majority, many of whom were of British descent or had
married into local families, were absorbed into the local community, either as
farmers or craftsmen.

The early years of the fifth century will have been characterized by a continual
movement of population: country people moving to the safety of towns or the
refortified hillforts of their ancestors; refugees escaping from massacres such as
that experienced at Caistor-by-Norwich, where excavations uncovered the
skeletons of thirty-five men, women and children huddled under the ruins of
one house; escaping slaves taking advantage of the confused times; unemployed
craftsmen looking for work; foreign mercenaries hired by townspeople to aid
their defence; soldiers making their way home or to a new posting. Throughout
the country there would be people on the move, with their women trying to
retain some semblance of family routine as they abandoned their homes and
belongings through fear or necessity, and struggled to feed and clothe their
children and ensure their safety.

So ended a unique period in British history – a period which had seen Britain
at its most cosmopolitan, part of an empire which covered most of the then
known world. It is difficult to imagine the impact of Roman rule on the native
women of Britain (68), as evidence for their way of life in the periods immediately
before and after the occupation is limited. Iron Age Britain was a somewhat
introspective country with little interest in the rest of the world; the social unit
was the extended family which formed part of a tribe, but there was little sense
of the tribes making up a larger entity. Some groups in the south-east had had
trading and cultural links with Gaul but these links had not opened up the
country to merchants or travellers to any great extent.

Women at the time held a respected position as wives and mothers; some,
such as Cartimandua, had political status. The Bath curse tablets suggest that
British women in the Iron Age may have had a stronger position at law than
their contemporaries in Rome, or even their descendants until the twentieth
century, and the evidence from excavations might suggest that this position
was based on their involvement in the production and supply of food. Despite
these possibilities, however, their horizons were strictly limited. The country
was then invaded by an army which represented a major power, and within a
generation everything had changed. At first most of the invaders may have been
of Italian descent but within a few years the full cross-section of the Roman
populace would have been found in the new province. Some of the side-effects
of the Boudican revolt suggest that it took at least a generation for intermarriage
between invaders and the native women to be accepted, but once accepted,
liaisons between Britons and Africans, Pannonians, Gauls, Italians, Germans,
Greeks and Syrians became commonplace.

The result was an extraordinary mixture of races and languages. Within a
generation a woman whose mother would never have met anyone outside her

own tribe would have become acquainted with women from all over the world. Even if their facility with the Latin language was limited the great sisterhood of women will have ensured that they would have been able to communicate on the subjects of most interest to them. Conversations in the privacy of the baths during the hours open to women must have been fascinating as they exchanged their common experiences and opinions. With only a towel around them the differences in race or between free, freed or slave may have been of little importance.

We have sparse evidence as to whether there was any racial prejudice in Britain at this time. It is likely that those of Italian descent would have regarded themselves as superior but the attitude of the other races to each other is not well recorded. A reference to 'Brittunculi' – possibly a disparaging term – on one of the Vindolanda writing tablets[4] may suggest that Britons were not highly thought of by the army. A poem published by the Bordeaux poet Ausonius in AD 382, about the British poet Silvius Bonus, makes a play on his name:

> What? Silvius Good?
> No Briton could
> Be – better he had
> Been Silvius Bad

Again, the implication is that the Britons did not enjoy a good reputation in other provinces, but there is no reason to believe that the incoming women shared these views or that the natives looked down on the newcomers.

Despite the possible camaraderie, the feature which has emerged most strongly from this study is the sense of loneliness which many women will have experienced in Roman Britain. The extended family system provides support for every member of the group, each of whom is aware of their place in the order of things. Young wives can draw upon the experience of their mothers and grandmothers and their children grow up with their cousins: the system may be introspective but it has its strengths. The undermining of the tribal system and the introduction of towns broke up the extended family units and the native women who moved to the towns would have found themselves in strange surroundings with foreign neighbours, cut off from the back-up of their families. The isolation of many mothers of small children on today's housing estates might be seen as a close parallel. The phenomenon will have been particularly noticeable in the first century AD but may have continued throughout the centuries of Roman rule as the population shifted.

Women from other parts of the Empire who emigrated to Britain will have found much that was familiar, but would not necessarily have been able to find women from their own province or background to turn to for advice or to exchange reminiscences. They may have found their dress, hairstyles or diet different from those with whom they were in daily contact, and in particular they may have been isolated by their religious beliefs and practices. It is only too easy to overestimate the ease with which a provincial used the Latin language or the extent to which it was used. To the majority of women it would have been a second language, with all the frustrations inherent in having to use a second language all day and every day. Many women will not even have shared a first language with their husbands or children. They may have been able to make themselves intelligible when shopping or in general conversation but in more complex situations misunderstandings may have been a regular hazard.

The impact of the invasion on the physical appearance of the country is undeniable. The building of roads, forts, towns, frontiers and villas were obvious changes. The long-term cultural impact is less easy to evaluate and the speed with which the trappings of Roman domination broke down in the early years of the fifth century may suggest that Romanisation to most people was at best only skin deep. Even after four centuries the bulk of the population rapidly returned to the ways of their ancestors: even the new religion of Christianity disappeared so effectively that it had to be reintroduced several generations later. In the process the average woman may have lost a great deal. With the breakdown of the Roman legal system the women did not regain the position they appear to have enjoyed in the Celtic code, but became even more subservient to the men in their family. Power was now estimated in terms of land owned, and a woman's place in the scheme of things was to provide land by means of her dowry. The collapse of the coinage system meant that there was less to spend on fripperies and the closing of the trade routes deprived them of many materials, semi-precious stones, spices and foreign ideas that had previously been imported into the country. Britain retreated into itself once more and the horizons open to women were drastically reduced. Many generations had to pass before women in Britain could once again have an extensive knowledge of the world and a balanced view of their place in it.

Women mentioned in the text

Any letters in the names which are uncertain due to the incomplete state of the stone or to abbreviations used by the inscriber are in brackets.

ABUDIA MEGISTE: seller of grain and pulses at the Middle Stairs, Rome. *CIL* VI.9683 (tombstone)

AELIA AELIANA: died in York. *RIB* 682; *CSIR* I.3, no. 40 (tombstone)

AEL(IA) AMMILLUSIMA: widow of Marcus Trojanius Augustinus. Lived at Stanwix. *RIB* 2029 (tombstone)

AELIA AUGUSTINA: co-dedicator of an altar to the Mother Goddesses Ollototae with Julius Secundus, at Heronbridge. *RIB* 574

AEL(IA) COMINDUS: wife of Nobilianus, a decurion. Died at Carrawburgh aged thirty-two. *RIB* 1561; *CSIR* I.6, no. 194 (tombstone)

AEL(IA) MATRONA: wife of Julius Maximus, *singularis consularis* of the Cavalry Regiment of Sarmatians; mother of Marcus Julius Maximus; daughter of Campania Dubitata. Died at Ribchester aged twenty-eight. *RIB* 594 (tombstone)

AEL(IA) PROCULINA: dedicator of an altar to the Emperor's Fortune at Risingham. *RIB* 1211

AEL(IA) SEVERA: widow of Caecilius Rufus. Died at York aged twenty-seven and her coffin paid for by her husband's freedman, Caecilius Musicus. *RIB* 683; *CSIR* I.3, no. 64 (coffin)

AEL(IA) TIMO: dedicator of an altar to Diana at Risingham. *RIB* 1209

AHTEHA: daughter of Nobilis. Died at Corbridge aged five. *RIB* 1180; *CSIR* I.1, no. 66 (tombstone)

AICETUOS: wife of Limisius; mother of Lattio. Died at Old Penrith aged forty-five. *RIB* 936 (tombstone)

ALBIA FAUSTINA: widow of Flavius Agricola, soldier of VIth Legion Victrix. Lived in London. *RIB* 11 (tombstone)

ALOGIOSA: presumed wife of Decentinus; sister-in-law of Uricalus and Docilosa; aunt of Docilis and Docilina. Swore on oath against perjury at Bath. *Tab.Sul.* 94 (lead tablet)

AMANDA: widow of Julius Julianus, soldier of IInd Legion Augusta. Lived at Caerleon. *RIB* 360 (tombstone)

ANNIOLA: accused of stealing six silver coins at Bath. *Tab.Sul.* 8 (curse tablet)

ANTONIA: daughter or slave of Strato who dedicated an altar to Fortune the Preserver at Kirkby Thore 'following a vision'. *RIB* 760

ARMEA: girlfriend of a tile-maker at Binchester. *Britannia* IX (1978), 477, no. 27 (tile graffiti)

ATINIA TYRANNIS: seed seller at the Porta Triumphalis in Praeneste, Italy. *CIL* XIV, 2850 (altar)

AUR(ELIA) AIA: daughter of Titus from Salonae in Dalmatia; wife of Aurelius Marcus in the century of Obsequens. Died at Carvoran aged thirty-three. *RIB* 1828 (tombstone)

AUR(ELIA) AURELIA(NA): wife of Ulpius Apolinaris. Died at Carlisle aged forty-one. *RIB* 959; *CSIR* I.6, no. 493 (tombstone)

AURELIA CAULA: sister of Aurelia S...illa. Died at Great Chesters aged fifteen. *RIB* 1745 (tombstone)

AURELIA CENSORINA: widow of Aurelius Super, centurion of VIth Legion. Lived at York. *RIB* 670 (tombstone)

AUREL(IA) CONCESSA: died on a villa estate at Branston. *Britannia* VI (1975), 212 (tombstone)

AURELIA E(G)LEC(T)IANE: wife of Fabius Honoratus, tribune of 1st Cohort of Vangiones; mother of Fabia Honorata. Lived at Chesters. *RIB* 1482 (tombstone)

AUR(ELIA) LUPUL(A): mother of Dionysius Fortunatus. Died at Risingham. *RIB* 1250 (tombstone)

AURELIA NAIS: wholesale fish-seller at the warehouses of Galba in Rome. *CIL* VI.9801 (inscription)

AURELIA PHILMATIO: child bride. Died in Rome aged forty. *ILS* 7472 (tombstone)

AURELIA ROM(ANA): sister of Aurelia Sabina. Lived at Greta Bridge. *RIB* 749 (tombstone)

AURELIA SABIN(A): sister of Aurelia Romana. Lived at Greta Bridge. *RIB* 749 (tombstone)

AUR(E)LIA S. . .ILLA: sister of Aurelia Caula. Lived at Great Chesters. *RIB* 1745 (tombstone)

AURELIA . . .ILLA: widow of Gracilis, centurion of XXIInd Legion, from Upper Germany. Lived at Piercebridge. *RIB* 1026 (tombstone)

AURELIA VICTOR(I)NA: daughter of Aurelius Victor. Died at Halton Chesters. *RIB* 1435 (tombstone)

AVITA: daughter of Carinus, a citizen of Rome, and his wife Romana; sister of Rufinus and Carina. Lived at Dorchester (Dorset). *RIB* 188 (tombstone)

BASILIA: victim of theft who petitioned Mars at Bath for the return of her silver ring. *Tab.Sul.* 97 (curse tablet)

BELLICIA: owner of a pottery *syrinx* at Shakenoak. *Britannia* IV (1973), 332 (graffiti)

BOUDICA: wife of Prasutagus, king of the Iceni; mother of two daughters. Tacitus *Annals* XIV; Tacitus *Agricola* 16; Cassius Dio LXII.2.7

BRICA: daughter of Januaria with whom she dedicated an altar to the Nymph Neine at Greta Bridge. *RIB* 744

CALPURNIA TRIFOSA: freedwoman and widow of Gaius Calpurnius Receptus, priest of Sulis. Lived at Bath. *RIB* 155 (tombstone)

CAMPANIA DUB(I)TATA: mother of Aelia Matrona; grandmother of Marcus Julius Maximus; 'most steadfast mother-in-law' of Julius Maximus, *singularis consularis* of the Cavalry Regiment of Sarmatians. Died at Ribchester aged fifty. *RIB* 594 (tombstone)

CANDIDA BARITA: mother of Mantinia Maerica; mother-in-law of Marcus Aurinius Simnus. Died at York. *RIB* 689 (tombstone)

CANDIEDINIA FORTUNA(TA): died at Adel aged fifteen. *RIB* 632 (tombstone)

CARINA: daughter of Carinus, a citizen of Rome, and his wife Romana; sister of Avita and Rufinus. Lived in Dorchester (Dorset). *RIB* 188 (tombstone)

CARSSOUNA: wife of Sacer, a citizen of the Senones (Gaul); daughter-in-law of Bruscus; presumed mother of Quintus. Died at Lincoln. *RIB* 262 (tombstone)

CARTIMANDUA: Queen of the Brigantes; wife of Venutius; mistress of Vellocatus. Tacitus *Histories* III.45; Tacitus *Annals* XII.36, 40

CATIA MARIA: owner of a *mortarium* at Brockley Hill. *JRS* LIX (1969) 237 (graffiti)

CLAUDIA CATIOTUOS: mother or second wife of Aurelius Senecio, a member of the *ordo* of Lincoln. Died at Lincoln aged sixty. *RIB* 250 (there translated as Claudius Catiotus); Birley 1979, 117 (tombstone)

CLAUDIA CRYSIS: died at Lincoln aged ninety. *RIB* 263 (tombstone)

CLAUDIA MARCIA CAPITOLINA: widow of Petronius Fortunatus, centurion of VIth Victrix among other legions; mother of Petronius Fortunatus. Lived at York, in Arabia, the Upper Euphrates and on the Danube. Died at Cillium in Tunisia. *ILS* 2658 (monumental inscription)

C(LAUDIA) MARTINA: wife of Anencletus, slave of the province. Died at London aged nineteen. *RIB* 21 (statue base)

CLAUDIA RUFINA: wife of a friend of the poet Martial. Lived in Rome but of British origins. Noted for her charm. Martial *Epigrams* 11.53

CLAUDIA SEVERA: wife of Aelius Brocchus, cohort commander at one of the Stanegate forts in the early years of the second century AD. Mother of one son. Her birthday was on the third day before the Ides of September; friend and correspondent of Sulpicia Lepidina. Bowman and Thomas 1987, no. 5 (writing tablet)

CLAUDIA TURI(A)NILLA: daughter of Vettia Mansueta with whom she dedicated an altar to the Nymph Goddesses at Carvoran. *RIB* 1789

COCCE(IA) IRENE: wife of Gaius Valerius Justus, *actarius* (record clerk) of XXth Legion. Died at Chester aged thirty. *RIB* 507 (tombstone)

CORELLIA OPTATA: daughter of Quintus Corellius Fortis. Died at York aged thirteen. *RIB* 684; *CSIR* I.3, no. 52 (tombstone)

COSC(ONIA) MAMMIOLA: wife of Aurelius Serenus. Died at Sutton-under-Whitestone Cliff. *JRS* XLVII (1957) 228 (coffin)

CURATIA DINYSIA: died at Chester aged forty. *RIB* 562 (tombstone)

DECIMINA: daughter of Decimus. Died at York. *RIB* 692; *CSIR* I.3, no. 45 (tombstone)

(D)IANA HERMIONE: daughter of Quintus. Dedicated an altar to Juno (*RIB* 813), and an altar to the Emperor's Virtue (*RIB* 845) at Maryport

DIODORA: priestess of the cult of Heracles of Tyre at Corbridge. *RIB* 1129 *CSIR* I.I, no. 49 (altar)

DOCILINA: daughter of Uricalus and Docilosa; sister of Docilis; niece of Decentinus and Alogiosa. Swore an oath against perjury at Bath. *Tab.Sul.* 94 (lead tablet)

DOCILOSA: wife of Uricalus; mother of Docilis and Docilina; sister-in-law of Decentinus and Alogiosa. Swore an oath against perjury at Bath. *Tab.Sul.* 94 (lead tablet)

DOMITIA SATURNINA: died at Chester aged forty-one. *RIB* 564 (tombstone)

EGERIA: occasionally known as Etheria or Silvia. Nun who wrote travelogue of her journeys through Egypt, Syria, Turkey and the Holy Land in fourth century AD. Thought to have originated in one of the western provinces on the Atlantic coast. *Egeria's Travels*, trans. J. Wilkinson 1971.

EMI(LIA) THEODORA: mother of Valerius Theodorianus. Lived at York. *RIB* 677 (tombstone)

ERTOLA: nicknamed Vellibia; presumed daughter of Sudrenus. Died at Corbridge aged four. *RIB* 1181; *CSIR* I.I, no. 71 (tombstone)

ET(T)ERNA(A) (AETERNA): the female member of a love triangle with Timotneus and an anonymous man, at Old Harlow. *Britannia* IV (1973), no. 3 (lead tablet)

FABIA HONORATA: daughter of Fabius Honoratus, tribune of the 1st Cohort of Vangiones, and his wife Aurelia Eglectiane. Died at Chesters. *RIB* 1482 (tombstone)

FLAVIA AUGUSTINA: wife of Gaius Aeresius Saenus, veteran of VIth Legion Victrix; mother of Saenius Augustinus and a daughter. *RIB* 685; *CSIR* I.3, no. 39 (tombstone)

FLAVIA BAETICA: widow of Afutianus, centurion of 2nd Cohort of Tungrians; daughter-in-law of Bassus. Lived at Birrens. *RIB* 2115 (tombstone)

FLA(VIA) INGENUA: widow of Flavius Helius, a Greek. Lived at Lincoln. *RIB* 251 (tombstone)

FLAVIA PEREGRINA: widow of Crotus, veteran of the 4th Cohort of Gauls; daughter-in-law of Vindex. Lived at Templebrough. *RIB* 620 (tombstone)

FL(AVIA) VICTORINA: widow of Titus Tammonius. Lived at Silchester. *RIB* 87 (tombstone)

GRATA: wife of Solinus, daughter of Dagobitus. Died at Lincoln aged forty. *RIB* 22 (tombstone)

GRECA: sister of Crotilo Germanus and Vindicianus. Died at Old Penrith aged four. *RIB* 934 (tombstone)

INNOCENTIA: co-dedicator of a piece of Christian silverware at Water Newton with Viventia. *Britannia* VII (1976), 385, no. 32

IVIXA: dedicator of an altar to the Viteres at Carvoran. *RIB* 1804

JANUARIA: daughter of Brica with whom she dedicated an altar to the Nymph Neine at Greta Bridge. *RIB* 744

JANUARIA MARTINA: widow of Vivius Marcianus of the IInd Legion Augusta. Lived at London. *RIB* 17 (tombstone)

(JAVOLENA) MONIME: dedicated an altar at Netherby. *RIB* 967; Birley 1979, 112

JULIA: wife of Lurio, a German; mother of Canio; sister-in-law of Ursa. Died at Chesters. *RIB* 1483 (tombstone)

JULIA BRICA: presumed wife of Sepronius Martinus and mother of Sepronia Martina. Died at York aged thirty-one. *RIB* 686; *CSIR* I.3, no. 41 (tombstone)

JUL(IA) FORTUNATA: Sardinian wife of Verecundius Diogenes, *sevir* of York and a tribesman of the Bituriges Cubi (from Bourges). *RIB* 687; *CSIR* I.3, no. 60 (stone coffin); see also *RIB* 678

JUL(IA) INGENUILLA: died at Horsley aged twenty. *RIB* 133 (tombstone)

JULIA LUCILLA: widow of Rufinus, prefect of the 1st Cohort of Vardulli, 1st Cohort Augusta of Lusitanians and 1st Cohort of Breuci, sub-curator of the Flaminian Way and Doles in Rome as well as sub-curator of Public Works. An altar to Silvanus Pantheus was set up on their behalf by their freedman Eutychus and his dependents. A senator's daughter. Lived at High Rochester. *RIB* 1271 (altar); *RIB* 1288 (tombstone)

JULIA PACATA I(NDIANA): widow of Gaius Julius Alpinus Classicianus, procurator of Britain; daughter of Indus; daughter-in-law of Gaius. Lived in London. *RIB* 12 (tomb inscription)

JUL(IA) SECUNDINA: widow of Julius Valens, veteran of the IInd Legion Augusta; mother of Gaius Julius Martinus. Died at Caerleon aged seventy-five. *RIB* 363; 373 (tombstones)

JUL(IA) SIMILINA: widow and heiress of Titinius Felix, *beneficiarius* of the legate of XXth Legion Valeria Victrix. Lived at Chester. *RIB* 505 (tombstone base)

JULIA VELVA: relation or freedwoman of Aurelius Mercurialis. Died at York aged fifty. *RIB* 688; *CSIR* I.3, no. 42 (tombstone)

LATTIO: daughter of Limisius and Aicetuos. Died at Old Penrith aged twelve. *RIB* 936 (tombstone)

LOLLIA BODICCA: widow of Titus Flavius Virilis, who died at Lambaesis in Algeria. He was a centurion of five legions including IInd Augusta, and may have been a Briton or a Numidian. She was British. *ILS* 2653 (tombstone)

LOVERNISCA: victim of theft who petitioned Sulis Minerva at Bath for the return of her cape. *Tab.Sul.* 61 (curse tablet)

MAGUNNA: dedicator of an altar to Jupiter Dolichenus at Birrens. *RIB* 2099

MANTINI(A) MAERICA: wife of Marcus Aurinius Simnus; daughter of Candida Barita. Died at York. *RIB* 689; *CSIR* I.3, no. 43 (tombstone)

MARITIMA: relation or freedwoman of Julius Marinus, a centurion. Lived at Maryport. *RIB* 858 (tombstone)

MARTIOLA: daughter and heiress of Flavius Martius, *senator* of the Carvetii. Lived at Old Penrith. *RIB* 933 (tombstone)

MATUGENA: owner of a pottery flagon at Neatham. *Britannia* VI (1975), 286, no. 10 (graffiti)

MELANIA: Italian heiress who owned large estates in Britain. *Vita Melania* (10) Latin; (11) Greek.

MENIMANE: widow of Blussus, a ship's captain; daughter of Annius Brigionis. Lived at Mainz-Weisenau, Germany. Espérandieu 1922, no. 5815

MERC(ATILLA): freedwoman and foster-daughter of Magnius. Died at eighteen months at Bath. *RIB* 162 (tombstone)

MINERVINA: presumed wife of Cunomolius and daughter-in-law of Minicus. A witness on a petition or curse at Bath. *Tab.Sul.* 9 (lead tablet)

MOCUXSOMA: dedicator of a silver plaque to the god Veteris at Thistleton. *JRS* LII (1962), 192

NIGRA: a married woman to whom Vinicius wrote from Wroxeter. *Trans. Shropshire Arch. Soc.*[3] V, i–ii (writing tablet)

OCONEA: victim of a theft who petitioned Sulis Minerva at Bath for the return of her pan. *Tab.Sul.* 60 (curse tablet)

ONERATA: widow of Valerius Verecundus, veteran of IInd Legion Augusta. Lived at Caerleon. *Britannia* VIII (1977), 429, no. 15 (tombstone)

PERVICA: died at Great Chesters. *RIB* 1747; *CSIR* I.6, no. 216 (tombstone)

PERVINCA: daughter of Quartio; benefactress of Delfinus from Upper Germany. Possibly a member of a burial club. Died at Housesteads. *RIB* 1620 (tombstone)

PLACIDA: died at Wroxeter aged fifty-five in the thirtieth year of her marriage. Possibly related to Deuccus. *RIB* 295 (tombstone)

POMPONIA GRAECINA: wife of Aulus Plautius who led the invasion force to Britain in AD 43. Tacitus *Annals* XIII.32

PUSINNA: widow of Dagvalda, soldier in the 1st Cohort of Pannonians. Lived at either Housesteads or Great Chesters. *RIB* 1667 (tombstone)

REGINA: freedwoman and wife of Barates of Palmyra, a flag maker or standard bearer. She was a Catuvellaunian by tribe but died at South Shields aged thirty. *RIB* 1065; *CSIR* I.1, no. 247 (tombstone); see also *RIB* 1171

ROMANA: dedicator of an altar to the Veteres at Great Chesters. *RIB* 1729

(R)OMANA: widow of Carinus, a citizen of Rome; mother of Rufinus, Carina and Avita. Lived at Dorchester (Dorset). *RIB* 188 (tombstone)

RUSONIA AVENT(I)NA: benefactress of Lucius Ulpius Sestius and tribeswoman of the Mediomatrici (centred on Metz in France). Died at Bath aged fifty-eight. *RIB* 163 (tombstone)

SALVIENA METILIANA: widow of C. Julius Maritimus of Cologne, centurion of the three legions of the British army of occupation in turn before his death whilst attached to IIIrd Legion Augusta at Lambaesis in Algeria. *CIL* VIII. 2907 (tombstone)

SATURNINA: victim of theft who petitioned Mercury at Uley for the return of her linen cloth. *Britannia* X (1979), 343, no. 3 (curse tablet)

SECUNDA: owner of a greyware pot at Billericay. *Britannia* IV (1973), 330, no. 19 (graffiti)

SENOVARA: presumed wife Cunitius, the slave of Cunomolis and Minervina. Witness of a petition or curse at Bath. *Tab.Sul.* 9 (lead tablet)

SEPRONIA MARTINA: daughter of Sepronius Martinus and Julia Brica. Died at York aged six. *RIB* 686; *CSIR* 1.3, no. 41 (tombstone)

SIMPLICIA: dedicator of a statuette to Mars Corotiacus at Martlesham; customer of the metalworker Glaucus. *RIB* 213 (bronze statuette base)

SIMPLICIA FLORENTIN(A): daughter of Felicius Simplex of VIth Legion Victrix. Died at York aged ten months. *RIB* 690 (stone coffin)

SOSIA JUNCINA: wife of Quintus Antonius Isauricus, imperial legate. Dedicator of an altar to Fortuna at York. *RIB* 644.

SULICENA: died at Lasborough, aged fourteen. *RIB* 134 (tombstone)

SULPICIA LEPIDINA: wife of Flavius Cerialis, prefect of 8th or 9th Cohort of Batavians at Vindolanda. Correspondent of Claudia Severa. Bowman and Thomas 1987, no. 5 (writing tablet)

TACITA: cursed by an anonymous enemy at Clothall. *RIB* 221 (curse tablet)

TADIA EXUPERATA: daughter of Tadia Vallaunius; sister of Tadius Exuperatus. Lived at Caerleon. *RIB* 369 (tombstone)

TADIA VALLAUN(I)US: mother of Tadia Exuperata and Tadius Exuperatus. Died at Caerleon aged sixty-five. *RIB* 369 (tombstone)

TANCORIX: died at Old Carlisle aged sixty. *RIB* 908 (tombstone)

TIBERIA: heiress of (Ti)berius. Lived at Chester. *RIB* 554 (tombstone)

TITIA PINTA: wife of Valerius Vindicianus; mother of Valerius Adjutor. Died near Eastness aged thirty-eight. *RIB* 720

TITULLINIA PUSSITTA: a Raetian who died at Netherby aged thirty-five. *RIB* 984 (tombstone)

TRANQUILA SEVERA: dedicator on behalf of herself and her family of an altar to the 'Goddess Mother of the Gods' (Cybele) at Carrawburgh. *RIB* 1539

TRETIA MARIA (or Maria Tretia): cursed by an anonymous enemy at London. *RIB* 7 (curse tablet)

URSA: sister of Lurio, a German; sister-in-law of Julia; aunt of Canio. Died at Chesters. *RIB* 1483; *CSIR* 1.6, no. 192 (tombstone)

VACIA: sister of Aelius Mercurialis, a staff clerk (*cornicularius*). Died at Great Chesters. *RIB* 1742; *CSIR* 1.6, no. 213 (tombstone)

VACIA: died at Carlisle aged three. *RIB* 961; *CSIR* 1.6, no. 495 (tombstone)

VAL(ERIA) FRONTINA: widow of Macr..us, an equestrian. Lived at Colchester. *RIB* 202 (tombstone)

VED...IC..: tribeswoman of the Cornovii. Died at Ilkley aged thirty. *RIB* 639; *CSIR* 1.3, no. 98 (tombstone)

VELORIGA: head of a Bath family. *Tab.Sul.* 53 (lead tablet)

VERECUNDA: actress and girlfriend of Lucius, a gladiator at Leicester. *CIL* VII, 1335, 4 (graffiti)

VERECU(N)D(A) RUFILIA: wife of Excingus; tribeswoman of the Dobunni. Died at Templebrough aged thirty-five. *RIB* 621 (tombstone)

VERINA: gave a buffware flagon to 'little Vrilucolus'. *Britannia* VIII (1977), 444, no. 10 (graffiti)

VETTI(A) MANSUETA: mother of Claudia Turianilla with whom she dedicated an altar to the Nymphs at Carvoran. *RIB* 1789

VIBIA PACATA: wife of Flavius Verecundus, centurion of VIth Legion Victrix. He was a Pannonian, while she may have been an African. Dedicated an altar to the Silvanae and the Quadruviae at Westerwood on the Antonine Wall. *JRS* LIV (1964), 178; *CSIR* 1.4, no. 86

VITELLIA PROCULA: mother and heiress of a thirteen-year-old child who died at York. *RIB* 696 (tombstone)

VITIA: illiterate owner of a greyware jar at Darenth villa ('Vitia X: her mark'). *Britannia* II (1971), 298, no. 54 (graffiti)

VIVENTIA: co-dedicator with Innocentia of a piece of Christian silverware. *Britannia* VII (1976), 385, no. 32.

VIVENTIA: wife or daughter of Victoricus. Owner of a pewter plate at Verulamium. *JRS* XLVII (1957), 232

VOLUSIA FAUSTINA: wife of Aurelius Senecio, a decurion. She was a citizen of Lincoln where she died aged twenty-six. *RIB* 250 (tombstone)

DAUGHTER OF BLESCIUS DIOVICUS: died at Risingham aged one year and twenty-one days. *RIB* 1254 (tombstone)

DAUGHTER OF CRESCENS, an *imaginifer*; died at Kirkby Thore. *RIB* 769 (tombstone)

DAUGHTER OF SABINUS: presumed relation of Regulus, who set up an altar to Jupiter Dolichenus at Great Chesters. *RIB* 1726; *CSIR* 1.6, no. 119.

WIFE OF CASSIUS SECUNDUS, a veteran who died at Chester when he was eighty. *RIB* 526 (tombstone)

WIFE OF FABIUS: set up an altar to the Nymphs at Risingham after being 'forwarned in a dream' by an anonymous soldier. *RIB* 1228.

WIFE OF MARCUS AURELIUS NEPOS, centurion of the XXth Legion Valeria Victrix. Lived at Chester. *RIB* 491 (tombstone)

CHESTER 2: Wright and Richmond 1955, no. 117, pl. XXX (tombstone)

CHESTER 3: Wright and Richmond 1955, no. 119, pl. XXXI (tombstone)

CHESTER 4: Wright and Richmond 1955, no. 120, pl. XXXI (tombstone)

CHESTER 5: Wright and Richmond 1955, no. 118, pl. XXXI (tombstone)

CHESTER 6: Wright and Richmond 1955, no. 112, pl. XXIX (tombstone)

CORBRIDGE: *CSIR* 1.1, no. 15 (relief of Maenad)

HALTON CHESTERS 1: *Britannia* V (1974), 462, no. 61 (tombstone)

HALTON CHESTERS 2: *CSIR* 1.1, no. 261 (tombstone)

HIGH ROCHESTER: *CSIR* 1.1, no. 271; *RIB* 1293 (tombstone)

ILKLEY: *CSIR* 1.3, no. 99 (tombstone)

LLANIO: *CSIR* 1.5, no. 56 (wooden sculpture)

MIDLOTHIAN: *CSIR* 1.4, no. 61 (relief of three mother goddesses)

YORK 1: *CSIR* 1.3, no. 59 (tombstone)

YORK 2 (Fishergate): *CSIR* 1.3, no. 71 (sculpture)

YORK 3: *CSIR* 1.3, no. 132 (sculpture)

YORK 4 (Micklegate): *CSIR* 1.3, no. 54 (tombstone)

Anonymous women

ALDBOROUGH: *CSIR* 1.3, no. 15A (sculpture)

BATH 1 (Landsdown): *CSIR* 1.2, no. 144 (sculpture)

BATH 2 (Winterslow): *CSIR* 1.2, no. 94 (sculpture)

BATH 3 (R. Avon): *CSIR* 1.2, no. 2 (sculpture)

BATH 4 (Walcot): *CSIR* 1.2, no. 1 (sculpture)

BEWCASTLE: *CSIR* 1.6, no. 180 (relief of a mother goddess)

BIRRENS: *CSIR* 1.4, no. 20 (sculpture)

BOWNESS-ON-SOLWAY: *CSIR* 1.6, no. 233 (tombstone)

CAERWENT: *CSIR* 1.5, no. 14 (sculpture)

CARLISLE: *CSIR* 1.6, no. 497 (tombstone)

CASTLESTEADS: *CSIR* 1.6, no. 228 (tombstone)

CHESTER 1: Wright and Richmond 1955, no. 66, pl. XIX (tombstone)

Abbreviations and notes

The majority of the classical authors referred to below have been translated into English in the Loeb Classical Library volumes.

CIL Corpus Inscriptionum Latinarum 16 vols (Berlin, 1863–)

CSIR Corpus Signorum Imperii Romani (London)

ILS Inscriptiones Latinae Selectae 3 vols (Berlin, 1892–1916)

JRS Journal of Roman Studies (London)

RIB The Roman Inscriptions of Britain (Oxford 1965)

Tab. Sul. Tomlin (Oxford 1988)

Introduction

1 Tacitus *Annals* II.24
2 Strabo *Geography* IV.v.2
3 Caesar *De Bello Gallico* II.4
4 The popular spelling 'Boudicea' was the result of the miscopying of Tacitus' text. Kenneth Jackson has recently shown that the correct spelling is 'Boudica'
5 Cassius Dio *Roman History* LXII.2.4
6 Cicero *Pro Murena* 27
7 Tacitus *Histories* III.45
8 Tacitus *Annals* XII.36
9 Tacitus *Histories* III.45
10 Tacitus *Histories* III.45
11 Tacitus *Annals* XII.40
12 Tacitus *Annals* XIV.30
13 Ruffus, Article 40 in C. E. Brand *Roman Military Law* (1978)
14 Cassius Dio *Roman History* LXII.2.2
15 Cassius Dio *Roman History* LXII.2.2
16 Cassius Dio *Roman History* LXII.3–6; Tacitus *Annals* XIV
17 *Henry V* Act III, Scene 1
18 Tacitus *Agricola* 31
19 *Antiquaries Journal* XXXIII (1953), 207; *British Museum Quarterly* XX (1967), 102–3
20 *RIB* 560; see also Birley 1979, 146
21 Justinian *Digest* 37.15.11

1 Birth, marriage and death

1 Soranus *Gynecology* II.10 (see also Temkin 1956)
2 Soranus *Gynecology* II.12
3 Soranus *Gynecology* I.20
4 Soranus *Gynecology* I.23
5 Soranus *Gynecology* I.20,24
6 Soranus *Gynecology* I.29
7 Soranus *Gynecology* I.26
8 Tacitus *Annals* III.28
9 *ILS* 7472
10 Tacitus *Germania* 20
11 Caesar *De Bello Gallico* VI.21
12 Caesar *De Bello Gallico* V.14
13 Cassius Dio *Roman History* LXXVII.16.5
14 Soranus *Gynecology* I.34
15 Aulus Gellius *Noctes Atticae* 3.10.8; 3.16
16 Soranus *Gynecology* I.48
17 Soranus *Gynecology* I.55
18 Claudia Trophima: *CIL* VI.9720; Poblicia Aphe: *CIL* VI.9723
19 Tacitus *Germania* 20
20 Soranus *Gynecology* II.19
21 Soranus *Gynecology* II.19
22 Soranus *Gynecology* II.49–54; 46; 45
23 Hopkins 1967, 126
24 Aristotle *Historia Animalium* 583a
25 Hippocrates *Natura Mulierum* 98; *Muliebria* 1.76
26 Pliny *Naturalis Historia* XXIV.11.18
27 Pliny *Naturalis Historia* XXIX, 27.85
28 Dioscorides *De Materia Medica* 3.34; 1.77.2; 3.130; 5.106.6
29 Caelius Aurelianus *Gynaecia* (ed. Drabkin, 29, 1.83)
30 Lucretius *De Rerum Natura* IV.1265ff.
31 Soranus *Gynecology* I.60
32 Soranus *Gynecology* I.61
33 Soranus *Gynecology* I.60
34 St John Chrysostom *Epistle to the Romans* 24.4
35 Dioscorides *De Materia Medica* 2.159.3
36 Pliny *Naturalis Historia* XXV.37.75; XXVII.55.80
37 Soranus *Gynecology* II.10
38 Plautus *Casina* prol. 41, 79; *Cistellaria* i.3, 17, 31
39 Tacitus *Germania* 19
40 Columella *De Re Rustica* 1.8.19
41 Soranus *Gynecology* II.10

42 *RIB* 681
43 *RIB* 1292
44 *RIB* 937
45 Oribasius *Ecloga Medicamentorum* 132.1
46 Galen *On Prognosis* 6

2 Women and the army

1 Tacitus *Annals* III.34
2 *Scriptores Historiae Augustae Hadrian* 11.3
3 Tacitus *Annals* III.33
4 Tacitus *Agricola* 29
5 Juvenal *Satires* VI.398ff.
6 *ILS* 1092
7 Cassius Dio *Roman History* LX.24.3
8 Herodian *Histories* 3.8.4–5
9 Justinian *Digest* XLIX.17.13
10 Cassius Dio *Roman History* LVI.20.2–5
11 [Caesar] *De Bello Africo* 75
12 *RIB* 1700
13 *RIB* 369: Tadius Exuperatus is presumed to have born in the *canabae* of Caerleon but this is not explicitly stated. For references to people born *ex castris* elsewhere in the Empire see J. C. Mann (ed. M. M. Roxan) *Legionary Recruitment and Veteran Settlement during the Principate* (London 1983)
14 *RIB* 1064
15 Justinian *Digest* 49.15.6
16 *RIB* 2059
17 *RIB* 2182

3 Women of town and country

1 Nennius *Historia Brittonum* 31; see also Gildas *The Ruin of Britain* 25, and Bede *Ecclesiastical History* I.16
2 Tacitus *Annals* XIV.32
3 Cassius Dio *Roman History* LXII.2.7
4 Caesar *De Bello Gallico* IV.20
5 *RIB* 69; 70; 71
6 *Britannia* VIII (1977), 430–1
7 *Britannia* IV (1973), 332
8 *Britannia* III (1972), 359
9 *JRS* LI (1961), 195
10 *CIL* VII.1238; *Britannia* II (1971), 297
11 *CIL* VI.9846; 9848; 37820
12 *CIL* VI.10006; 33928; X.1965
13 *CIL* III.153
14 *CIL* VI.9488
15 *CIL* VI.9855
16 Horace *Epistles* 1.14.21
17 Horace *Satires* 1.2.36; Ovid *Fasti* 4.134; Ovid *Ars Amatoria* 1.31ff.
18 *Scriptores Historiae Augustae Hadrian* 18.8
19 Suetonius *Caligula* 40

4 At home

1 Justinian *Digest* 47.2.12
2 *CSIR* I.1. no. 248
3 Wright and Richmond 1955, pl. XXXVII.156
4 *CSIR* I.2. no. 41
5 Unfortunately, the marble tombstone from London which shows a female resting her feet on a small elaborate footstool is now considered to be a recent import. R. E. M. Wheeler, *London in Roman Times* (London 1930), pl. XVIII
6 Lucretius *De Rerum Natura* IV.1029; IV.1123
7 Strabo *Geography* X.1.6; Pliny *Naturalis Historia* XIX.19
8 Apicius *The Art of Cooking*
9 Caesar *De Bello Gallico* V.12
10 Martial *Epigrams* XIII.103
11 Pliny *Naturalis Historia* XXI.93
12 Petronius *Satyricon* LXVI
13 Pliny *Naturalis Historia* XVIII.12.68; 26.102–4
14 Pliny *Naturalis Historia* XI.240–2
15 Athenaeus *Deipnosophistae* IV.152
16 Ovid *Ars Amatoria* III.765
17 Plutarch *Moralia* 244A
18 Diodorus Siculus *Library of History* XXIII.21
19 Pliny *Naturalis Historia* XXVIII.4.19

5 Fashion

1 Suetonius *Augustus* 73
2 Wild 1984. 404
3 Soranus *Gynecology* II.ix.14
4 *Tab.Sul.* no. 61
5 *Scriptores Historiae Augustae Alexander Severus* 27
6 *Tab.Sul.* no. 55
7 Palladius *De Re Rustica* i.42(43)4; Ionas *Vita Columbari* 1.15
8 *Tab.Sul.* 5
9 Woad, dog's mercury, bilberry, whortleberry
10 Elder bark, meadowsweet
11 Rhizomes of bracken, the flowering shoots of heather, pine-cones, pear leaves and gorse
12 Flowerheads of reeds
13 Onion skins
14 Whelks
15 Orchil lichen
16 Madder
17 Tacitus *Annals* XIV.30
18 Ovid *Ars Amatoria* III.170–83
19 Ovid *Ars Amatoria* III.190
20 Tacitus *Germania* 17
21 Tertullian *On Female Dress* VIII
22 Cassius Dio *Roman History* LXII.2.4

23 Aulus Gellius *Noctes Atticae* 10.10
24 Tertullian *On Female Dress* X
25 *CIL* VI.1527
26 Pliny *Naturalis Historia* XXXVII.30
27 Artemidorus *Onirocritica* 2,5
28 Tacitus *Agricola* 12
29 Pliny *Naturalis Historia* XXXVI. 141–2
30 Lucian *Amores* 39
31 Ovid *Ars Amatoria* III.10ff.
32 Ovid *On Painting the Face* 75–80
33 Ovid *On Painting the Face* 100
34 Juvenal *Satires* 6.461–74
35 Plautus *Truculentus* 294; *Mostellaria* 258; Tertullian *On Female Dress* V; Ovid *Ars Amatoria* III.200
36 Ovid *On Painting the Face* 66–71
37 Tertullian *On Female Dress* II
38 Pliny *Naturalis Historia* XXVIII.46.166
39 Ovid *Ars Amatoria* III.202
40 Juvenal *Satires* 2.93
41 Propertius *Elegies* II.18B, 1–4
42 Ovid *Ars Amatoria* III.197
43 Ovid *Ars Amatoria* I.505–6
44 Pliny *Naturalis Historia* XXVIII.249 and 255
45 Ovid *Ars Amatoria* III.215
46 Lucian *Amores* 39
47 Ovid *Ars Amatoria* III.193
48 Ovid *Ars Amatoria* III.149
49 Ovid *Ars Amatoria* III.140
50 Tertullian *On Female Dress* VII
51 Ovid *Amores* I.14.45
52 Tertullian *On Female Dress* VI
53 Ovid *Ars Amatoria* III.165
54 Pliny *Naturalis Historia* XXVIII.191; Martial *Epigrams* 8.33.20; 14.26
55 Propertius *Elegies* II.18B
56 Diodorus Siculus *Library of History* V.28
57 Tertullian *On Female Dress* VI
58 Tacitus *Agricola* 11
59 Cassius Dio *Roman History* LXII.2.4

6 Religion

1 Tacitus *Annals* XIV.31
2 Tacitus *Annals* XIV.31
3 Diana is known to have been entreated to increase the population of Rome on occasions: Horace *Carmen Saeculare* 17.20
4 Ovid *Ars Amatoria* I.400–40
5 *RIB* 1270
6 *RIB* 1253; see also Henig 1984
7 Tacitus *Annals* XIV.30
8 Strabo *Geography* IV.4.6
9 Suetonius *Claudius* XXV.5
10 *RIB* 246
11 Cassius Dio *Roman History* LXII.7
12 *Britannia* XIII, 1982, 408–9
13 Tacitus *Annals* XIV.30
14 Anicius Ingenuus at Housesteads: *RIB* 1618; Abrocomas at Binchester: *RIB* 1028; Hermogenes at Chester: *RIB* 461
15 *RIB* 1028
16 *Victoria County History: Somerset* (1906), 283, no. 46
17 Apuleius *The Golden Ass* XI.4
18 Ovid *Ars Amatoria* III.636
19 C. Hill, M. Millett and T. Blagg *The Roman Riverside Wall and Monumental Arch in London* 1980, 196–8
20 Tertullian *On Female Dress* VIII
21 Lactantius *Institutiones Divinae* 6, 20, 18ff.

7 Entertainment and recreation

1 Ovid *Ars Amatoria* III. 355–63
2 Pliny *Naturalis Historia* X.59
3 Suetonius *Augustus* 44
4 Tacitus *Annals* XIV.32
5 *RIB* 707
6 Ovid *Ars Amatoria* I.90
7 Soranus *Gynecology* I.22
8 Ovid *Ars Amatoria* III.320–5
9 Tacitus *Agricola* 21
10 *RIB* 662; 663; Plutarch *On the Cessation of Oracles* 410A
11 *Ephemeris Epigraphica* VII.1141
12 Ovid *Ars Amatoria* III.620–30
13 *RIB* 265
14 *ILS* 6891; *CIL* II.5181
15 Pliny *Naturalis Historia* XXXIII, 54.152
16 Seneca *Epistulae Morales* 56
17 Martial *Epigrams* VI.93
18 Diodorus Siculus *Library of History* V.40
19 Pliny *Naturalis Historia* XXI.10.14–22
20 Varro *De Re Rustica* I.39ff.
21 Pliny *Naturalis Historia* XIX, .19.57
22 Soranus *Gynecology* 47

8 Finale

1 Zosimus *Historia Nova* VI. 5–2
2 *RIB* 235
3 Ammianus Marcellinus *History* XXVII, 8, 1–3, 5–8
4 Bowman and Thomas 1987, 136

Bibliography

To cover adequately the topics discussed would require a bibliography of enormous size. The list is, therefore, confined to those modern authors cited in the text and a selection of general works which will lead interested readers to more specialised works.

ALCOCK, J. 1980. 'Classical religious belief and burial practice in Roman Britain', *Archaeological Journal* CXXXVII, 50–85

APPLEBAUM, S. 1975. 'Some observations on the economy of the Roman villa at Bignor, Sussex', *Britannia* VI, 118–32

BALSDON, J. P. V. D. 1962. *Roman Women* (London)

BARRETT, A. A. 1978. 'Knowledge of the literary classics in Roman Britain', *Britannia* IX, 307–13

BIRLEY, A. 1979. *The People of Roman Britain* (London)

BIRLEY, A. 1981. *Life in Roman Britain* (London)

BLAGG, T. F. C. AND KING, A. C. 1984. *Military and Civilian in Roman Britain: Cultural Relationships in a Frontier Province* (Oxford)

BOON, G. C. 1974. *Silchester: the Roman Town of Calleva* (London)

BOON, G. C. 1983. 'Potters, Oculists and Eye Troubles', *Britannia* XIV, 1–12

BOON, G. C. 1983. 'Some Romano-British domestic shrines and their inhabitants', in *Rome and her Northern Provinces*, ed. B. Hartley and J. Wacher (Gloucester)

BOWMAN, A. K. AND THOMAS, J. D. 1987. 'New texts from Vindolanda', *Britannia* XVIII, 125–42

BRAUND, D. 1984. 'Observations on Cartimandua', *Britannia* XV, 1–6

BREEZE, D. 1982. 'Demand and supply on the northern frontier', in *Rural Settlement in the Roman North*, ed. P. Clack and S. Haselgrove (Durham)

BROTHWELL, D. 1972. 'Palaeodemography and earlier British populations', *World Archaeology* 4.1, 75–87

CAMPBELL, B. 1978. 'The marriage of soldiers under the Empire', *Journal of Roman Studies* LXI, 153–66

CARCOPINO, J. 1956. *Daily Life in Ancient Rome*, trans. E. O. Lorimer (London)

CASSON, L. 1974. *Travel in the Ancient World* (London)

CLAYTON, J., in L. Allason-Jones. 1985. *Coventina's Well* (Chollerford)

COCKS, A. H. 1921. 'A Romano-British homestead in the Hambledon valley, Bucks.' *Archaeologia* LXXI, 141–98

CUNLIFFE, B. 1981. 'Roman gardens in Britain. A review of the evidence', in *Ancient Roman Gardens*, ed. E. B. MacDougall and W. F. Jashenski (Washington)

CUNLIFFE, B. 1988. *The Temple of Sulis Minerva at Bath.* II *The Finds from the Sacred Spring* (Oxford)

DAVEY, N. AND LING, R. 1982. *Wallpainting in Roman Britain* (London)

DIMBLEBY, G. W. 1978. *Plants and Archaeology* (London)

DIXON, S. 1988. *The Roman Mother* (London)

DRIEL-MURRAY, C. VAN 1987. 'Roman footwear: a mirror of fashion and society', *Recent Research in Archaeological Footwear*, Technical Paper 8, Association of Archaeological Illustrators and Surveyors

DUDLEY, D. R. AND WEBSTER, G. 1962. *The Rebellion of Boudica* (London)

ESPÉRANDIEU, C. 1907–38. *Recueil Général des Bas-Reliefs, Statues et Bustes de la Gaule Romaine* 10 vols (Paris)

EVANS, M. M. 1906. 'Hairdressing of Roman ladies as illustrated on coins', *The Numismatic Chronicle* 4th series, VI, 37–65

FLOWER, B. AND ROSENBAUM, E. 1958. *Apicius: The Roman Cookery Book* (London)

FRERE, S. S. 1987. *Britannia* (London)

GARBSCH, J. G. 1965. 'Die Norisch-Pannonische Frauentracht im 1. und 2. Jahrhundert', *Münchener Beiträge zur Vor- u. Frühgeschichte* XI

GARDENER, J. F. 1986. *Women in Roman Law and Society* (London)

GREEN, M. 1986. *The Gods of the Celts* (Gloucester)

GUIDO, M. 1979. 'Beads and necklaces', in G. Clarke *Pre-Roman and Roman Winchester* II *The Roman Cemetery at Lankhills* (Oxford)

HANLEY, R. 1987. *Villages in Roman Britain* (Aylesbury)

HARRIS, E. AND HARRIS, J. R. 1965. *The Oriental Cults in Roman Britain* (Leiden)

HENIG, M. 1984. *Religion in Roman Britain* (London)

HOPKINS, K. 1965. 'Age of Roman girls at marriage', *Population Studies* XVIII, 309–27

HOPKINS, K. 1967. 'Contraception in the Roman Empire', *Comparative Studies in Society and History* VIII (1965–6), 124–51

JACKSON, K. 1953. *Language and History in Early Britain* (Edinburgh)

JACKSON, R. 1985. 'Cosmetic sets from the late Iron Age and Roman Britain', *Britannia* XVI, 165–92

JACKSON, R. 1988. *Doctors and Diseases in the Roman Empire* (London)

JOHNSON, P. 1982. *Romano-British Mosaics* (Aylesbury)

JOHNSON, S. 1980. *Later Roman Britain* (London)

JONES, G. D. B. 1984. 'Becoming different without knowing it. The role and development of vici', in Blagg and King 1984

KILBRIDE-JONES, H. 1938. 'Glass armlets in Britain', *PSAS* LXXII, 366–95

KING, A. 1984. 'Animal bones and the dietary identity of military and civilian groups in Roman Britain', in Blagg and King 1984

LETHBRIDGE, T. C. 1936. 'Further excavations in the early Iron Age and Romano-British cemetery at Guilden Morden', *Cambridge Antiquarian Communications* XXXVI (1934–5), 109–20

LEWIS, M. J. T. 1966. *Temples in Roman Britain* (Cambridge)

LING, R. 1985. *Romano-British Wallpainting* (Aylesbury)

LIVERSIDGE, J. 1955. *Furniture in Roman Britain* (London)

LIVERSIDGE, J. 1957. 'Kitchens in Roman Britain', *Archaeological Newsletter* VI, 82–5

LIVERSIDGE, J. 1973. *Britain in the Roman Empire* (London)

LLOYD-MORGAN, G. 1977. 'Mirrors in Roman Britain', in *Roman Life and Art in Britain*, ed. J. Munby and M. Henig (Oxford)

MACDONALD, G. 1919. 'A sculptured relief of the Roman period at Colinton', *Proceedings of the Society of Antiquaries of Scotland* LII (1917–18), 38–48

MACGREGOR, A. 1985. *Bone, Antler, Ivory and Horn* (London)

MANN, J. 1971. 'Spoken Latin in Britain as evidenced in the inscriptions', *Britannia* II, 218–24

MATTHEWS, C. L. 1981. 'A Romano-British inhumation cemetery at Dunstable', *Bedfordshire Archaeological Journal* XV, passim

MILNE, G. 1985. *The Port of Roman London* (London)

NEAL, D. S. 1981. *Roman Mosaics in Britain* (London)

OGDEN, J. 1980. Note in *The Society of Jewellery Historians Newsletter* IX

PEACOCK, D. P. S. 1982. *Pottery in the Roman World: an Ethnoarchaeological Approach* (Harlow)

PIGGOTT, S. 1968. *The Druids* (London)

POTTER, T. W. 1983. *Roman Britain* (London)

PRITCHARD, F. A. 1986. 'Ornamental stonework from Roman London', *Britannia* XVII, 169–89

RANSOM, C. L. 1905. *Studies in Ancient Furniture. Couches and Beds of the Greeks, Etruscans and Romans* (Chicago)

RHODES, M. 1980. 'Leather footwear', in *Excavations at Billingsgate Buildings, Lower Thames Street, London, 1974* ed. D. M. Jones (London)

RICHMOND, I. A. 1954. 'Queen Cartimandua', *Journal of Roman Studies* XLIV, 43–52

RIVET, A. L. F. 1964. *Town and Country in Roman Britain* (London)

ROSS, A. 1974. *Pagan Celtic Britain* (London)

SALWAY, P. 1981. *Roman Britain* (Oxford)

SMITH, J. T. 1963. 'Romano-British aisled houses', *Archaeological Journal* CXX, 1–30

SOMMER, C. S. 1984. *The Military Vici in Roman Britain* (Oxford)

STEPHENS, G. R. 1985. 'Civic aqueducts in Britain', *Britannia* XVI, 197–208

STEVENSON, R. B. K. 1957. 'Native bangles and Roman glass', *Proceedings of the Society of Antiquaries of Scotland* LXXXVIII (1954–6), 208–21

STRONG, D. AND BROWN, D. 1976. *Roman Crafts* (London)

SWAN, V. 1988. *Pottery in Roman Britain* (Aylesbury)

TEMKIN, O. 1956. *Soranus' Gynecology* (Baltimore)

THOMAS, C. 1981. *Christianity in Roman Britain to AD 500* (London)

TOMLIN, R. S. O. 1988. 'The Curse Tablets', in Cunliffe 1988

TOYNBEE, J. M. C. 1952. 'A Roman (?) head at Dumfries', *Journal of Roman Studies* XLII, 63–5

VERMASEREN, M. J. 1977. *Cybele and Atys: The Myth and the Cult* (London)

WACHER, J. 1974. *Towns of Roman Britain* (London)

WACHER, J. 1979. *The Coming of Rome* (London)

WALTHEW, C. V. 1975. 'The town house and the villa house', *Britannia* VI, 189–205

WEBSTER, G. 1978. *Boudica: The British Revolt against Rome AD 60* (London)

WEBSTER, G. 1986. *The British Celts and their Gods under Rome* (London)

WILD, J. P. 1968. 'Clothing in the North-west provinces of the Roman Empire', *Bonner Jahrbucher* CLXVIII, 166–240

WILD, J. P. 1970. *Textile Manufacture in the Northern Roman Provinces* (Cambridge)

Index